THE HAPPY CAMPER

THE HAPPY CAMPER

AN ESSENTIAL GUIDE TO LIFE OUTDOORS

Kevin Callan

The BOSTON MILLS PRESS

To my daughter, Kyla, who is absolute proof that miracles do happen.

A BOSTON MILLS PRESS BOOK

Second printing 2007

Library and Archives Canada Cataloguing in Publication

Callan, Kevin
The happy camper : an essential guide to life outdoors / Kevin Callan.

Includes bibliographical references and index.
ISBN-10: 1-55046-450-7
ISBN-13: 978-1-55046-450-4

1. Camping. I. Title.

GV191.7.C24 2005 796.54 C2004-906227-1

Publisher Cataloging-in-Publication Data (U.S.)

Callan, Kevin.

The happy camper : an essential guide to life outdoors / Kevin Callan.—1st ed.
[320] p. : col. photos.; cm.
Includes bibliographical references and index.

Summary: Basic wilderness instruction and campsite advice; how to plan the trip, how to pack, how to prevent insect bites, stake a tent, build a fire, ward off wildlife, paddle a canoe, etc.

ISBN-10: 1-55046-450-7 (pbk.)
ISBN-13: 978-1-55046-450-4

1. Camping. I. Title.

796.54 22 GV191.7.C35 2005

Published in 2005 by
BOSTON MILLS PRESS
132 Main Street,
Erin, Ontario N0B 1T0
Tel 519-833-2407
Fax 519-833-2195
books@bostonmillspress.com
www.bostonmillspress.com

Editors: Janes Gates, Kathleen Fraser
Text design & production: PageWave Graphics Inc.
Cover design: Gill Stead

IN CANADA:
Distributed by Firefly Books Ltd.
66 Leek Crescent
Richmond Hill, Ontario L4B 1H1
IN THE UNITED STATES:
Distributed by Firefly Books (U.S.) Inc.
P.O. Box 1338, Ellicott Station
Buffalo, New York 14205

The publisher acknowledges the financial support of the Government of Canada through the Book Publishing Industry Development Program (BPIDP) for its publishing efforts.

Photo page 2: Prime beachfront property on the shores of Lake Superior.

Printed in China

CONTENTS

INTRODUCTION

I submit the above as good advice. I know it is good advice for I did not follow it. I have never followed good advice — I have only given it.

ALBERT BIGELOW PAINE, *THE TENT DWELLERS* (1908)

THIS ISN'T A NEW BOOK. It's a revised edition of something I wrote over ten years ago titled *Ways of the Wild*. The initial printing did well. It was even used as a textbook for a junior high school in Newfoundland. (I'm quite proud of that.) But for the past few years I've been bursting to rewrite it.

In the original version I was more concerned with having a wealth of past information for the reader, listing all the new-age gadgets and gizmos and lecturing them about how important it is to have the right skill level before heading out. I've recently changed my tune, however. Through my countless trips out there, some good and some horrible, I now realize that the reason for spending time in the wilderness has more to do with inspiration than information.

Don't get me wrong — I spend a lot of time browsing the aisles of outdoor stores, maxing out my credit card so I can have the latest gear. I go to seminars and continue to take courses to improve my skills. And I still think it's vital that everyone knows how to play it safe before they embark on any major expedition. I also believe it's crucial that a book such as this makes things like trip planning, compass navigation, and food preparation (and everything else that seems like an ordeal) feel less daunting for the first-time camper. But in between all that is an important element that I think I missed out on the first time around. It's a philosophy that's based on the simple belief that it's far more important that you head out hiking, canoeing, kayaking or even car camping than it is to spend all your time thinking about it and preparing yourself for it. This enlightenment came to me the day I was robbed.

My wife and I had just finished a three-day canoe trip down a not-so-remote urban river in southwestern Ontario. Somehow we managed to arrive three hours early for our shuttle, and rather than hang around the take-out point, we decided to ditch our gear in the nearby bushes and take a walk up to the outfitters. Of course, that was a foolish move. The trip into town took an hour, and by the time we got back, all our gear had been stolen.

◀ *Wet, bug-bitten, and carrying a heavy load across yet another portage, but still a happy camper — author Kevin Callan.*

▲ *A group of true happy campers.*

Words cannot describe the effect this incident had on us. I was furious. It wasn't just a pile of camping equipment that had been taken from us, it was part of our life. The three-season sleeping bag Alana bought me for my birthday, a Therm-a-Rest I bought her for Christmas, a compass I received from my father the day I graduated from college as a forest technician, a coffee pot that I had used since high school — all were now sitting in some idiot's car. And, believe it or not, this was the second time I'd been robbed that summer! Just a month before, the door of my truck was pried open with a crowbar while it sat in the parking lot in Algonquin Provincial Park. I was canoeing the interior at the time, so my gear was safe. But everything else, including my collection of John Denver tapes, was stolen.

The worst part of this dilemma was that Alana and I had planned to go on a much longer canoe trip in northwestern Ontario just two days after our quick weekend jaunt. Our ordeal had left me feeling ill-equipped and unprepared for it, though, and I immediately cancelled. My wife, however, wasn't as willing to give up that easily. When we arrived back home she gathered all the old gear we had stopped using over the years: musty canvas packs, a cheap nylon tent patched with duct tape, a severely weathered plastic rain tarp, and a blackened set of cooking pots. We even borrowed worn-out sleeping bags from the neighbors, packed our threadbare wool sweaters instead of new-age fleece, and picked up another antique coffee pot at a garage sale. We didn't care what we had, we just knew that we had gathered enough essentials that we would be content and safe, and we knew we had gained enough experience over the years to deal with whatever came up. It ended up being one of the best trips we've ever had. And when all was said and done, it was our desire to go traveling in the wilderness, not the gear that we happened to bring along with us, that made the trip so perfect. It was definitely inspiration rather than information that made Alana and me "Happy Campers."

This winter Alana and I reminisced about our mishap on the urban river, and a few days later I began preparing the new rendition of my previous "how-to" book. I hope I have changed it for the better. I certainly didn't want to exclude any information on the types of gear and techniques needed to get you started. But I wanted to make sure that I mixed in some reflective or even revealing elements about my newfound philosophy wherever I could. After all, practical things such as how to light a fire in a rainstorm or protect yourself from biting insects may be integral parts of any camping trip. But having the inspiration to go camping in the first place is far more important. Hope to see you out there.

▲ *Finding inspiration for the next trip.*

ROUND RIVER
ALDO LEOPOLD

TRIP PLANNING

"There's one thing that bothers me," Drew said. "We don't really know what we're getting into."

JAMES DICKEY, *DELIVERANCE (1970)*

THERE'S NO DOUBT that organizing a trip can sometimes be more fun than the actual trip itself. It's so exhilarating to bring the smoke-scented packs down from the attic, give the blackened cooking pots a quick scrub, and unroll the tent out in the backyard to check for any signs of mildew. At the same time, however, the organizational part can quickly become a real headache.

First there's the pre-trip planning party hosted by the proclaimed leader of the so-called expedition. It begins with a show and tell of all the new gear purchased for the upcoming season, with each item being heavily scrutinized and debated over. Then all the maps and relevant guidebooks are spread out or displayed on the kitchen table and route choices discussed. Arguments begin to erupt almost immediately, of course, usually due to the fact that each member has a totally different reason for tagging along.

The squabbling continues when the host serves samples of new camp recipes, none of which taste as good as last year's. By the time dessert is served (washed down with a generous quantity of rum), the route has been altered, the length has been changed, the scheduled date has been rescheduled, and somehow a couple of new members have been added to the list without the consent of half the group. It's obvious at this point that the trip is destined to fail.

◀ *It's important that* all *members of the group pay close attention during the trip planning session.*

My regular companions know this scenario all too well. For the past fourteen years we've met in mid-February to plan our spring outing. For the first few years it was disastrous. We constantly argued over where we were going, how we were going to get there, who was going, and most important, why we were going in the first place. However, we've changed our ways. Our pre-trip planning party now has some strict rules applied to it, and we make darn sure they're seriously followed. Our trips, of course, still have their problems. But at least we can't blame poor planning.

RULES AND REGULATIONS

Here are some important tips to keep in mind when planning your trip:

- Who is going is definitely the first thing decided upon, since it has a direct bearing on everything else. Group dynamics is number one. When choosing the crew, always lean toward skill and the ability to communicate with the other team members rather than going with the age-old friendship thing. Obviously, friendship is one of the reasons groups go out together in the first place. But not having the proper skills, friends or not, can get you into some real jams out there.
- The group should consist of at least four but no more than six people. Any fewer and it's not a safe trip. Any more and you're just asking for compatibility problems (not to mention being unable to find a large enough campsite).
- The mode of travel — that being hiking, canoeing or kayaking — is voted on by all members, with the newest member in the group being the tiebreaker.
- Selecting gear (who is bringing what) is carefully planned out. And remember, no belittling someone else's new gear during show and tell. If you do happen to make fun of the gear you are definitely not permitted to borrow it while out on the trip.
- Members are split up into small cooking groups (two or three). For each meal, the team leader taste-tests the individual recipes, and the group with the worst meal does the dishes while the group with the best meal gets to tease the losers unmercifully while they're doing the dishes.
- Cooking groups share items such as a tent or a canoe. However, each member must be self-sufficient when it comes to everything else. Borrowing items such as toilet paper is strictly forbidden.
- The route chosen best depicts, as closely as possible, the group's general "trip philosophy." Are we going for a real adventure or just to relax? Do we want to fish along the way or travel as much as possible? Is there a rest day

What is a good trip leader?

- well organized
- honest but compassionate
- decisive
- able to deal with stress under pressure
- able to change with the conditions
- exuding a positive attitude
- possessing excellent communication skills
- possessing excellent outdoor skills (but doesn't try to prove it all the time)
- enthusiastic
- owner of a great sense of humor

planned halfway through or a side trip added on? Will it be a circular route or a linear trip requiring a car shuttle? Achieving total agreement is next to impossible, of course. The important thing is that you've at least tried to accommodate everyone's needs. This process will help control the frustration (and reduce the blame) when something goes wrong — and something definitely will go wrong.

- A trip leader is chosen and agreed upon by all members of the group, as well as by the leader. The voyageurs always had a trip leader, titled the *bourgeois,* who made all the important decisions. Remember, good judgment and fair consensus, especially between groups of friends, can be easily swayed by fatigue or bravado. A trip leader can quickly solve this issue. Or, at best, be the one to complain to.
- Each crew member is given a separate task or duty so the leader knows who to blame when it's not properly done, or not done at all.
- Once the date of departure is set, it's set. Period!

A CONTACT PERSON...

One of the most important things to put on your to-do list before heading out on a trip is to leave detailed information about your route with a neighbor or family member. If you ever find yourself lost or injured out there, it's a comforting feeling to know that someone at home knows when and where to send the search party. A contact person may save your life.

It also makes total sense to check in with your contact person the moment you arrive home. Just recently a canoeist returning from a trip down Lake Superior's Pukaskwa River failed to tell his contact person that he had returned. This not only cost him the embarrassment of having his family members watch the search-and-rescue attempts on the six o'clock news, but he was also forced to pay a portion of the price tag ($30,000) it cost the government to look for him while he was sitting at home.

Best ways to start an argument out there

- not agreeing to pay your fair share of trip costs
- being late at the pick-up point
- getting up late when everybody else gets up early – or vice versa
- forgetting a "very important" piece of group tripping gear such as a first-aid kit or rain tarp
- never consulting with your partner(s) on any decision, or consulting but never using any of the other person's ideas
- carrying less than everyone else but complaining about the weight more than anyone else
- constantly stopping to collect items (rocks, unique driftwood, tree stumps), then being unable to keep up because you are overloaded
- constantly comparing gear choices and extolling yours over everyone else's
- sneaking food and gear from someone else's pack
- using someone else's toothbrush and not telling them until the last day
- running out of toilet paper then using everyone else's, in generous amounts
- constantly critiquing your camp mates on how they run rapids, start the fire, hang the food, make meals . . . .
- not doing your fair share of camp chores
- using a metal knife to cut the dessert baked in the Outback Oven nonstick pan
- going poop too close to camp
- complaining about the weather
- talking all day and all night for the entire trip
- singing the same song over-and-over-and-over-and-over
- yelling, "There's a moose," and watching it run away before the group photographer gets a chance to get a picture of it
- showing off, getting hurt, and then having everyone else take care of you
- stopping to fish every ten minutes when no one else bothered to bring fishing gear
- always being well ahead of the rest of the group
- always being well behind the rest of the group
- being obsessed about completing the route sooner than later

ROUTE PLANNING

To make the difference between a memorable trip and one to forget, keep the following points in mind.

- Attempt to have the route meet each member's objectives for the trip. (Good luck.)
- Provide each member a copy of the route map.
- Create a contingency plan (what to do if something goes wrong).
- Make the first day the easiest so everyone can get used to carrying heavy loads.

- After estimating travel time, always add an extra hour or two per day for unexpected circumstances.
- Include a rest day every five days of the trip.
- Plan a few alternative routes to shorten or lengthen your trip.
- Make a list of possible side routes and make them a highlight of the trip.
- Make the last day the shortest so you have plenty of time to get home.

And don't forget to . . .

- Provide each member with an estimate of the trip's cost.
- Provide each member with a list of regulations that may be in place where you are going (can and bottle bans, group size, fire bans, fishing species in season, fish sanctuaries, or restricted camping areas).

▲ *Alana looks over the "contingency plan" after a black bear steals half our food and we're forced to take a shortcut home.*

▲ *"Are we there yet?" Len Lockwood checks the map once again.*

Who's taking notes?

A trip journal is a great way to record the happenings of a trip, both for reminiscing later and to help others who want to follow in your footsteps. Apart from your personal feelings, make sure to routinely write down things such as where you camped, the sites you liked, wildlife sighted, unique features visited, fishing success, confusing sections of the trail while backpacking, or the difficulty of rapids while canoeing.

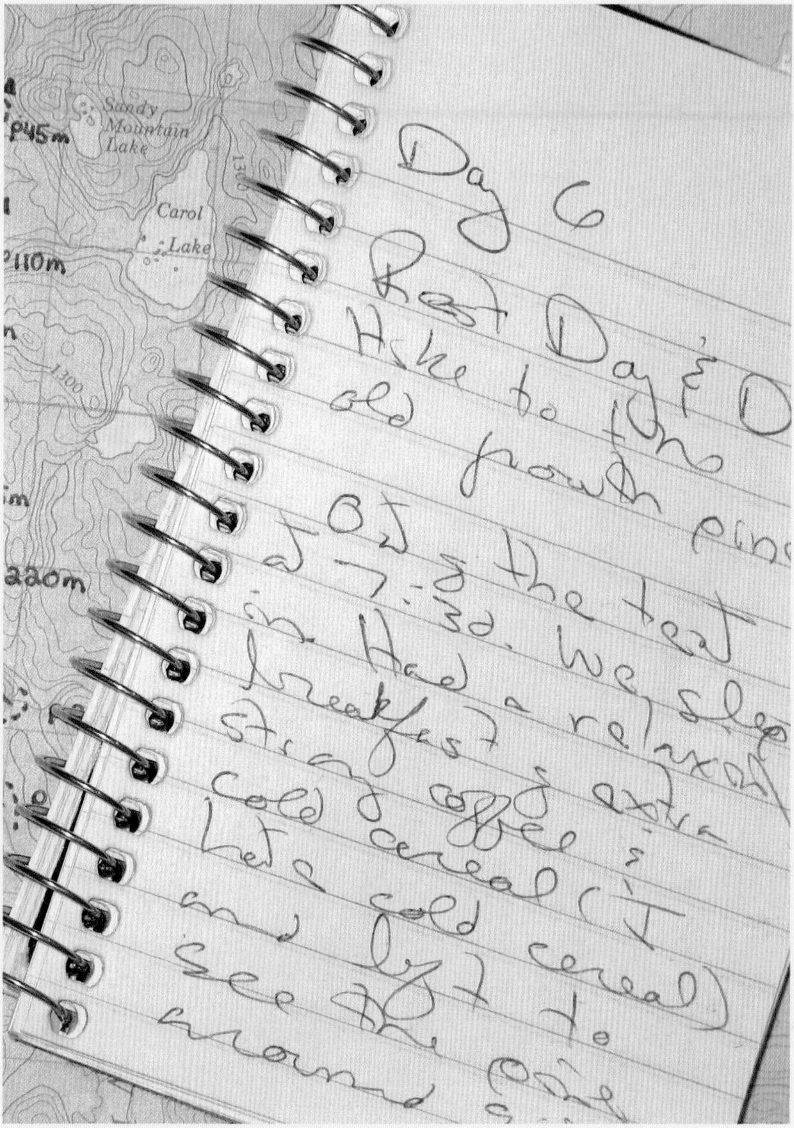

PACKING THE ESSENTIALS

The human is the only creature who fares badly in the wilderness without tools. Yet, if he overburdens himself with equipment, he impedes his freedom to travel.

CALVIN RUTSTRUM, *NORTH AMERICAN CANOE COUNTRY* (1964)

I'M DEFINITELY NOT one of those gear gurus who go on and on about their choice of camping equipment for the entire trip. People like that drive me bonkers. It's true that some gear is essential for any type of trip in the woods. The problem is, however, that people have various ways to define "essential." I figure as long as you use think practical, safe, basic and cost efficient when choosing what gear to purchase, then you're going to be fine. Start talking cool, high-tech, better-than-yours and cost me a fortune, and you're definitely out there for the wrong reasons. Here are a few essentials I like to pack along.

CAMP STOVES

Fire or stove? I once guided for a very traditional outfitting company. They insisted that I cook all three meals a day on a campfire. It absolutely made no sense. I must have spent close to four hours a day cooking. The group's paddling time was obviously reduced considerably because of this. Also, due to the hazards of cooking over an open flame, I served burnt offerings to the clients more often than not. But the biggest issue about using a campfire rather than a cook stove was that when traveling in

◀ *"You can't cook a decent fish cake without a good camp grill."*

the busier canoe areas it was next to impossible to find enough dry wood to boil up a pot of water for tea, let alone cook three full-course meals a day.

Now don't get me wrong. I'm not trying to start one of those age-old fire-versus-stove debates. I'm not one of those campers who insists on everyone huddling around a candle lantern at night, gawking up at the stars, rather than gathering around the warmth of a cozy campfire. I believe that campfires are a key ingredient to any outdoor trip, and that the process of extracting and refining stove fuel can be just as harmful to the environment as collecting a bundle of dead wood from the forest floor. I just prefer cooking on a camp stove, that's all.

So, halfway through the summer I began packing a small camp stove, without the consent of my employer, and by the end of the season I had every other guide doing the same. Eventually, the owner of the company broke down and ordered in half a dozen stoves.

Recognizing the benefits of cooking on a camp stove rather than a campfire is much simpler than figuring out which stove to buy. You've got your two-burners and single-burners. You've got gas-fueled, liquid-fueled and multi-fueled. There are stoves that need to be primed and some that switch on with an electronic ignition. You have some stoves that cost a small fortune, and some homemade versions that can be made out of a tuna can and a piece of cardboard.

Here's a general breakdown to help you decide which one to purchase, based mainly on fuel types, boiling times, and cost.

Butane

So many campers find butane models such as the Camping Gaz Turbo ideal. It is a clean-burning, reliable and trouble-free stove, and operates on a pressurized canister (butane) that is attached to the stove and punctured to let loose the vaporized gas. The flame can be controlled easily and set at a simmer, unlike many of the other stove models. It also sells at a good price. The only disadvantage, apart from butane not working well in cold temperatures, is that you have to carry the empty canisters out with you and drop them off at a designated recycling center (finding replacement canisters at outdoor stores can also be an issue). The problem with the empty canisters is that far too many people don't even bother carrying them out, let alone recycling them. Personally, I've found enough empty butane canisters left behind out there, usually thrown down an outhouse hole, to believe that these types of stoves should be totally banned from the interior. They're great for car camping or a weekend jaunt in the summer, but in no way do they make sense for wilderness travel.

▲ *Left: Primus (butane/propane) stove. Right: Swiss Trangia (alcohol) stove.*

Propane

Propane outperforms butane in cold temperatures. It also produces one of the cleanest flames, which is also incredibly easy to adjust. The stove owners still have to deal with the empty canister dilemma; however, propane stoves such as the Coleman Two Burner make a good, inexpensive stove for car camping. But don't pack one into the interior: it's big and heavy.

Butane/Propane

This blend of fuel offers a much higher octane performance than butane alone, which means it will run in temperatures as low as 14 degrees F (-10 C). A butane/propane stove such as the Coleman Peak or the Primus is also more compact than the regular propane stoves, easy to light and control, and has a quiet burner. Again, it has the problem with replacement cylinders. The cost of the stove, and each cylinder, are also a little too high for my liking.

Alcohol

It's not that easy to find these stoves anymore. But in the mid-1980s almost every Scout group owned a Swiss Trangia. The stoves came equipped with a set of easy-to-clean nesting pots and a nonstick frying pan. More important, the stove ran on alcohol instead of a petroleum product. This made it one of the most environmentally friendly stoves available. It's got a big price tag, though. It also has too short a burning time to cook an entire meal without refueling, and takes more than ten minutes to boil a pot of water. The very worst, however, is the added danger of having to reach into the stove, slide a metal disc over the burner, and adjust a flame you can hardly see. Not my personal choice of stove, but I know people who swear by them.

White Gas

White gas is my personal choice (it was also what the owner of the outfitting company went for). The stove models (for example, Optimus Climber, Optimus Hunter, Coleman Feather One, MSR) are more expensive than

▲ *The Optimus Hunter is one of the most reliable stoves out there.*

most other fuel-type designs. However, since white gas is relatively inexpensive to buy, and there are no separate cylinders to purchase, they are actually less expensive in the long run. White-gas stoves also require priming, which can be a real hassle. But they're also far more efficient in cold temperatures. For most models it's possible to spend a bit more and have them burn more than one type of fuel (i.e., unleaded gas, kerosene, diesel or jet fuel). However, unless you're going to countries where white gas is unavailable, this option is a waste of money.

The real trick to using white gas is figuring out which model is best for you. To help, here's a look at a few models I've tried over the years.

Optimus Hunter 8R I picked one of these up at a garage sale for $5. Clearly the previous owner had no idea how valuable the stove was. A new model would go for well over $100. I also had no idea why someone would sell such a stove. Since its first patent in 1927, the Optimus stove has never seemed to break down and is one of the most reliable white-gas stoves available. It's easy to set up and brings water to a boil in good time. My only complaint is the weight, and that it has one of the most rudimentary priming procedures ever invented.

Coleman Feather One This is one of the best stoves for the money. There's also an assortment of models, ranging from multi-fuel types to lightweight models with a separate attachable gas cylinder. It does a reasonable job of getting the meal cooked in a hurry, especially with the windscreen attachment.

▲ *Left: Optimus Climber (white gas) stove.*
Right: Coleman Feather One (white gas) stove.

Winter Storage

Before you put your white-gas stove away for the winter, take time out to fill the tank up with fuel, add a capful of carburetor cleaner, and then burn the stove dry. The carburetor cleaner should do a good job of cleaning the fuel jet.

It's stable, with wide-stance legs. The flame is also easy to adjust, which is why it's one of the best models for slow cooking and baking. Coleman's ad campaign, "We've made them easy to use and hard to abuse," also holds true. The only problem is that if they actually do end up breaking down on a trip, it's almost impossible to fix them.

MSR Whisperlite/Dragonfly I just recently upgraded from an MSR (Mountain Safety Research) Whisperlite to the advanced MSR Dragonfly. Both stoves are praised for being extremely light, efficient (boils a pot of water in three minutes), and easy to repair in the field. But the Whisperlite had no flame control at all. It was either off or on full throttle. The new Dragonfly model, with its innovative dual-valve design, doesn't have that problem at all. But like the Whisperlite, it still is a pain to prime. I've singed far too many eyebrow hairs due to its constant flare-ups. It is also extremely loud. Seriously, you can't even hear yourself think when this thing is on.

▲ *The MSR Whisperlite (left) lacks good flame control. If you do a lot of baking, choose the MSR Dragonfly (right).*

Stove Repair Tip

Don't use the old white gas that's been sitting in your garage all winter. (Be sure to dispose of it at a proper recycling center.) Splurge on a fresh container. It will greatly improve your stove's performance and eliminate the need to repair the stove when you need it most.

▲ *Cooking with a camp stove eliminates the hassle of searching out available firewood, especially in overused areas.*

How Much Fuel Do I Bring Along?

The amount of fuel required has so many variables: fuel type, air temperature, wind and design of windscreen used, maximum heat output (BTU) of the stove, even the type of pots and pans used. Overall, however, the best way to judge your fuel consumption is to plan forty minutes of cooking time for dinner and twenty minutes for preparing a hot breakfast. Let's say you're going on a five-day trip. That adds up to four dinners (two hours and forty minutes of burning time) and four breakfasts (one hour and twenty minutes). Now add an extra hour for a couple of hot soups for lunch or an unexpected cold-weather snap that will rob you of extra fuel. So, to be on the safe side, you can say you need a little more than five hours of fuel for a five-day trip. If your stove runs on white gas and burns quick and hot like the MSR models, with a pump or fuel bottle it will use up a 1-quart (1L) bottle of fuel every three days, which means you bring 2 quarts for five days to be on the safe side. If you have butane or propane stoves, which run on pressurized canisters, then two canisters should be enough, with a little to spare.

Is It Done Yet?

There's no need to keep lifting the pot lid to see if the water is boiling yet. To increase boiling time, and to save fuel, position the pot lid on upside down and place a small amount of water in the depression. When the water in the lid begins to form small bubbles, then the water inside the pot has reached a rolling boil.

Reducing Flare-Ups

A flare-up, which happens only on stoves fueled by white gas or kerosene, is a large yellow flame that forces everyone in camp to run for cover while the stove operator fiddles with the control to reduce it to a much safer, stunted blue flame. This occurs when liquid gas exits the stove while the burner is cold. To control this on stoves such as the MSR Whisperlite or Dragonfly, make sure to put enough fuel in the priming cup and check that it has almost burned away (to properly preheat the burner), before turning the switch to "on." Stoves that have no priming cup are ignited by spraying a mixture of air and gas into the chamber below the burner, ready to be set alight. To have the mixture properly exit the stove, you must pump up the stove enough to create pressure to form the spray. If it's not pumped enough, then liquid fuel leaks into the chamber, flooding and then flaring up until the extra fuel burns off. Once the flame calms down, the stove's pressure must be pumped back up before a second attempt is made.

More Stove Tips

Canister Stoves The main problem with canister stoves is that they don't like working in cold temperatures. Not only are they difficult to start, but when the stove is turned on, the temperature of the liquefied gas in the canister drops significantly. As the fuel evaporates to feed the burner, the fuel remaining in the canister cools to a point where it has difficulty evaporating, so the flow of gas to the burner is limited.

- Warm the cylinder up by placing it under your armpit for a few minutes or rubbing it in your palms. Storing it in your sleeping bag during the day can also be a plus. If frost forms on the canister itself, stand it in a dish of cold water and agitate the water slightly. This will stop the canister from cooling below 32 degrees F (zero Celsius).
- Try to boil when the canister is full and simmer when it's nearly empty. The full canister has greater mass, so the cooling of the liquefied gas is less of a problem. And the close-to-empty canister doesn't put out much gas while simmering, making cooling less of an issue.

▲ *Flare-ups are a common occurrence with all white gas stoves.*

Don't Singe Your Eyebrows!

If you're worried about getting too close to the flare-up when lighting a gas stove, save your eyebrows by using a utility lighter.

- If at all possible, attempt to boil small amounts of water at one time. The stove will then only push for peak output for a few minutes and not allow enough time for the liquid gas in the canister to cool down.
- Wind is just as much an issue with canister stoves as it is with white gas; however, watch that the windshield is tall enough to protect the entire stove without allowing the canister to heat up.

White Gas Stoves Wind can rob the stove of unbelievable amounts of fuel. Make sure to place an aluminum windscreen around and under the stove — even on warm, windless days, the screen will cook up dinner far more quickly.

- Only fill the fuel container to three quarters. No pressure can be created if it's full, and the stove will refuse to light properly.
- Make sure to oil or replace the rubber gaskets inside the pressure cap at least once a season. After continual use the gaskets have a tendency to break down and leak. To check for leakage, squirt a drop of liquid detergent around the pressure cap. If bubbles form, you have a problem.
- Make sure to pack along replacement parts and a mini toolkit for the stove. To help familiarize yourself with your stove, as well as to help you fix it when the darn thing breaks down, it helps to take the stove completely apart and put it back together again prior to your trip.
- Some models may need priming paste to light the stove when it's cold outside.

SLEEPING BAGS

Consider What You Need

A cozy night's sleep is absolutely priceless after a long day on the trail. I suffered for years shivering away in a cheap, bulky bag, and grew jealous of my other campmates who had saved up enough for a high-quality sleeping bag. Thankfully, however, a friend borrowed it for a weekend of camping and accidentally burned it to a crisp while trying to dry it over the campfire. I wasn't too pleased at first. I mean really, who the heck would try to dry out a sleeping bag over open flames? But it was as good an excuse as any for me to finally upgrade.

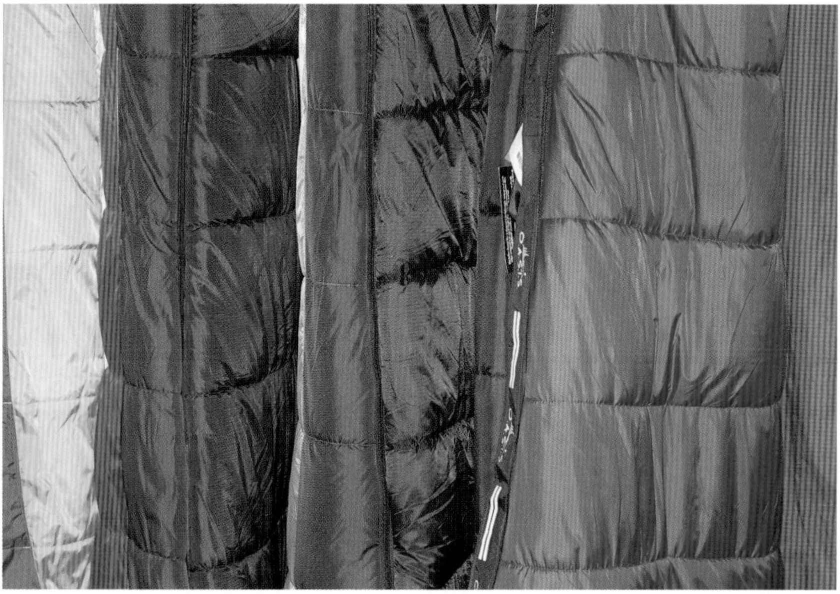

▲ *Shopping for the perfect sleeping bag can leave even the most experienced camper dazed and confused.*

The main problem with my original bag was that it was only suited for midsummer snoozing. I needed a good three-season bag, something rated for 15 to 20 degrees F (-12 to -7 C). I also went for the mummy bag shape rather than rectangular. The original square-shaped bag is well-suited to people who squirm around a lot while sleeping. The mummy bag, however, offers less space to heat up and cuts the weight down half a pound at least. Of course it was a little more complicated to zip it up to another person's bag (that being my wife's), whereas rectangular bags can be easily attached to each another. With a mummy bag I had to make sure my wife's bag had an opposite zipper. It's not a perfect system either — I found that only extended mummy bags had left zippers and regular-sized bags had right zippers (and our feet had to be separate since the two bags didn't zip up completely together!).

Homemade Liner

To rid the sleeping bag of that clammy feeling when you crawl in, insert a homemade liner. Simply fold a regular cotton or fleece bedsheet in half, sew the bottom and halfway up the open side. Insert the liner with the half-sewn side toward the zipper. The extra weight is minimal and the liner adds extra warmth for early- and late-season camping. It can also be easily removed for cleaning.

"No mystery here: If it packs small and keeps you warm, it's good enough."

CLIFF JACOBSON, *CANOEING WILD RIVERS* (1984)

Sleeping Bag Maintenance

After spending a small fortune on a high-quality bag, I'm also determined to keep it as long as possible. So, apart from never letting my friend borrow it so he can singe it over the campfire, as soon as the trip is over I hang the bag out in the sun to dry. Sunshine and fresh air is the best way to keep bad smells from lingering. And whenever I'm not using the bag it's stored in an oversized storage bag or hung up on a hanger. If the bag is left constantly compressed, it will eventually lose its loft and start collecting mildew.

To wash my bag I definitely stay away from dry cleaners, as their powerful solvents will destroy the insulation. I also stay away from my washer at home, a top-loading machine that dances across the floor when turned on that would certainly twist my bag to pieces. The downtown laundromat's front-loading washing machine is what I use. It temperately tumble washes the bag around when placed on gentle cycle in cold water.

To dry the bag in the dryer I set it on low or just shake it out well and hang it out to dry. I've heard that some campers even place tennis balls inside the bag while it's drying. It's supposed to keep the loft intact. It's worth a try, I guess, but it sure opens you up to some odd questions if someone catches you doing it.

Solving the Insulation Debate

Choosing the insulation was the most complex thing I've ever had to deal with when buying a new piece of camp gear; the debate over down and synthetic bags is a very complex one. One store owner had me convinced that down (the soft plumage of a goose or duck) is lighter, warmer and can be compressed far more than any synthetic bag. Another store owner was strongly against using down and much preferred synthetic bags (Polarguard 3D being the more popular model). He informed me that if I ever got a down bag wet its insulation ability would be reduced more than 80 percent; however, if a synthetic bag gets wet, it retains most of its loft and continues to keep you warm. They're also resistant to mildew, are better for people who suffer from allergies, can be cleaned much more easily and have a much lower sales price.

In the end I went for the down bag. I also splurged on a model that had a strip of fabric behind the zipper to stop it catching (I absolutely hate when

▲ *A good sleeping bag means nothing if you don't have a dry, flat spot to sleep on.*

that happens), a miniature pocket for my miniature alarm clock, and of course, a good quality waterproof storage bag.

Sleeping Pads

Gone are the days when a camper layers the floor of the tent with a bed of conifer boughs. Not only is it bad for the environment, it's also not the most comfortable sleeping arrangement. Now for a cozy night's sleep, a plastic tarp or nylon groundsheet is placed on the inside of the tent, followed by either a foam sleeping pad or foam-filled air mattress (Therm-a-Rest). I'd

Insulation Alternative

Make sure to fill the dead-air space in your sleeping bag with next day's change of clothes before going to bed at night. Not only will the clothes add more insulation, the clothing will be a lot warmer to put on in the morning.

A Stitch in Time . . .

For greater warmth take note of how close the stitching is on the bag; the closer the stitching the more effective the insulation.

▲ *Peter and Scott prepare to sleep "between a rock and a hard place."*

spend the extra money and purchase the Therm-a-Rest (especially the ones that double as a camp chair). The simple strips of open or closed foam are okay, but they're a little bulky in your pack and don't seem to help eliminate back pain as much as the fancier models. Also, make sure to construct your own cotton shell cover for your sleeping pad, as the regular slippery nylon covers will slide out from under you, and there's nothing worse than waking up in the morning to find the pad halfway across the tent floor.

How to Repair a Leaky Air Mattress

When a self-inflating mattress springs a leak, it's usually impossible to figure out where the puncture is. You can squeeze the air out and listen for a telltale hiss, but for the best results, blow the mattress up, submerge it under water, and watch for air bubbles. Once you've found and marked the leak, follow these instructions:

- Place a pot of water on the camp stove to boil.
- Clean the area with an alcohol swab from your first-aid kit.
- Open the valve on the mattress.
- Most self-inflating mattresses come with their own patch material (a strip of duct tape is a good short-term substitute). Cut the patch, making sure it's at least triple the size of the hole and has rounded edges to stop it from peeling off.
- Glob on a liberal amount of seam sealer to the puncture area.
- Place the patch on the adhesive and then set the pot of boiled water on top to act as a quick sealer.
- Leave the pot on the patch until the water cools.

How Is Body Heat Lost?

RADIATION • Over 30 percent of body heat can be lost by not having your head covered. Wear a wool toque to bed or purchase a sleeping bag with a hood.

RESPIRATION • Breathing in cold air and breathing out warm can give you extreme chills, so make sure to purchase a tent with good ventilation.

EVAPORATION • The body can lose 1.5 pints (1L) of water overnight. Drink warm liquids before going to bed.

CONVECTION • Dead-air space on exposed skin can chill the body. Make sure your sleeping bag is snug.

TRANSMISSION • Having contact with the cold ground can zap an incredible amount of body heat. Use a high-quality sleeping pad.

PACKS

Hiking Backpacks

An external-frame backpack has a lightweight aluminum or aluminum alloy frame outside the main body that holds your equipment. As the frame is external, the weight of your gear is held away from your body and is evenly distributed between your shoulders and hips. Since the load is held up on a frame, however, the pack will tend to sway back and forth while you walk along the trail, decreasing your freedom of movement. The majority of backpackers are now switching to internal-frame packs, which place the weight snug against your back. With the load hugging your body it's much easier to scramble up a hillside or cross-country ski across a frozen lake without losing your balance. The disadvantage of short-term comfort, however, is long-term back pain.

▲ *Most backpackers prefer an internal-frame pack to an external-frame pack.*

▲ *It's not what you carry, it's how you carry it that's important.*

Given the variety of both external- and internal-frame backpacks, along with the assorted travel packs, rucksacks, and converted luggage bags, the only safe advice I can give to help pick an appropriate pack is to ask yourself if the pack is for short weekend jaunts, a month-long hiking expedition, or just some leisure time spent hitchhiking across Europe. How much gear has to be stored on your back? And how much room is left on your credit card?

In the store, make sure to properly size the pack to your weight and build. If you purchase a cheaper, one-size-fits-all pack, make sure the adjustment straps have a little give. A hip belt should conform to your hips, not your hips to the belt. Padded shoulder straps should have extra padding that provides comfortable cushioning and shape retention. Before you hike out with your new purchase, ask the salesperson to load the pack up with weight, and walk around the store, just to make sure it's nice and snug. Out on the trail is no place to discover you've made the wrong choice.

Canoe Packs

You'd think choosing a canoe pack, since it's generally only used for carrying a large volume of gear for a short period of time, would be quite a simple task. It's the complete opposite, however. There's an endless assortment of designs and models, and each one seems to have a bunch of overzealous followers who think their system for hauling equipment around is far better than all the rest. Here's a general breakdown, but just remember that no matter which one you pick I can guarantee that a fellow canoeist will take the time out to challenge your selection when you meet on the trail.

Canvas Packs The canvas pack, more commonly known as the "Duluth Pack," has been claimed by some canoeists to be the most traditional canoe pack, and their story is hard to beat. After all, the original patent by Camille Poirer (a shoestore owner in Duluth, Minnesota) dates as far back as 1882.

The traditional canvas pack (left) and pack basket (right) have one huge advantage over the rest of the the pack choices — they look great in photos.

It came with a buckled flap, fancy leather shoulder straps, a conventional tumpline (a strap running from the top of the head to the bottom of the pack), a new-age sternum strap, and even an umbrella holder. Woods Canada also produced a similar style of pack in 1909. Both styles haven't changed much since.

The canvas pack is a large-volume, frameless pack, with almost unlimited space to stuff things in. They fit perfectly in a canoe. They're also extremely durable and can take years of abuse. They absolutely won't break, period.

However, other canoeists think that canvas packs are a thing of the past — a sack with straps used only by a bunch of nostalgia freaks who force themselves to be uncomfortable for the sake of tradition. The canvas eventually rots, the leather breaks down, and it's impossible to waterproof your gear without using layer after layer of heavy-duty garbage bags.

I'm not sure who's right. There's no doubt that better bags have been designed since 1882. But I will say that I've abused mine for over twenty years now and it's still going strong.

Pack Basket The woven ash pack basket is still used extensively in Maine and the Adirondacks. It's another one of those traditional packs that doesn't make much sense to many canoeists. These packs are not waterproof and can be quite uncomfortable to carry; however, I've used one for years. Pack baskets are hard to beat for keeping fragile gear from breaking or those gawky items from jabbing you in the spine. Of course, they're not as effective as a barrel pack (see page 40), but they sure are nicer to look at.

Wanigan Another age-old packing device is the wanigan. The word, loosely translated, comes from the Native term for "kitchen," and many youth camps are devoted to it for that very reason. The wanigan makes an excellent storage bin for a large group's cook set. Basically, it's a wooden box, usually made of quarter-inch (0.6 cm) plywood measuring 25 inches long, 12 inches wide, and 15 inches deep (64 by 30 by 38 cm) that's used to carry all the pots, pans, utensils and some food items. The lid makes a perfect cutting board, and the box itself comes in handy as a serving table. It's a perfect system for keeping everything organized, eliminates shuffling through packs for last-minute items, protects breakables, fits snugly in the canoe, and will even float in the event of an upset. The portaging technique also makes good use of the tumpline, a system that's considered by many expert canoeists the only true way to carry a heavy load across the trail. You just place the tump on your head, making sure not to rest it directly on your forehead or so far back that the weight wrenches your neck muscles. If only kitchen gadgets are stored in the box then it's usually light enough to even toss a small canvas pack on top as well.

▲ *The best way to take a wanigan across a lengthy portage is to have someone else carry it for you.*

I made good use of a wanigan while working for a traditional camp in the Temagami region. I'll be honest though, I hope to never see one again. Some of the guides swore by them, I swore at them. I could never understand the reasoning for carrying a big, heavy wooden box with only a strip of leather lashed across your head. To each his own, I guess.

Barrels The plastic olive barrel is today's waterproof version of a wanigan. In the mid-1980s a few canoeists began picking them up at yard sales or delicatessens after realizing that the watertight containers were perfect for keeping gear dry, especially on river trips. Now you can pick them up at almost any outdoor store. Just like using the traditional wanigan, however, it's a love-hate relationship. The barrel has all the advantages of the conventional wooden box — even having the lid serve as a cutting board — but in no way is the thing comfortable to carry. At least it doesn't rely exclusively on a tumpline system. The barrel comes with shoulder straps, or can be slipped inside an old canvas pack. I strongly recommend, however, that you pay the extra cost for a high-quality barrel harness, like Ostrom Packs' Voyager model. You'll thank me when you hit the portage.

When purchasing a barrel, make sure the O-ring seal and the metal snap ring that fastens the lid are not damaged. Also, get the ones that come with handles; they make it a lot easier to get the barrels in and out of the canoe. Stores usually sell them in 8- or 16-gallon (30 or 60 L) sizes.

You can also pick up smaller surplus olive barrels by visiting any place that buys olives in bulk (large chain grocery stores, delicatessens, restaurants). Either ask for them or wait until garbage day and pick them out of the recycle bin! Two of them, resting side-by-side in a regular canoe pack, works well. I also place my sleeping pad between the barrels and my back for more comfort. They have a screw-on top with a rubber washer, making the container waterproof. But the opening is a little too tight for my liking.

▲ *Small surplus olive barrels are completely waterproof and can usually be found free of charge any place olives are sold in bulk.*

▲ *Using a barrel to carry gear is like using the traditional wanigan: it's a love-hate relationship.*

Internal-Frame Hiking Backpack An internal-frame hiking backpack isn't necessarily used by canoeists. The frame itself always seem to make the pack fit oddly inside the canoe, taking up way too much valuable space. However, a backpack happens to be fantastic to carry on the portage. Some solo canoeists even find it a perfect option when attempting to carry the canoe and pack together in one trip. So, if you think about it, there's no strong reasoning behind not using one, especially if that's the only kind of pack you happen to own.

▲ *A nylon pack (left) or a waterproof carrying pack (right) are two very comfortable ways to haul your gear over the portage.*

Nylon Packs In the past few years there's been a lot of hype about high-tech nylon canoe packs. They're based on one main compartment rather than several separate pockets, like a backpack. But they still come with a top-notch system of shoulder straps and a hip belt, making them just as comfortable to carry as a top-of-the line internal-frame hiking pack. Lots of buckles and straps help compact everything and keep the weight centralized. An individual waterproof sack keeps everything dry. And because there are so many companies developing different models, prices seem to stay competitive as well. The only thing they don't have going for them is tradition. However, my custom-made Ostrom pack, the 26-gallon (115 L) Wabikimi design I purchased just a year ago, is such an excellent product that I'm positive it's destined to create its own legacy. It's one of the most durable and comfortable-fitting canoe packs on the market.

Waterproof Packs Rather than using various bagging devices to waterproof gear inside the pack, you can now purchase a pack that's already waterproof. PVC-coated packs were first made by Cascade Design and developed by Dennis Hill of the Seattle Sports camping equipment company. Hill, while hospitalized for a knee injury, was inspired to combine the roll-down closure on an ice pack placed on his knee with the bottom design of a grocery bag.

Packs for Women

A woman's physique is obviously different from a man's. So why is it that so many companies ignore this when manufacturing packs? Thankfully things are beginning to change. Some businesses make specific packs for women. However, fitting a pack is more a matter of matching pack size and shape to body size and shape, not gender. Still, it doesn't hurt to take note of these main differences:

- Women tend to have narrower shoulders and therefore tend to need narrower shoulder straps.
- Women typically require a shorter torso length and need a pack with a shorter frame.
- Women's hips do not generally fit well into a man's waist strap. They need more curve or flare to the hip belt. The hip belt also needs to be narrower, since the distance between a woman's ribs and hips is shorter than a man's.
- Women's center of gravity is lower, and an external pack design needs to be mounted lower on the frame.

The pack uses a suspension system reminiscent of internal-frame backpacks. It offers detachable, padded shoulder straps and an anatomically shaped, padded hip belt. The only thing it lacks is a padded back and vertical stays, making it extremely uncomfortable to carry with a heavy load. And due to the fact that the PVC coating keeps the pack from breathing, your dirty socks will smell up the interior something fierce.

Packing Your Pack

A few years back I helped lead a group of high-school students on a week-long hiking trip. It was their first backpacking trip, so I made sure to spend some quality time going over important tips with them before heading out, including how to properly pack a backpack. Disappointingly, however, the pre-trip planning seemed like a waste of time. We weren't even an hour from the trail head when they starting complaining about all the weight strapped to their backs.

I called a break and began checking each student's pack to see if I could suggest ways to lessen their load. Some had only cheap hand-me-down packs. But, on average, the design of the pack wasn't a huge issue. Neither was the fact that a few too many had completely ignored my advice (leave all the nonessentials at home). It was how they packed their gear that actually was causing bruised shoulders and lower back pain.

The method used to load up your gear depends a lot on the style of pack used. For an external pack it's better to keep the weight low to help keep your balance. But for an internal pack, or even a canoe pack, the

Equipment for Two Canoeists

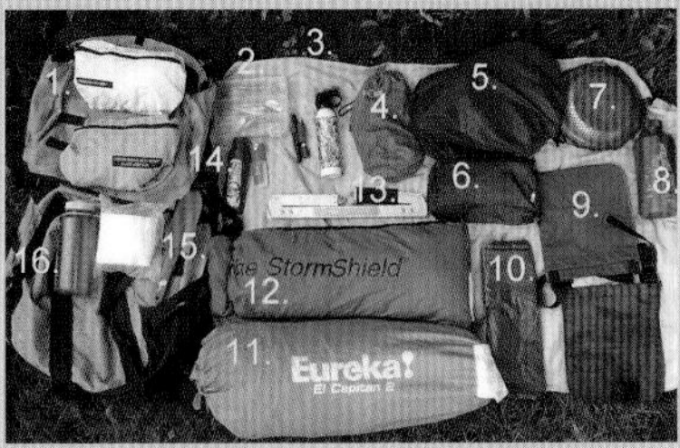

Contents of first pack:

1. bug jacket
2. assorted fishing lures
3. bear spray and bear bangers
4. water filter
5. cooking pots and camp stove
6. kitchen cutlery
7. Outback Oven
8. stove fuel (white gas)
9. pole holder for center of tarp
10. plastic ground sheet
11. two-person tent
12. rain tarp
13. saw
14. bug repellent and sunscreen
15. T.P. and trowel
16. water jug

Contents of second pack:

1. Therm-a-rest with compact chair
2. Therm-a-rest
3. sleeping bag (synthetic)
4. sleeping bag (down)
5. clothes
6. partner's clothes
7. camera equipment in waterproof Pelican case
8. repair kit, flashlight and odds and ends
9. first-aid kit
10. two rain suits
11. rope for hanging food from bears

weight must be kept to the middle. Since the design is made to hug the body more, the weight is kept closer to the center of gravity. That means the sleeping bag and clothes go first. Then the cook set, food, stove and fuel bottle are placed in the middle. Just make sure not to have a hard-edged frying pan or a plastic peanut butter container jabbing you in the spine.

The lighter items, along with gear you'll need in a hurry (such as rain jacket, camp shoes, extra socks and camera) then get layered on top or get stuffed into all the empty corners or gaps and spaces found along the edge. The tent goes last, due to the fact that it's usually the first thing you unpack when arriving at camp and the last item that goes away. The more separate waterproof sacks, resealable containers or even garbage bags the better;

they keep everything waterproof and organized. Your sleeping bag and clothes, the two bulkiest items, should also be stored in compression bags (a stuff sack with straps on the side that cinch down to reduce the size). Most backpacks come with small side pouches. These are great for all the odds and ends: map, compass, bug repellent, water bottle, sunglasses, first-aid kit and munchies. Just make sure not to dangle your favorite camp mug, or anything else for that matter, on the outside of the pack. It will eventually free itself and become lost forever. And make sure that roll of toilet paper is handy — you never know when nature will call.

How to Lighten Your Load

I believe that all outdoor enthusiasts go through various stages in preparing and packing for their trips. Usually they begin by taking almost everything imaginable. Then, after a few years of pain and suffering, they most likely give up packing beyond the essentials and either learn ways to cut down the weight considerably or just give up on tripping altogether. If they do decide to continue on, they'll definitely stop toting such a meager existence and go back to loading up on some luxury items.

There's nothing wrong with any of these particular strategies. What is important is to understand which one best reflects the reasons you're out there in the first place, and then match it accordingly.

Which level am I? At this point in my life I'm beyond my earlier days of packing silly, useless items, such as a latrine shovel or a separate wardrobe for each and every day. But I've also left all that ultra-light weirdness behind. No longer do I remove the cardboard roll from the center of the toilet paper, cut the end off my toothbrush, or trim down the edges of my topographic maps. I'm somewhere in between, and would rather do a double carry across a portage if it means having an extra glass of wine at dinner or relaxing on a cozy camp chair while watching the sun set.

A Few Points from the Pros

- It's recommended that the weight of your pack be no more than 33 percent of your own body weight. You might push it to 40 percent, but that's going to hurt a lot. That said, voyageurs were known for carrying well over their full body weight. So what are you complaining about?
- If your camping partner constantly complains about the weight of his pack, and you happen to be carrying the biggest part of the load, it is common practice to toss a few rocks into his pack when he's not looking. It works every time.
- To a canoeist, a hiking trail is just a really long portage.

P. G. Downes

P. G. Downes, author of *Sleeping Islands,* wrote "To travel at all, one must travel fast. To travel fast, one must travel light." He packed this meager equipment list for his 1939 canoe trip from Pelican Narrows, Saskatchewan, to Nueltin Lake Post, Northwest Territories:

- lightweight feather sleeping bag (8 lb.)
- axe (manufactured in 1811)
- copper tea pail of unknown age
- two shirts, one with the tail badly scorched
- medical kit consisting of a small bottle of iodine done up in adhesive tape and some surgical needles
- a 7-by-9-foot piece of balloon silk – used for a tent and a sail
- some twine
- trolling hooks
- collapsible frying pan and spoon
- jackknife
- stout pack with leather tump to carry everything in

What I do is look at each trip individually and then decide what to bring along. After all, there's a big difference between a portage-free canoe trip and one where you have to drag all your gear from lake to lake, and the essential gear differs considerably for a weekend hike in the summer and a month-long trek in the winter.

What also helps is to learn to embrace various tripping techniques, and at the same time purchase all the new-age lightweight gear that you can possibly afford. Here are a few tips that seem to work for me when trying to find a balance between comfort and minimalism:

- The major bulk inside your pack usually comes from three essential items: tent, sleeping bag, and clothes. When it comes to tents your choice is simple — aim for the smallest and lightest you can afford and spend more quality time huddled under a rain tarp during foul weather. Go for the down-filled rather than synthetic when comparison shopping for sleeping bags; the down bag is unmatched when it comes to warmth, weight and its ability to be compressed to the size of a miniature football. Just make sure it's packed in a watertight stuff sack. The amount and type of clothing is a little more complex. Your choice of garments is totally dependant on the season. You have to bring an extra fleece, long johns and wool toque during spring and fall outings. In this case, remember to choose clothing with the highest possible performance-to-weight ratio. In warm summer conditions, however, you only need to pack one extra set of clothes. That's all you'll really need. Just hope for a hot, sunny day halfway through your trip so you can do laundry.
- The weight of cookware can also add up, especially for a large group. The problem is that most of what you bring is essential. Items such as a camp stove, fuel, and cooking pots are indispensable. There are ways to limit the

weight, however. First, spend the extra money and purchase the lightest stove possible and make good use of a windscreen to reduce your fuel consumption. Second, a cheap lightweight pot set bought at a discount store is a far better bet than one of those new-aged titanium sets. You can pack a fork if you want, but each person needs only a plastic spoon and a handy Swiss Army knife for eating. Scrub pads can also be left at home — they end up becoming a breeding ground for bacteria anyway. A handful of pine needles and sand works just as well and is far more sanitary.

- Food can add up. But if you keep to homemade dehydrated food for at least 80 percent of your meals you can really reduce the weight of your food pack. This doesn't necessarily take away the taste either. I've made better dinners out there than in the comfort of my own kitchen. And, just as in grocery shopping, don't pack your food when you're hungry. Keep portions for staples like rice and noodles to a science, and measure.
- The final and probably best advice is to place every item in your pack that you would normally bring along on a trip. Then weigh the pack on a good-quality scale. Now, take everything back out, and begin considering which items could be left at home or replaced by a newer and lighter version. Take special note of all those little extras you decide to pack along, as they can cause real problems. You don't think they mean much, but when added together, all those gadgets and gizmos can really put on the pounds. Start off by thinking multitasking — each item should have two or more jobs. Also, limit the size of containers of sunscreen, toothpaste and bug repellent. You'll never go through it all on one trip. So use smaller containers or shop for those convenient trial packs. Store-bought first-aid kits also have a tendency to have lots of useless items. By making your own you not only reduce the weight but you produce a much better kit. A repair kit can be made of duct tape and one of those handy multi-tools. A pocket-size disposable camera can easily replace a 35 mm single lens reflex camera if you're just taking photos to share with friends and family. A small orienteering compass is just as good as a Global Positioning System (GPS) if you're traveling in a well-used area. A monocular can easily replace binoculars. Light-emitting diode (LED) headlights are far superior to packing along cheap flashlights that need extra bulbs and a supply of AA batteries.

Stress Relief

A hike in the woods has proven to be very effective in treating people for common anxiety and depression disorders. It creates a steady rate of spirited breathing and a release of endorphins that can positively affect moods.

DAY HIKING

Whether you're lounging around an organized campground or spending a week trekking through the interior, make sure to keep a day free for breaking away from your regular itinerary. Some of my favorite times have been spent clambering up a hilltop behind camp to view the surrounding landscape or walking to some isolated trout pond in search of a trophy fish. At times I even think that heading out from home to take a walk through the local park can be just as uplifting. After all, a day hike has that one advantage that can't be ignored; if anything bad happens, like a rainstorm or being attacked by hordes of mosquitoes, the pain and suffering can be easily ended by walking back to the car and driving home.

Take note, however, that even though it's easier to escape the elements while out on a day hike, this is definitely not an excuse to go out unprepared. The well-equipped day pack, weighing somewhere between 10 and 12 pounds (4.5 to 5.5 kg), should contain enough gear to help battle bugs, blistering sun, sudden storms, and an unexpected night in the woods.

Items for a Day Pack

- rain jacket and rain pants
- extra sweater or fleece top
- spare socks
- sunscreen and lip balm
- hat
- sunglasses
- bug repellent
- Swiss Army knife
- nutritious lunch (plus a few high-energy snacks)
- butane lighter and waterproof matches
- water bottle
- flashlight
- lightweight nylon tarp and ball of twine
- map and compass
- whistle

Optional gear:

- binoculars
- journal
- fishing gear
- camera
- paperback novel
- walking stick

TENTS

The basic aim when purchasing a tent is to choose the one that is lightest and smallest when packed but spacious enough for occupants and gear. You also want it to shed water without serious leaking, hold together during hurricane winds, be well ventilated, and be a breeze to set up. Basically, buying the perfect tent is not easy! What is possible, however, is to choose a tent that at least meets the needs of your type of camping as well as your pocketbook.

▲ *The bigger the better when choosing a tent for campground camping.*

So where to start? First, what type of camping are you most likely to do? The bigger the better if it's just car camping for the weekend. Just make sure it has a good fly system that gives full weather protection but also excellent ventilation. It should also be easy to set up and provide sleeping space for at least six people. Huge, oversized vestibules are a great addition, or splurge for a separate screen house with no-see-um netting and the most rugged aluminum pole set you can afford.

If you are heading to the interior it becomes a little more complicated. There is no roomy tent that is light to carry. So you must decide what is more important to you: space or weight. Backpackers should obviously go for the smallest and lightest tent possible. It's going to be a tight fit, but you also have to lug the darn thing around all day. Canoeists, however, only have to worry about the weight issue while portaging, and can usually get away with something with a little more elbow room. Winter campers really need to choose carefully. They need a sturdy structure, with at least three poles and tough fabric that can withstand snow loads and heavy winds. Good ventilation is also a key factor.

Tents come in all shapes and sizes, all of which have their merits. You've got the cabin style, which is extremely roomy but strictly for campground use. Then there's the A-frame or "pup tent." It's a classic design that gives you lots of headroom and works well for large canoe groups. But make sure it's well staked down during heavy winds. There's also the oddball tunnel tent. Its hoop design is reminiscent of the old covered wagon, giving you a light, compact tent with maximum floor space. It's not without its disadvantages, though. Most types are not free-standing and can feel quite flimsy when a strong wind hits the wrong way. My choice is the geodesic dome. Its crossing-pole structure makes it free-standing (perfect for pitching on top of solid granite) and quite stable in a windstorm. It also gives you the best space-to-weight ratio.

The fabric used is also an important feature. Most designs have the fly (basically your tent's rain parka) made of polyester. Compared to nylon, this material gives the tent less stretch when wet and lasts longer against the onslaught of UV rays. Beneath the fly there should be lots of ventilation, usually by way of a double door and a mesh roof. Don't bother with expensive tents that have special panels that zip up over the mesh ceiling; if the fly is a good one, you won't need the extra weight and cost. Also make sure the

▲ *The A-frame tent design gives you lots of headroom and is a great choice for large groups.*

▲ *Above: The tunnel tent design is reminiscent of the old covered wagon. Below: A geodesic dome is the most stable tent during a heavy wind.*

Storm Proofing Your Tent

- Place a ground sheet inside your tent to prevent water from soaking your sleeping bag, making sure it's big enough to ride up the tent walls at least 6 inches (15 cm). Don't place it on the outside. This will only trap water and cause more problems than using no ground sheet.
- Waterproof the seams of a new tent with seam seal (Thompson's Water Seal works well).
- Face the door away from wind. This area, especially the zipper, is the least storm-proofed part of the tent.
- Use shock cords rather than the regular nylon cords to tie the tent down. This will help relieve stress on the nylon fabric during heavy windstorms.
- Attach (sew) extra loops to the fly, especially at the front and rear of the tent (attached to tent poles). This will help stop the fly from rubbing against the tent walls, which will definitely cause condensation and leakage.

fly reaches to the very bottom of the tent. A tent that has its fly only halfway usually leaks like a sieve, and not surprisingly these are the ones you'll see on sale.

The tent fabric should also be well-coated. The thicker the fabric the better for average use, especially if the tent's seams are factory taped. Tight-stitched seams are also a good indicator that the tent wasn't mass-produced. The tent floor should be made of tough waterproof material and extend a good distance up the wall. Even then, make sure to put a ground sheet down. Don't put it on the outside of the tent — it will just collect the water that way. Place it inside. You have to assume, no matter how good the tent is, that the floor will eventually leak. And having a ground sheet between the floor and your sleeping pad is an extra bonus (if used outside, to protect the floor from abrasion, it must not extend past the floor as it will gather rain and possibly channel the water beneath the floor where leakage can occur).

Extra-large-sized vestibules are also great. You can store lots of gear outside the tent, especially those smelly sneakers. But make sure never to use a vestibule as a miniature kitchen; the tent can easily burst into flame, and adding food smells to the fabric is just asking for trouble with nuisance bears.

Aluminum collapsible poles are the cat's meow. Stay away from fiberglass. They're lighter but are brittle and can give you some painful splinters that are impossible to pull out. They're also cheaper than aluminum, but the replacement parts, which you will surely end up needing, are expensive.

Keep an open mind when looking at those silly diagrams of stick figures laying side-by-side inside the tent. They're used to indicate the number

▲ *No matter how much you pay for it, your tent will eventually leak.*

Clean and Dry Storage

Most tent damage is caused by campers not airing them out the moment they get back from a trip. A tent can be rained on for days during the trip and not develop any mold. However, the moment it's stored wet for three or four days back home it can look like a piece of cheese left on the kitchen counter for a month.

The Zen of Tent Packing

There are the "rollers" and then there are the "crammers." The rollers painstakingly lay out the tent, fold it in thirds, place the poles at one end, and then roll everything up in a cigar shape. The difficulty always remains in getting the darn thing to fit in the storage bag. To eliminate the hassle, use a large-sized bag and then compact it by wrapping bungee cords around it. Or you could convert to cramming. Simply open up the storage bag and start stuffing everything in. Hard-core campers even have two separate compression sacks – one for the main tent and another for the fly. It's not a bad idea to separate the two, considering that the tent fly is always wetter than the tent body.

Zipper Maintenance

Before your trip make sure to rub a bar of soap along each zipper. This will reduce the stress placed on the zipper and limit the chance of it sticking. If it does break, hope for a coil zipper rather than a toothed zipper. Coil zippers are usually self-healing by slipping the slider back and forth. Once a tooth is broken in a toothed zipper, however, it's usually game over. The only way to repair it is to sew together the section where the tooth is missing and have the zipper work from there.

of people that can comfortably fit inside the given design (standard measure is that a 20-by-72-inch [51-by-183 cm] mat equals one person, and is the measure used by tentmakers). Take note, however, that no stinky socks, spare clothing, soggy rain gear, or especially a pet dog are stuffed in there with them. The day my wife and I picked up our canoe dog, Bailey, from the pound, we upgraded from a two-person to a three-person tent and haven't looked back since.

Look for those little extras such as side pockets and a ceiling hammock for gear storage, a center hook from which to dangle your flashlight or candle lantern, quick clips for poles rather than sleeves, color-coded clips and poles for easier setup, secondary guy lines for tightening the tent down in harsh conditions, and a light-colored fabric that allows in more light and brightens up your camp photos.

One final bit of advice: if the store you are dealing with can't provide any solid answers to your questions, doesn't have any tents set up so you can have a good look-see, or doesn't give a good warranty with their product, then I suggest you move on to another store. Of course, you must understand what the warranty means. Lifetime, for example, does not mean you get a new tent when this one wears out. Warranties cover defects only, not wear and tear, not stupidity!

AN OUTDOORS TOOLKIT

Lots of duct tape. That's what I recommend for any repair kit you pack along. I've used it to fix broken tent poles, snapped fishing rods, ripped rain jackets, leaking cookpots, cracked drinking mugs, and split paddles. I've even used it to splint a broken finger and wrapped the tape around my left sneaker when the sole fell off. I've patched three of my own canoes so far and come to aid of two other canoe groups who had abandoned their wrecked boat and were walking out from a remote river trip.

Make sure not to buy the cheap knockoffs like "duck tape," that you see on sale. The stuff doesn't work when it gets wet. And bring a whole roll with you. You'll eventually discover it's just as essential as matches or a pocketknife.

Other Items for the Toolkit

- a small container filled with an assortment of screws , bolts, nails and rivets to put back together split yokes, broken backpack straps. . .
- epoxy glue for those "sticky" situations
- a strip of leather for replacing broken pack straps
- a roll of copper wire or dental floss for lacing up canoe seats or even snaring the odd rabbit in a pinch
- compact needle-nosed pliers (or a multi-tool) for fixing anything and everything
- a needle and thread (those portable sewing kits are great)
- safety pins are almost as good as duct tape at times
- a spare flashlight bulb
- spare backpack snaps
- A Swiss Army knife with all the extra gadgets one can afford.
- twist-tie — a great replacement for that tiny screw holding your eyeglasses together, an eye missing from your fishing rod, or used to clean out your gas stove
- it wouldn't hurt to pack a little ingenuity as well

Who Stinks?

Most people focus on the trip itself and not on the journey home. Always remember to pack a separate set of clean clothes and extra footwear for the return trip. There's something to be said about improving the aroma in the vehicle during the long drive home, not to mention looking a little more respectable when you stop to eat at some restaurant along the way.

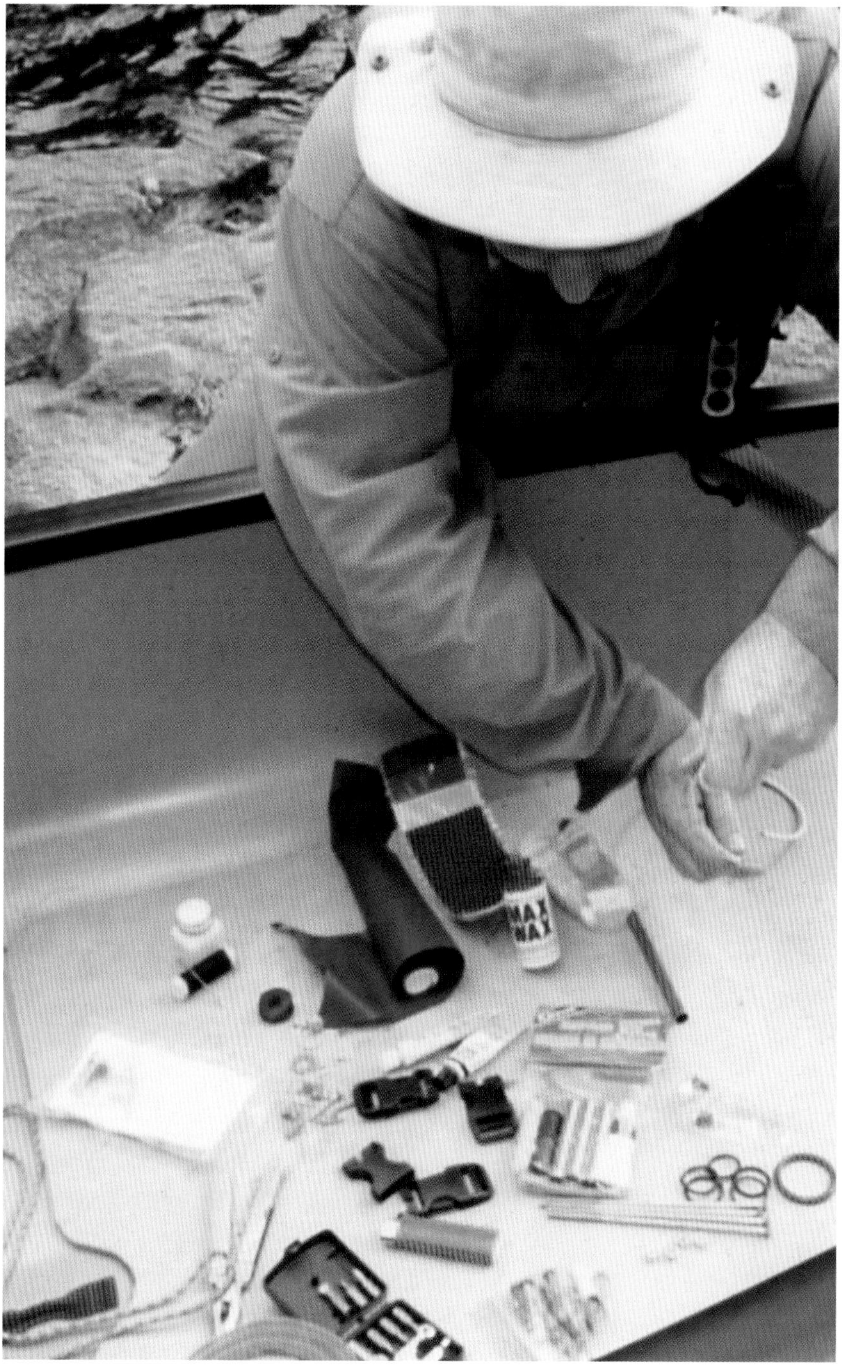

▲ *Andy attempts to fix his canoe seat, again.*

HAVE YOU FORGOTTEN ANYTHING?

Every camper goes through that anxious moment the night before the trip when they spread all the gear out across the living room floor, stuff it tight into packs, and then yank it back out seconds before departure because they're unsure if they remembered essentials such as flashlight batteries, toothpaste or bug repellent. Usually a trip doesn't go by without something being forgotten. The worst thing I've ever done was to head out on a two-week canoe trip without paddles. The only way to deal with this dilemma is to prepare an equipment list and then check and recheck it at least a thousand times before heading out. What follows on the next few pages is a sample packing list for a five-day trip during moderate weather conditions.

The History of Duct Tape

The story behind the development of duct tape is sketchy. It apparently was developed for the military during the Second World War by the Johnson and Johnson Company. What was needed was a strong tape that was waterproof, and the combination of cloth mesh, a rubber adhesive, and a rubberized coating was the answer. It was originally called "silver tape" or "gray tape." But once furnace installers caught on to the product after the war, its common name changed to duct tape.

Clothes

- two cotton or canvas shirts
- two T-shirts
- one wool sweater or fleece top
- three extra pairs of socks
- one extra pair of underwear
- two pairs of pants (no blue jeans)
- one pair of shorts (doubles as a swim suit if you're not into skinny dipping)
- hiking boots
- sneakers, moccasins or sport sandals for around camp
- bug hat (finer mesh for blackfly season)
- bandanna (useful for spraying bug dope on rather than directly onto your skin)
- wide-rimmed hat
- rain gear (make sure to keep handy on the top of your pack)
- good sunglasses

Toiletries

- beach towel
- portable toothbrush and toothpaste (small travel sizes can usually be purchased at drug stores)
- toilet paper (store in a resealable plastic bag)
- hairbrush
- biodegradable soap
- hairband
- razor
- contact lens solution
- glasses case and extra pair of glasses
- birth control
- any medications needed

Kitchen Set

- one large, one medium and one small cooking pot with lids, and nonstick frying pan (to avoid expensive cooking sets, purchase all three separately at a department store and simply remove handles)
- Outback Oven
- plastic travel mug
- plastic plate
- hard plastic spoon and metal fork

- metal spatula
- aluminum foil
- camp stove with extra fuel container and funnel
- waterproof matches in a waterproof container plus a butane lighter
- tea towel
- pair of garden gloves for grabbing the cooking pot off the fire
- lightweight saw
- water bottle
- water purification gadget
- spices, jam, peanut butter, coffee, sugar, maple syrup, honey, margarine, as well as various sizes, shapes and styles of plastic containers
- meals packed in separate containers within one large food bag

Sleeping Gear

- tent
- ground sheet that fits inside the tent
- large rain tarp
- sleeping bag
- sleeping pad

Packs

- external- or internal-frame pack
- various stuff sacks for clothes and other items
- separate pack or barrel for food
- day pack
- camera bag

Individual Items

- maps with waterproof map case
- compass
- insect repellent
- bug jacket
- hand lotion
- sunscreen
- camera, film and extra batteries
- playing cards, cribbage board, etc.
- fishing licence
- camping permit
- first-aid kit
- repair kit

- roll of duct tape
- extra resealable bags
- a couple of strong garbage bags
- journal and pencil
- paperback novel
- flashlight and candle lantern
- hammock
- bird, tree, animal track identification guide
- binoculars
- star chart
- fishing rod and small compact tackle box
- pocketknife

Luxury Items

- collapsible camp chair
- camp pillow
- extra-long sleeping pad
- solar-powered radio
- propane-fired hot-shower gadget
- two-burner camp stove
- miniature espresso maker
- coffee Bodum
- Thermos
- cast-iron frying pan
- reflector oven
- bug screen
- lantern
- hammock
- various field guides to flora and fauna
- cooler packed with ice and an endless assortment of fresh food, spirits of choice, and ice cream
- oversized tent
- fold-out picnic table

Major Innovations in Outdoor Gear

1884 • Carl Elsener invents a pocketknife that was approved by the Swiss Army and became an instant success. Thirteen years later Elsener patented another pocketknife that opened on both ends, containing six separate blades, and required only two springs. Elsener called it the "Officer's Knife," but we know it today as the Swiss Army knife.

1907 • Primus stoves, originally developed in 1884, were mass-produced in North America and replaced the inefficient wick-type stoves.

1910 • The zipper, first invented by Whitecomb I. Judson in 1893, was used on outdoor clothing and not long after on tents, packs and sleeping bags.

1923 • William C. Coleman introduces his first camp stove, a two-burner design featuring a hot-blast starter, eliminating the need for priming.

1925 • Government surveys begin for the development of the National Topographic Mapping System.

1933 • The Silva Company is established and produces the first navigational instrument combining a compass and a protractor.

1939 • Nylon becomes a hot item, especially for making climbing rope, lightweight tents, packs and clothing.

1945 • The Grumman Aircraft Company replaces the traditional heavy wood-and-canvas canoe with aluminum to construct a new lightweight model.

1948 • Velcro is invented, inspired from seed burrs caught on wool socks.

1967 • The Lowe Company revolutionizes the use of internal frames for backpacks.

1968 • Uniroyal begins the development of Royalex ABS plastic hulls for canoes.

1974 • The first effective polyester synthetic insulation (Polarguard) is used for sleeping bags, replacing the old-style down-filled bags.

1975 • North Face comes out with a lightweight geodesic dome tent, the first tent to have flexible aluminum poles.

1975 • Lifa polypropylene long underwear takes over classic cotton.

1976 • W.L. Gore company introduces a new breathable rainwear fabric called Gore-Tex.

1977 • Therm-a-Rest mattresses begin relieving campers' bad backs across North America.

1980 • Alex Tilley begins to sell his prototype sailing hat at Toronto outdoor shows.

1987 • A bear repellent product called "Bear-Off" is invented by Ed Cesar, consisting of a red-pepper-based powder stored in a resealable plastic bag. The idea is to throw the powder in the face of the attacking bear, impairing its sense of smell and sight long enough for the victim to escape. Not long after a spray repellent replaced the powder in the bag.

1994 • Global Positioning System (GPS), first conceived by the USAF in 1960, becomes available for outdoor enthusiasts.

Items (required by law) for the canoe or kayak

- two 100-foot (30 m) lengths of floating rope stuffed in a throwbag
- flashlight
- sounding device (whistle)
- approved PFD (personal flotation device)
- bailer
- extra paddle

Top Ten Items Usually Left Behind

- matches
- rain gear
- tent poles
- pot gripper
- camp mug
- sunscreen
- water purification system
- bug repellent
- extra bulb for flashlight
- toilet paper

> *"By now the crisis had hit one canoe-team. Jim Matthews suffers from hay fever, and the pine tree pollen had been causing him trouble all the way. After exhausting his supply of handkerchiefs and tissues, he turned to toilet paper, and finally run through all his own and that of his partners, Johnny Davis. The crisis has been hastened by the fact that both of them were rather lavish in their use of this important commodity. The rest of us put on a show of heartlessness in their plight, charging them with profligacy. Toilet paper became precious currency, to be bartered for. A plea for help from John Bayly, portaging a canoe, to get a blackfly out of his eye, was answered by Jim only at the price of ten sheets of toilet paper. Hard bargaining was the order of the day, but neither Jim nor Johnny could bring themselves to barter away their evening daiquiris, though there were several offers."*
>
> ERIC MORSE, *FRESH WATER SAGA*

CAMP COOKING

It is a source of no amusement to the genuine woodsman to witness the vast quantity of supplies the amateur feels it necessary to take with him for a few days . . . the boxes of bread, biscuits, and cheese; the bottles of pickles and spices; the cans of condensed milk and prepared fruits; the rolls of spiced bacon and tins of fresh beef and pressed vegetables; and last, but by no means least, the demijohns of gin and brandy, bottles of old rye, and boxes of cigars.

JAMES DICKSON, *ALGONQUIN ADVENTURE* (1886)

FOOD HAS TO be one of the most important items to pack for a camping trip. A combination of protein, fats and carbohydrates has long been the key to refueling the body while venturing out in the wilds, especially when you are forced to go past your physical and mental limits to gain that extra distance before sundown. Basically, camp meals should be nourishing, lightweight, easy and quick to prepare, and most important, palatable.

Thankfully the days are gone when dried meals consisted mostly of beans and green-colored powdered eggs. Even the dehydrated foods sold at outdoor stores are now pretty close to capturing a miniature lightweight and bacteria-free replica of homestyle meals. But don't stop there. I find it far better to create your own recipes. It's cheaper than buying a week's supply of pre-packed meals, and a lot more fun. By combining visits to the local supermarket and bulk-food store, and by drying your own food, some real masterpieces can be created.

◀ *"I think I eat better on a camping trip than I do at home." Scott Roberts.*

SUPERMARKET TOUR

The first part of food preparation is to check out the local supermarket. You will be surprised at what you can pick up cheaply at the grocery store that is relatively lightweight, nutritious, and nonperishable. You may have to go to the smaller specialty stores for those hard-to-find items. Here are a few to keep an eye out for:

- Kraft mini packets of mayonnaise
- Freybe dried salami (the best dried meat available)
- Quaker Oats hot cereal packets
- Thai Kitchen's Bangkok Curry Noodles
- Kraft Dinner
- Potatoes au Gratin with Cheddar Cheese Sauce
- Uncle Ben's Zesty Tomato Rice
- Uncle Ben's Bistro Express
- Lipton's Pasta and Sauce
- Knorr Soups
- Bear Creek Soup Mixes
- Ramen Noodles
- Ready Crisp Bacon
- Clover Leaf Tuna (now sealed in a foil packet rather than a can)
- Tyson Chicken (also sealed in a foil packet rather than a can)
- RyKrisp Crackers
- Thomas English Muffins
- Kashi Breakfast Pilaf
- Amare Tortellini
- Black Bear Chili
- Kraft a La Carte
- Del Monte Vegetable Classics
- Nescafé House Cappuccino instant beverage mix (try blending half of the regular French Vanilla with half the new Rolo flavor).

BULK-FOOD BONANZA

Bulk-food stores are the saving grace for any camper. You'll find all the ingredients necessary to make up your own meals. The prices are always cheaper than the supermarket, and the meals you can make are far better than the store-bought freeze-dried stuff, which for some reason has a tendency to give you gas. Here are some of the basics you can pick up at any bulk-food store.

Lentils The common Egyptian lentil is more widely used than the decorated lentil, which is split and has its outer husk removed. However, use the decorated type, since its cooking time is far shorter and saves precious stove fuel.

Rice There is an endless assortment of rice that can be used in many different recipes. Precooked white rice (Minute Rice) is the less nutritious variety, but it saves a lot on boiling time and fuel consumption. Mixing rice with lentils is a good idea. Together they provide a richer balance of protein.

Pasta Regular pastas can be bought at any supermarket and bulk-food store. But so can whole-grain and vegetable pastas, which are far better for you.

Beans Dried beans really add to a meal. There are countless varieties, but to reduce cooking time it is crucial that they are pre-soaked well before mealtime. Place them in a sealed container and let them soak in water a full day before using them in a meal. If you plan on using beans for an evening meal, make sure to place them in a closed resealable bag stuffed in your cook set or a small Nalgene bottle in the morning. By the time you cook up dinner the boiling time has been reduced to twenty minutes rather than two hours.

Textured Vegetable Protein (TVP) This is a product commercially dried and used regularly by vegetarians as a meat substitute. It comes in granular or cubed form, and is easily rehydrated.

Soy Grits For a quick, high-protein dinner, try soy grits. They're similar to soy flour except the soybeans have been toasted and cracked into tiny flakes and not ground into a powder.

Bulgur Bulgur is made up of wheat kernels that have been cooked and dried. It has a nutlike flavor, which makes it a good breakfast meal, but also makes an excellent substitute for any recipe calling for ground beef.

Toasted Buckwheat Buckwheat is not in the wheat family. It's a seed produced by a grasslike herb and is high in potassium and phosphorus.

Soft Wheat Kernels Wheat produces a one-seeded fruit called a kernel, often called wheat berries, that is extremely high in protein. It's the simplest form of wheat and was the main crop in Egypt and Palestine.

Millet Millet does not contain gluten and is ranked as the least allergenic of grains. It's also extremely high in B-complex vitamins and the most balanced in essential amino acids.

Couscous This is a favorite for camp meals. It's a grainlike pasta, made by mixing flour and water to form a paste, which is formed into small grains and then dried. Couscous you find at the bulk-food store is most likely made from 100 percent durum wheat, but rice or corn can be used as well.

Quinoa (pronounced keen-wa) This "mother grain" is found in Andean Mountain regions of South America. It contains more protein than any other grain and is even a complex protein by itself. It is also high in fiber, minerals and vitamins, which made it an ancient food staple for the Inca civilization, as well as the present-day hungry camper. It takes no time to cook (even shorter than couscous) and will turn from white to transparent when done.

▲ *Bulgur is an excellent substitute for ground beef in shepherd's pie.*

▲ *Alana prepares one of her "one-pot-wonders."*

HOW MUCH FOOD TO BRING?

The quantity of food to bring is one of the most confusing elements of camp cooking. You have so many variables to consider, like the size of the group, eating habits of each individual, the length and difficulty of the trip. The National Outdoor Leadership School (NOLS) cookbook offers one of the best ways to rationalize the amount to bring. It states that an average person on a normal trip will consume 1.5 to 2 pounds (2,500 to 3,000 calories) of food per day. On a more strenuous trip the weight increases to 2 to 2.5 pounds (3,000 to 3,700 calories). The problem is that using this to try to budget for each individual recipe can be confusing. I handle meals and the amount of food taken by to splitting each group into two (perfect for canoe trips). Each group is responsible for organizing all meals, as well as cooking gear and stoves, for their own group. I find this is much easier than for one person to try to figure out (not to mention to cook) meals for everyone else. It also creates fun in camp. My regular friends have a cook-off the first night out. Each group tries to outdo the others for the main meal. The winners get an extra drink of spirits and the losers wash the dishes for the remainder of the trip.

Food to Last Six Fellows One Week

(Ernest Thompson Seton, *The Book of Woodcraft*, 1912)

- oatmeal – 6 lb.
- rice – 2 lb.
- crackers – 10 lb.
- cocoa – 3 lb.
- tea – ½ lb.
- coffee – 3 lb.
- lard – 5 lb.
- sugar – 6 lb.
- condensed milk – 12 tins
- eggs – 3 dozen
- bacon – 15 lb.
- prunes – 3 qt.
- potatoes – 3 qt.
- white beans – 3 qt.
- flour – 25 lb.
- baking powder – 1 lb.

* Fresh fish and game are pleasant variations, but seem to make little difference in the grocery bill.

However, it's still a given that you'll either pack too little or too much food on the trip, and not having enough is dangerous. But at least by spreading out the organization of meals there's less chance of everyone going hungry. Having too much is usually the main problem. Storing the waste in a garbage bag or sealed container can quickly become a smelly mess if temperatures rise. So it's best to try and utilize the leftovers in other meals. Cold rice left from dinner makes an excellent rice pudding for breakfast, porridge can be added to your bread mix, and noodles can be tossed into soups for a hearty lunch.

DRY IT, YOU'LL LIKE IT

Drying your own food is by far the best way to prepare camp meals. You can pick up a good dehydrator for less than $100 (my wife and I received one as a wedding gift). But you can also place items on racks in your oven (use a cookie sheet for sauces), set on the lowest temperature possible, for six to eight hours.

Sauces are the best to practise on. One jar of spaghetti sauce placed in the dehydrator or oven is reduced to a thin slice of what looks like fruit leather. Then, once at camp, you simply place the dried sauce in a small amount (1/2 cup) of boiling water and it turns right back to the original spaghetti sauce.

Vegetables are also quite easy to dehydrate. My wife and I routinely spend the winter months buying up different veggies on sale and then drying them in bulk for use later on. Some of our favorites are broccoli, celery, green and red peppers, mushrooms, zucchini, corn, peas and eggplant.

▲ *One can of corn takes approximately seven to eight hours to dry on a commercial dehydrator.*

Meat takes a lot more preparation. It first must be cooked before drying. Some meats, such as cooked ground beef, should also be rinsed over and over again with hot water to eliminate the grease content and reduce the chances of bacteria forming. Alana and I prefer drying ground turkey or ground venison. It has less fat and therefore less chance of spoiling while we are out on the trip.

We also prefer to buy some dried foods at the bulk-food store. Onions really stink up the house when dried in the dehydrator, and we can't seem to get our banana chips or pineapple slices to look as appetizing as the ones you can pick up at the store.

Blackened Cooking Pots Have Character

An age-old method to stop your cooking pots from getting blackened when cooking over an open fire is to coat them with a bar of soap. It works. But why bother? A blackened pot will absorb the heat from the fire much better than a shiny one. It also has more character. Just keep the pot set in a separate storage bag to keep everything else clean.

Turkey Jerky

You'll be surprised how easy it is to make your own jerky. Start off by purchasing meats with the least fat; a round roast or chicken works well. Even tofu can be done. But by far the best is turkey. Slice the meat, across the grain, and marinate for 2 to 4 hours in $^{1}/_{2}$ cup Worcestershire sauce, $^{1}/_{2}$ cup soy sauce, and $^{1}/_{4}$ cup red wine vinegar. Then lay the slices across the oven racks and dry overnight (8–12 hours) at 150 degrees F. If it snaps in half when bent, it's done. You can simply snack on it or add it to soup or stew.

▲ *A bag of pasta combined with dehydrated mushrooms and red and green peppers, all of which were done in a conventional oven, is a great first-time practice recipe.*

THINKING BEYOND CAMP GRUEL

If you're car camping, or the portages on your interior canoe trip happen to be short, or better yet, nonexistent, then you definitely have the privilege of taking along a few luxury food items. After all, some dehydrated meals taste a little like munching on a cardboard box. So there's nothing better than to be able to pack fresh meat and vegetables, at least for the first few days of your trip. Imagine ending your day and dining on a juicy steak, crisp salad, and chocolate ice cream for dessert.

Here are a few tips on keeping the fresh food fresh and the frozen food frozen:

- Some meats, like bacon and sausage, will last longer than other meats due to the high amount of preservatives.
- Vacuum sealing meat and vegetables will greatly increase their pack life. Don't go out and buy a vacuum machine right away, though. Most grocery stores will seal your purchase free of charge.
- Meat can be kept bacteria-free for up to four days by wrapping it up in a piece of J Cloth or cheesecloth that has been soaked (not saturated) in vinegar. The vinegar smell and taste disappears as soon as the meat is placed over the fire.
- Cheese can also stay fresh much longer by wrapping it up in a vinegar-soaked J Cloth or cheesecloth and then dipping it in paraffin wax.
- To keep frozen meat from thawing out too quickly, make sure to marinade it (liquid marinade acts as an ice pack), store it in a resealable plastic bag and then wrap it in newsprint, or better yet, the insulation material used for ironing boards.
- Frozen meat should be placed in the center of the food bag, which is always kept away from direct sunlight or stored in a small cooler. The soft-sided cooler bags don't necessarily work as well at keeping things as cool as plastic, but when empty they can easily be stuffed into your backpack for storage.
- Crushed ice you see at the grocery store holds the fish and other seafood, and is the best ice to pack in your cooler. It lasts longer than regular run-of-the-mill ice, and the store will probably give it away free.
- Dry ice works well to keep items completely frozen for up to six days. Also, as it melts it turns directly into carbon dioxide rather than a liquid, leaving no problems with freezer burn or wet food bags. It works well for meat, margarine, ice cubes and even ice cream. But it has a tendency to burst open pop or beer cans, weighs a fair bit, and can be a real hassle to find if you don't live near a major city with a medical supply business.

True Grit Camp Coffee

True camp coffee is nothing but real grounds-and-water-in-the-pot coffee. Bring water to a rolling boil, take it off the heat source, dump in one generous tablespoon of coffee grounds per cup of water, and let it steep (covered) alongside the campfire for approximately five to ten minutes. To settle the grounds, tap a spoon on the side of the pot three to five times.

The most crucial element of brewing "true grit" is to never let the coffee boil once you've taken it directly off the heat source. Old timers used to say that boiled coffee tastes like rotten shoe leather, and they're right! The bad taste of boiled coffee is in the bitter tannic acid and flavouring oils it contains. The tasty oils are released at 205 degrees F (86 C), just below boiling point. The bitter acids, however, are released right at or just above boiling point.

Another important factor is how to settle the grounds before serving the coffee. Some people throw in pieces of eggshell or toss in a few round pebbles. I've even witnessed campers take hold of the wire handle on the pot, swing it with the speed of an aircraft propeller, and have complete faith in centrifugal force. This suicidal action will pull the grounds to the bottom of the pot. Guaranteed. I merely tap the side of the pot with a knife or spoon and then make sure to offer the first and last cup of coffee to someone else in the group.

- Never break eggs from the shell and then store them in a container for liquids. This method is used by some to prevent their eggs from being broken in storage. Little do they know, however, that once the egg leaves the shell, it instantly becomes a breeding ground for bacteria and is one sure way to get massive food poisoning on your trip. Also, always buy fresh eggs from the farmer's market rather from than the grocery store. They haven't been sitting around as long, and they last at least three times longer. The best place to store them is in a styrofoam carton stuffed in the center of your pack or duct-taped firmly under the canoe seat.
- When making salads make sure to choose red cabbage or Japanese napa cabbage rather than the regular head of lettuce. They keep for weeks without refrigeration and make a tasty side dish when mixed with shredded carrots, red onion slices, red and green peppers, raisins and cashews.
- Vegetables such as tomatoes, peppers and celery will last much longer if you first float them in a sink of cold water and two tablespoons of chlorine bleach. Allow them to soak for a few minutes, air dry, and then pack them away. The bleach will kill any surface bacteria that promote spoilage.
- The best way to chill your wine for the evening meal is to store it in a collapsible water bottle like a Platypus, and then troll it behind you on a long rope for about half an hour before reaching camp.

Top Ten Wild Edibles

ARROW ROOT • This water plant, found across North America, grows along the edges of slow-moving rivers. The tubers at the end of the roots are high in starch and can be eaten raw or added to a stew. They're best picked after midsummer to avoid a bitter taste, and can even be dried and pounded into fine flour.

BIRCH • Found in most temperate forests of North America. The inner bark is quite bland but can be cut into strips and used as a substitute for spaghetti noodles. The young leaves can also be dried and made into a soothing tea, which is believed to be a cure for urinary infections and kidney stones.

BLUEBERRY • This is the preferred berry for most campers. It's located all across North America, including the far north. Huckleberries, which are also edible, are usually found growing alongside it. The berries are ripe around midsummer and can be eaten directly off the plant or used in pies, muffins and pancakes.

BUNCHBERRY • The range is north of California and New Jersey, with the plant preferring to grow along the forest floor of mixed woodland. The berries taste something like a bruised apple. They are also somewhat acidic, so don't overdo it.

CATTAIL • Another water plant that is found across North America but prefers more stagnant water. The entire plant is edible and is probably the best survival food out there. The fresh young shoots are the most palatable and are usually eaten raw. The roots make a great substitute for potatoes in a stew. They can also be dried and made into flour.

CRANBERRY • The plant, which has a wide range across North America, is found along the shores of lakes and ponds. The berries are traditionally picked after the first frost and made into a tasty sauce.

LABRADOR TEA • This is the tea of the north. It's found in sphagnum swamps across the northern United States and Canada. The leaves are dried and boiled. To cut the strong acidic taste, try adding a spoon of brown sugar and a shot of liqueur.

MILKWEED • The plant is found growing in old farmer's fields across the United States and southern Canada. The young sprouts are cooked and eaten like asparagus. The flower pods are also cooked and stuffed with rice. The bitter milky sap must be removed by boiling the plant in two or three changes of water.

WILD LEEK • Found all across North America, preferring deciduous woodlots. The root system is best eaten raw for nutrition value and makes an excellent additive to salads. The onion flavour and odour is so overpowering, however, that you may just want to cook them first.

WINTERGREEN • The range is more northerly, beginning in the St. Lawrence–Great Lakes region and the Mississippi. The leaves and berries, which remain on the plant throughout the winter months, make a soothing and refreshing tea.

Birch

Cattail

Milkweed

Wintergreen

Grow Your Own Sprouts

It's possible to dine on fresh greens halfway through a ten-day trip. On day one or two, soak the beans or seeds in water for half a day and then store them in a plastic bottle, capped with a J Cloth held on with an elastic band. Other than being rinsed with water daily, they need little care. On day five or six (depending on the temperature) you'll have a fresh additive for dinners or lunches. Alfalfa sprouts are the easiest to work with, mustard seeds add a great zip, and garbanzo beans or green lentils have the most flavor. Just make sure to take the sprouts to bed with you if it gets cold at night.

First-Ever Trail Snack

The Greek army was the first to use high-energy trip snacks. In 150 BC, Supply Officer Philon of Byzantium made up pellets mixed with sesame honey (for protein and carbohydrate), opium poppy (to control hunger pains), and a medicinal root called squill (acting as a stimulant). It probably tasted horrible but did the trick.

GORP EATING ETIQUETTE

GORP is commonly known as good old raisins and peanuts. But everything goes — salty, crunchy, sweet or chewy — for this traditional high-energy snack. Try adding M&Ms, Smarties, beer nuts, dried cranberries, dried mangoes, banana chips, mini marshmallows, salted pumpkin seeds, corn nuts, Goldfish, pretzels, chocolate-covered coffee beans, Grape-Nuts cereal, dried and spiced snow peas, or even dried jalapeno peppers. However you make it, though, it's crucial that the GORP-eating etiquette is followed. No "high grading" allowed, that is, nobody picks and chooses only the bits and pieces they like in the GORP bag. They must blindly grab a handful of the entire mixture and munch away.

Spice of Life

Here's a list of some top choices to add to a camper's spice kit:

- salt and pepper
- garlic salt
- chili powder
- curry
- basil
- oregano
- Spike (a brand-name combo of dried vegetables and herbs)
- cumin
- dillweed
- cayenne
- cinnamon
- nutmeg
- soy sauce (stored in a small plastic bottle)
- Tabasco (stored in a small plastic bottle)

▲ *The author gets caught high grading GORP.*

BAKING ON A CAMP STOVE

The Outback Oven is an excellent alternative to the traditional reflector oven for baking desserts or making fresh bread. They're lighter and are used with camp stoves rather than a messy campfire. You can make everything from blueberry pie to lasagne. The ultimate, however, is to use two ovens and two stoves (choose a stove that works well on simmer). Bake one chocolate cake in one and a second in the other. Then combine the two, placing raspberry jam in the centre and vanilla icing with shaved chocolate on top, to make the best double-layered cake ever.

▲ *The Outback Oven is the essential tool for baking on a camp stove.*

▲ *Color-coded oraganizers make it easy to find your lunch.*

ASSORTED CONTAINERS

A huge assortment of reusable containers can be used to store spices and food staples. Various sizes of wide-mouthed polyethylene bottles are also great. So are plastic vitamin bottles. But make sure to double pack everything in a resealable bag, just in case.

Also, stay away from anything that is not approved for food storage, like plastic 35 mm film canisters (film chemicals are deadly). And stay away from those darn squeeze tubes you can pick up at outdoor stores. They always crack and leak the contents all over your pack.

Color-Coded Organizers

There's nothing worse than looking through the entire contents of the food container before finding what you're looking for. To help eliminate the stress, try to organize everything in separate color-coded bags. For example, breakfast is blue, lunch is yellow, and dinner is red. That way you'll at least know which bag to start with before searching for the elusive peanut butter. You can easily make your own storage containers, but have a look at Ostrom's Barrel Bags for storing food in barrels. The company has even perfected a rounded (and crushable) cooler bag that fits perfectly into a barrel.

Five-Day Menu Plan

DAY 1
- Breakfast: On the road
- Lunch: Bagels with luncheon meat, cheese and tomato
- Dinner: Marinated steak (frozen), baked potatoes, fresh veggies, red wine, carrot cake

DAY 2
- Breakfast: Toasted English muffins with eggs and bacon, hash browns, coffee
- Lunch: Bagels with cheese and cucumber
- Dinner: Ham steaks, instant mashed potatoes, instant stuffing mix, frozen peas or beans, tea or cappuccino, brownies.

DAY 3
- Breakfast: Red River cereal with fresh apple slices, coffee flavored with Baileys Irish Cream
- Lunch: Crackers, cheese, orange slices and tabouli or humus mix
- Dinner: Pita pizza, chocolate pudding, hot chocolate flavored with Baileys Irish Cream

DAY 4
- Breakfast: Pancakes with real maple syrup, espresso
- Lunch: Soup mix with pita melts dipped in salsa
- Dinner: Pasta parmesan, white wine, corn bread sweetened with honey and cabbage salad

DAY 5
- Breakfast: Instant hot cereal with dried apricots and pears
- Lunch: Cinnamon bannock with peanut butter and jam
- Dinner: On the road

FIELD-TESTED RECIPES

Each recipe serves two hungry campers.

Chicken Curry

1 can	chicken, dehydrated
1 can	curry sauce, dehydrated (my favorite is Pataki's Korma or Vindaloo flavor)
½ cup	cashews or peanuts
1	small onion
2 cups	precooked white rice
2½ cups	water

Reconstitute curry sauce and dried chicken in ½ cup of boiling water, stirring constantly, over medium heat for 4 to 6 minutes, and then set aside. Cook rice in 2 cups of boiling water for 5 minutes. Pour curry sauce on top of rice and place nuts and chopped onion on top.

Tuna Casserole

1	can of tuna or tuna in vacuum pouch
1	single-serving package of cream of celery soup mix
1 cup	crumbled-up crackers
½ cup	dehydrated peas
½ cup	dehydrated onion
1 tablespoon	cornstarch
2 cups	egg noodles
3 cups	water

Mix soup package with 1 cup water. Add peas, tuna and onion. Cook, adding cornstarch, until it begins to thicken and peas soften (approximately 10 minutes). Serve over cooked noodles and sprinkle with crumbled-up crackers.

Meatless Chili

2 cups	spaghetti sauce, dehydrated
2 cups	kidney beans
1/4 cup	dehydrated red and green peppers
1/4 cup	dehydrated mushrooms
1/4 cup	dehydrated corn
2 tablespoons	chili powder
2–3 cups	water

Reconstitute spaghetti sauce in 2 to 3 cups boiling water. Add all remaining ingredients and let simmer for 30 minutes. Serve with tortillas.

▲ *Be warned! This chili recipe is recommended only if you are not sharing a tent with someone else.*

Spaghetti with Meat Sauce

1 cup	spaghetti sauce, dehydrated
1 cup	dehydrated hamburger (try turkey or even venison if you can get it)
1 cup	dehydrated vegetables (black olives, green peppers, red peppers)
1/4 cup	dehydrated mushrooms
2 cups	noodles (any style)
3 1/2 cups	water

Reconstitute dried hamburger by placing it in 1/2 cup of hot water and set it aside. Rehydrate spaghetti sauce, dried olives, peppers and mushrooms in 1 cup boiling water, stirring constantly over medium heat for 4 to 6 minutes. Drain water from reconstituted meat and add to the sauce. Cook noodles in 2 cups of boiling water, drain and add sauce.

Calzones

2 cups	Tea-Bisk or pizza crust mix
1 cup	shredded cheese (any kind)
1 cup	mixture of dehydrated eggplant, zucchini, red and green peppers and black olives
1	13-ounce can of tomato paste, dehydrated
1 tablespoon	olive oil
1 1/2 cups	water

* for best results use an Outback Oven

Reconstitute tomato paste and vegetables in 1/2 cup of boiling water. Mix Tea-Bisk and 1 cup water into dough and separate into four small bundles. Spread each bundle out and cover half with tomato paste, grated cheese and vegetables. Fold other half of bundle over and make sure the edges are sealed. Lightly grease deep-dish frying pan or Outback Oven and place individual calzones in pan. Cover and bake for 7 to 10 minutes, then turn the calzones over and bake 7 to 10 minutes more.

Hamburger Casserole

2 cups	dehydrated hamburger
1	package mashed potatoes
1 cup	dried corn
1 teaspoon	garlic powder
1 teaspoon	black pepper
½ cup	powdered skim milk
1 cup	water

* for best results use an Outback Oven

Mix skim milk powder up in 1 cup of water. Add all other ingredients and place in a deep-dish frying pan or Outback Oven and cook for 25 minutes over a moderate heat.

Hearty Stew with Herbed Dumplings

Stew

1	large package of minestrone soup mix
5 cups	water

Dumplings

1 cup	Tea-Bisk mix
1 teaspoon	dried cilantro
½ cup	water

Mix soup with water and set pot on medium heat. Form Tea-Bisk into dough (adding cilantro) and form it into small balls. Place dollops of Tea-Bisk on top of soup and cover. Cook (without peeking) for 20 to 25 minutes.

Variation

Many kinds of hearty soups (I actually prefer corn chowder) are delicious with dumplings and can make an excellent meal on a cold, miserable day.

Tomato Pesto Pasta

1 cup	noodles (any style)
1 cup	tomato pesto sauce (choose sauce without oil), dehydrated
1 cup	dehydrated celery, olives and mushrooms
1 tablespoon	Parmesan cheese
½ to 1 cup	water

Reconstitute tomato pesto sauce with ½ cup of boiling water. Slowly add more water as required until sauce thickens (approximately 10 minutes). Serve over cooked pasta and sprinkle on Parmesan cheese.

Cabbage, Carrot and Onion Stir Fry

1	small head red cabbage
1	small red onion
2	medium-sized carrots
1 cup	precooked white rice

Sauce:

1 teaspoon	ground ginger
1 teaspoon	garlic powder
1 teaspoon	ground pepper
1 tablespoon	cornstarch
1	cube vegetable bouillon
1 cup	water
1 tablespoon	olive oil

Add bouillon cube, cornstarch, and spices to 1 cup boiling water. Heat and stir until sauce thickens and then set aside. Lightly grease a frying pan with oil. Add chopped cabbage, onion and sliced carrots. Fry over medium heat until vegetables are softened slightly (5 to 7 minutes). Pour sauce over veggies and heat thoroughly. Serve over cooked rice.

Cheese and Onion Melts

4	tortillas
1 cup	shredded cheese (any kind)
1	red onion
1 cup	salsa sauce, dehydrated
1 tablespoon	olive oil
$\frac{1}{4}$ cup	water

Sprinkle shredded cheese and chopped onion on top of tortilla. Place in lightly oiled frying pan and cook over moderate heat until cheese is melted and tortilla is lightly browned on both sides. Slice tortilla into quarters. Reconstitute salsa sauce in $\frac{1}{4}$ cup boiling water and serve with tortillas.

▲ *Cheese melts with tabouli and salsa make an excellent snack before dinner.*

Refried Bean Burritos and Salsa

1	package refried bean mix
4	tortillas
1 cup	shredded cheese (any kind)
1 cup	salsa sauce, dehydrated
1 tablespoon	olive oil
¼ cup	water

Mix refried bean mix as described on package instructions. Scoop the bean mix onto the centre of a tortilla and cover bean mix with shredded cheese. Place in a lightly oiled frying pan and cook on moderate heat until cheese is melted (5 to 7 minutes). Reconstitute salsa sauce in ¼ cup boiling water and serve with burrito.

Sante Fe Fish Cakes

1	1-pound walleye or pike
1 cup	all-purpose flour
2 cups	dried potato flakes
2 tablespoons	cilantro
1 teaspoon	dehydrated jalapeno pepper
½ teaspoon	dried onion
½ cup	cornmeal
1	egg white (or ½ cup powdered egg)
1 cup	salsa, dehydrated
½ teaspoon	salt
½ teaspoon	pepper
¼ cup	water

* for best results use an Outback Oven

In a small pot combine reconstituted potato flakes, fish pieces, cilantro, jalapeno, onion, salt and pepper. Divide contents into small bundles and shape them into round cakes. Dredge in flour, dip in egg white (or reconstituted powdered egg), then dredge them in cornmeal. Bake in deep-dish frying pan or Outback Oven for 20 minutes. Reconstitute salsa sauce in ¼ cup boiling water and serve on top of fish cakes.

Baked Trout Amandine

4	small brook trout
1/4 cup	bread crumbs
1/4 cup	finely chopped almonds
1	lemon
1/2 teaspoon	pepper
1 tablespoon	dried lemon thyme
1 tablespoon	dried sage

In a small pot combine bread crumbs, almonds, lemon thyme, sage and pepper. Mix well. Sprinkle contents of pot over skin side of gutted trout. Roll trout in tinfoil with slices of lemon and bake in the coals of the campfire for 15 minutes.

Meatless Stroganoff

1	large package cream of mushroom soup mix
2 cups	noodles (any style)
2 tablespoons	dehydrated mushrooms
2 tablespoons	dehydrated leek
1 cube	beef bouillon
Pinch	paprika
Pinch	black pepper
Pinch	garlic powder
2 1/2 cups	water

Add bouillon cube to water and bring to a boil. Add the rest of the ingredients except for paprika, black pepper and garlic and let simmer until noodles are cooked and vegetables are rehydrated. Poor out excess water and add spices to desired flavor.

Shrimp Creole

1	can shrimp
1 cup	precooked white rice
½ cup	black beans
1 cup	dried tomatoes
½ cup	dehydrated celery
2	cloves of garlic
1	small onion
½ teaspoon	dried hot red pepper flakes
½ teaspoon	filé powder
½ teaspoon	pepper
½ cup	white wine
½	tomato juice drink box (the ones you use in the kids' lunches)
2 cups	water
1 tablespoon	olive oil

Presoak the beans in a container (a spare Nalgene bottle works well) for an entire day.Then combine black beans and tomatoes in wine and tomato juice. Lightly grease a frying pan with oil and cook celery, garlic, onion, hot pepper, pepper and filé powder over a medium heat for 10 minutes. Add tomato juice mixture. Cook and stir until it thickens (approximately 10 to 15 minutes). Add shrimp and cook for another 3 to 5 minutes. Cook rice in 2 cups of boiling water and add sauce.

Quinoa Curry

1 cup	quinoa (pronounced keen-wa)
1	fresh red onion
½ teaspoon	salt
2 teaspoons	curry powder
Handful	dried pears, dates, apricots, chopped almonds
3 cups	water

Bring three cups of water to a boil and add quinoa mixture. Grain is ready when it looks transparent. Let stand covered for 10 minutes.

Moroccan Couscous

1 cup	couscous
1½ teaspoons	curry powder
1	cube vegetable bouillon
¼ cup	dehydrated red and green peppers
4–5	diced, sundried tomatoes
¼ cup	pistachios
1	clove garlic
1½ cups	water

Bring water to a boil and mix in all ingredients. Over a moderate heat, cook 1 to 2 minutes. Let sit off heat for 3 more minutes.

Mexican-Style Couscous

1 cup	couscous
1	cube vegetable bouillon
2 tablespoons	dried vegetables
2 tablespoons	dried red and green peppers
2 tablespoons	dried corn
¼ cup	mixture of black beans and red organic beans
1 teaspoon	onion powder
1 teaspoon	parsley
Big dash	garlic
1	can of tomato paste, dehydrated
2½ cups	water

Presoak the beans in a container (a spare Nalgene bottle works well) for an entire day. Then, to prepare the dish, first reconstitute tomato paste in ½ cup of boiling water with the dried vegetables, dried peppers and dried corn. Set the sauce aside and boil beans in 1 cup of water for 20 minutes. Then, place the cooked beans in with the couscous, mixed with the vegetable bouillon, onion powder, parsley and garlic, and let boil in 1 cup of water for 1 to 2 minutes. Finally, add the tomato sauce and serve.

Mock Shepherd's Pie

1 cup	precooked rice
1 cup	bread crumbs
1 cup	mixed, dehydrated vegetables (peas, carrots, onion, green pepper)
¼ cup	dehydrated mushrooms
Pinch	parsley
Pinch	garlic powder
½ cup	bulgar
1 cup	potato flakes
1	beef bouillon cube
Dash	Worcestershire sauce
1 teaspoon	tomato or spaghetti sauce powder
4 cups	water

Combine the precooked rice, vegetables, mushrooms, parsley, garlic powder, beef bouillon cube, and tomato powder into 2 cups boiling water and let simmer for 5 minutes. Remove from heat and mix in bread crumbs. Let stand for 5 minutes. Then place bulgar into 2 cups boiling water and let simmer for 5 minutes. Add a dash of Worcestershire sauce and combine with the rice and bread crumbs. Finally, slowly add water to potato flakes until fluffy and place on top.

That's Italian

2 cups	noodles (any style)
1	13-ounce can of tomato paste, dehydrated
1 cup	spaghetti sauce, dehydrated
¼ cup	mixture of dehydrated egg plant, red and green peppers, onion, black olives and mushrooms
¼ cup	Parmesan cheese
4½ cups	water

Reconstitute tomato paste in ½ cup of boiling water with dried spaghetti sauce. Add noodles, vegetables and mushrooms to 4 cups boiling water and let simmer until noodles are cooked. Pour out excess water and add tomato paste. Sprinkle cheese on top.

Shrimp Alfredo

1	package of alfredo sauce, dehydrated
1	can small shrimp, dehydrated
2 cups	noodles (your preference)
1/4 cup	dried veggies
1 tablespoon	Parmesan
2 1/2 cups	water

Add noodles, shrimp and veggies to 2 cups boiling water and simmer for 12 minutes. Reconstitute dehydrated alfredo sauce in 1/2 cup boiling water and stir into noodles. Top with Parmesan cheese.

Easy Pasta Parmesan

2 cups	noodles (any style)
2 tablespoons	margarine
2 tablespoons	dried vegetables (green pepper, red pepper, carrots, onion flakes, etc.)
2 tablespoons	dried mushrooms
4	sundried tomatoes, chopped
1 teaspoon	red wine (optional)
1	package pasta parmesan noodle sauce
	Handful of shelled pistachio nuts
	(grated cheese is optional)
	4 cups water

Bring water to a boil in a pot. Add noodles, dried vegetables, mushrooms, pistachio nuts and tomatoes. Let simmer until noodles are cooked and vegetables have rehydrated. Pour out excess water and add margarine, red wine and noodle sauce, stir until well mixed and the margarine is melted. Serve with grated cheese.

Sweet-and-Sour Rice Dish

2 cups	water
½ cup	rice (brown rice is good)
1 cup	mixture of dried fruit (pineapple, apricot, apples and raisins)
¼ cup	mixture of walnuts and almonds
Dash	garlic
Dash	black pepper
2 tablespoons	brown sugar
1½ tablespoons	soy sauce (save a packet from your last take-out order of Chinese food)
1½ tablespoons	vinegar (pocket a packet from your local burger joint)
1 tablespoon	cooking oil

Place rice and fruit mixture into 2 cups boiling water and let simmer until rice is done (brown rice takes about 20 minutes). Drain excess water. Add nuts, sugar, spices, soy sauce and vinegar and then fry in oil for 5 to 7 minutes.

▲ *Be a little more creative and add TVP (textured vegetable protein) and dehydrated vegetables, with a side order of pappadums, to this sweet-and-sour dish.*

Pita Pizza

2	pita breads (more if needed)
1	can tomato paste, dehydrated
¼ cup	boiling water
2 tablespoons	green and red pepper
1	fresh red onion
1	dried salami (or other dried meats)
	Grated cheese (any kind)
1 tablespoon	olive oil

Coat pan with olive oil. Mix tomato paste with ¼ cup boiling water and spread on pizza, then add toppings. Place pizza in pan and cover for 5 to 7 minutes on a cook stove (longer over the fire). Cut up into pieces and share while the next pizza is being prepared and cooked. Toppings can be changed to suit personalities; just remember to keep it light and stick to food not easily spoiled.

▲ *The kids will love pita pizzas.*

SOME SIMPLE SALADS

Red Cabbage Salad

1	small head red cabbage
1 cup	dehydrated carrot slices
1	small red onion
½ cup	raisins
1 tablespoon	pine nuts or peanuts
1 tablespoon	sesame seeds

Dressing (made at home and placed in a sealed container)

½ cup	vegetable oil
¼ cup	rice wine vinegar
2 tablespoons	sugar
1 tablespoon	soy sauce

Shred or coarsely chop red cabbage. Add slices of onion, dehydrated carrot slices, raisins, sesame seeds and nuts. Mix in dressing.

Napa Cabbage Salad

1	small head napa cabbage
1	package Ramen Noodles (oriental flavour)
1 tablespoon	sesame seeds

Dressing (made at home and placed in a sealed container)

½ cup	vegetable oil
¼ cup	rice wine vinegar
2 tablespoons	sugar
1 tablespoon	soy sauce

Shred or coarsely grate napa cabbage. Add sesame seeds and uncooked noodles (broken up into small pieces) with flavouring. Mix in dressing.

Couscous Salad

1 cup	couscous
1 cup	dehydrated corn, black olives, red and green pepper
1	cube vegetable bouillon
2 cups	water
4	tortillas

Dressing (made at home and placed in a sealed container)

2 tablespoons	Club House Greek Seasoning
½ cup	vegetable oil
½ cup	balsamic vinegar

Boil 2 cups of water. Add couscous, dried vegetables and bouillon cube. Set aside for 5 minutes. Fluff with fork and pour dressing in couscous mixture. Serve warm or cold in a rolled-up tortilla.

DELIGHTFUL DESSERTS

Strawberry Turnovers

1 cup	dehydrated strawberries
1 cup	Tea-Bisk or Bisquick mix
	Flour for kneading
2 tablespoons	cognac
3 tablespoons	brown sugar
1 tablespoons	olive oil
1 cup	water

Let strawberries reconstitute in ½ cup of water, cognac and brown sugar. Mix Tea-Bisk or Bisquick with ½ cup water. Knead handful portions in flour, spread flat and place in an oiled deep-dish frying pan or shallow cooking pot. Add a glob of strawberries to one side of the dough and flip the opposite side over top. Press down on the corners, cover the pan and let it bake at a low temperature for 7 to 8 minutes.

▲ *A well-fed camper is a happy camper.*

Simple Cinnamon Rolls

3 cups	Tea-Bisk or Bisquick mix
½ cup	brown sugar
1 tablespoon	cinnamon
¼ cup	raisins
3 tablespoons	margarine
	Flour for rolling
1 tablespoon	olive oil
1½ cups	water

Slowly add water to Tea-Bisk or Bisquick to form dough, and roll out on floured canoe paddle. Spread margarine onto flattened surface (paddle works well), sprinkling on cinnamon, brown sugar and raisins. Roll into a log and slice 1-inch slices and place them in an oiled frying pan. Cover and bake over low heat for 7 to 8 minutes.

Tortilla Cinnamon Rolls

2	tortillas
2 tablespoons	margarine
½ cup	brown sugar
1 tablespoon	cinnamon
¼ cup	chopped nuts
1 tablespoon	olive oil

Spread margarine on tortilla and sprinkle on brown sugar, cinnamon and chopped nuts. Roll and fry in olive oil in a covered pan.

Rice Pudding

1½ cup	minute rice
¼ cup	raisins
3 tablespoons	brown sugar
¼ teaspoon	cinnamon
Dash	nutmeg
2 tablespoons	jam
¼ cup	powdered milk
1 cup	water
1 tablespoon	powdered egg
1½ teaspoon	flour

Cook ingredients (except for jam, flour and powdered egg) in 1 cup boiling water for 5 minutes. Add powdered egg and flour (mixed with enough water to make into a paste). Top with jam.

Couscous with Apricots and Almonds

1 cup	couscous
1 cup	dried apricots
¼ cup	almonds
1 bouillon	cube
1 teaspoon	nutmeg
1 tablespoon	honey or brown sugar
2 cups	water

Boil 2 cups of water. Remove from heat and add couscous, sliced apricots, almonds, nutmeg and honey. Stir and set aside for 5 minutes.

"It's rare to have people complain about eating seconds, but watch their patience disappear when there isn't enough for firsts."

BILL MASON, *SONG OF THE PADDLE (1984)*

Apple Crisp

1½ cup	dried apples, chopped
½ teaspoon	cinnamon or apple pie spice mix
	Hot water to just cover fruit in pot
½ cup	chopped walnuts or almonds
½ cup	raisins
¼ teaspoon	salt (optional)

Combine all ingredients except nuts in a pot and let soak until the fruit rehydrates — about 15 minutes.

Meanwhile, combine the following:

¼ to ½ cup	oatmeal
3 tablespoons	flour
4 heaping	tablespoons margarine
3 tablespoons	brown sugar
Pinch	salt (optional)

Mix together with hands to a crumbly consistency. Grease a fry pan. Add nuts to fruit mixture and pour into pan. (If there is a lot of liquid, stir in 1 tablespoon of flour.) Cover with oatmeal mix. Bake, using a twiggy fire, for about 15 minutes until heated through and browned on top.

Basic Bannock

½ cup	white flour
½ cup	whole wheat flour
1 teaspoon	baking powder
3 tablespoons	powdered milk
½ teaspoon	salt
¼ cup	water

Mix all dry ingredients and add water slowly until dough is slightly sticky. Separate into 3 or 4 patties and fry in an oiled frying pan over moderate heat until both sides are a golden brown.

Cajun Bannock

½ cup	white flour
½ cup	whole wheat flour
1 teaspoon	baking powder
3 tablespoon	powdered milk
½ teaspoon	salt
Pinch	garlic powder
Pinch	onion powder
Pinch	white pepper
Pinch	cracked black pepper
Pinch	cayenne pepper
Pinch	dried thyme
Pinch	dried oregano
1 tablespoon	unsalted sunflower seeds
1 tablespoon	olive oil
¼ cup	water

Mix all dry ingredients and add water slowly until dough is slightly sticky. Separate into 3 or 4 patties and fry in an oiled frying pan over moderate heat until both sides are a golden brown.

Super Pancakes

½ cup	white flour
½ cup	whole wheat flour
1 tablespoon	powdered eggs
1 tablespoon	powdered milk
½ teaspoon	baking powder
Pinch	salt
1 teaspoon	cinnamon
¼ cup	dried cranberries
1 tablespoon	olive oil
¼ cup	water

Mix dry ingredients. Add water slowly to make batter. Fry in an oiled pan at moderate heat. Serve with syrup.

CHOOSING THE PERFECT CAMPSITE

Somewhere between eighteen and twenty-five beaver dams later, we came to a large flat rock and a big patch of grass in a bend of the river. It was home for the night. We hung our wet pants on branches, cooked supper, and hit the hay.

JOYCE ALLENE STONE, *MUSKEG, MOSQUITOES AND MOOSE (1992)*

We've all been there. It's getting late in the day. The group spotted a perfect campsite a couple of hours ago but the overly keen trip leader pushed everyone to continue on. Now there's nowhere to pitch a tent, the bugs are getting bad, thunder can be heard in the distance, and the sun is close to setting. You're hoping for a scenic place with a nest of pines to protect you from the wind, but still enough out in the open to snag a breeze and keep the bugs at bay. Your preference is also to have it face west-southwest to catch the morning sun at its tip and also the last rays of the evening glow.

What you find, however, is a mound of sharp rock surrounded by swamp ooze. Even when you look for a flat place to pitch a tent, it's next to impossible. One spot would have your head lower than your legs, giving you a major headache by morning. Another is on a slope that would obviously cause all the occupants inside to pile on top of one another. A deep hollow would protect you from high winds, but with the coming rainstorm you stand a good chance of becoming the next Noah's Ark. The depression is also infested with blackflies, mosquitoes, and worst of all, bothersome ticks. You'd be free from the bugs if you pitch your tent on the mound of rock, but

◀ *A perfect campsite. Sweet serenity.*

▲ *Sometimes the whereabouts of a campsite is obvious, and sometimes it's not.*

a lone tree is rooted on top and is a perfect lightning rod. To make matters worse, the rock is such an exposed spot that if the sun happens to be shining the next morning it will beat down on the tent and quickly transform it into a sauna.

Well, what should you do? Make the best of it, I guess. And don't forget to ignore the trip leader the next day when you pass by another perfect site. Experience has taught me that all the good campsites are the ones you find around 3 to 4 P.M. The worst ones are always found around dusk.

Setting up camp is the next important issue. More times than not a group will arrive at their campsite and decide not to bother setting up until later in the evening. That's when trouble starts. It soon gets dark, not enough wood is gathered, the bear rope isn't hung up, the dishes have yet to be washed, some participants are even still out fishing, and tent sites haven't been chosen. It's almost inevitable that tension forms in the group and arguments soon erupt.

To avoid conflict, my wife and I have learned to make setting up camp an art form. The moment we arrive in camp Alana and I split up the duties and get right to them. She pitches the tent, unrolls the bedding, erects the rain tarp and puts the packs away. I locate the outhouse, hang the bear rope, gather firewood, filter water, boil water for tea and tie up the boat if it's

Top Ten Reasons to Avoid a Campsite

- You find a big pile of bear poop directly beside the tent space.
- You find a big pile of human poop directly beside the tent space.
- Park wardens have squared the site off with yellow caution tape.
- The camp chipmunk is friendlier than your neighbor's cat.
- The tent space is the size of a quarter.
- The nearest firewood is 20 miles away.
- Every third tree on the site has been hit by lightning.
- Every fourth tree has a dozen nails hammered into it.
- It's mosquito season and a stagnant pond circles the fire ring.
- It's already occupied by a group of youths equipped with a boom box and a cooler of beer.

a canoe trip. We then flip a coin to see who's preparing dinner and who's washing dishes. Half an hour later all the chores are done and we can start feeling at home.

In the morning it's the same routine, except in reverse. I'm the first out of the tent since Alana can hold her bladder longer than I can. After relieving myself I retrieve the food pack and boil water for coffee and cook up a quick breakfast. Alana packs up the gear and folds up the tent. It ordinarily takes us around forty minutes to get ready. Our record, however, is twelve minutes. We were camped on a big lake in Algonquin and woke up around 4:30 A.M. to the sound of a strong wind. Not wanting to become windbound the entire day, we got up and began our morning ritual. It only included a granola bar for breakfast, but I managed to make coffee and Alana and I got off the big lake just in time.

> *"Campsites are punctuation marks for a voyageur, signifying the end of the day. I may forget portages, rapids, and lakes, which merge into a nebulous montage of country traveled over, but there are some campsites that stand out vividly in my mind as special places remembered."*
>
> SIGURD F. OLSON, *OF TIME AND PLACE*

HOW TO BE A "GREEN" CAMPER

Wilderness is the feeling of enjoyment and peacefulness; once it is gone nothing artificial will ever replace it.

BRANDY STEWART, AGE 13, *ISLANDS OF HOPE* (1992)

DURING THE PAST decade more and more people have become environmentally friendly at home and at work. However, this change in attitude isn't necessarily as aggressive when it comes to camping. I'm not sure why. After all, you'd think that wild places, which provide us with the incentive to protect what we have at home, would be first on the list, not just an afterthought.

Government agencies have tried to lessen our damage of the land, as well as our impact on the wilderness experience of others, by creating strict regulations. In heavily utilized parks they've banned bottles and cans, insisted that campers use designated campsites, issued limited-use permits and handed out pamphlets urging campers to "take only photographs and leave only footprints." All have been effective, but all were developed only after the damage was already done. In my opinion, it's more effective to foster a strong environmental ethic than to manage everything with a bunch of rigid rules. This belief comes from the fact that in most cases it's not malice but ignorance that's the root of the problem. Here are a few suggestions that I think will help create a sense of what's wrong and what's right when it comes to being a green camper.

◀ *"Tree huggers" check out an old-growth forest in Temagami, Ontario.*

Cleaning Up a Mountain of Trash

Cleanup efforts initiated by environmental climbing expeditions have now successfully removed 7.7 tons (7 t) of the estimated 1,115 tons (1,012 t) of garbage left behind on Mount Everest by mountaineers. Items that have been hauled back include food containers, gas cartridges, ladders, batteries, bits of broken climbing gear and over four hundred oxygen bottles.

CHOOSING A CAMPSITE

A good number of canoe routes and hiking trails have been developed on non-park land, which means that campsites found along the way are not designated. There's no law stating you must stay at a particular spot; however, to lessen your impact on the area you should always make use of the more heavily impacted sites rather than "improve" on a new site.

Small island sites should be avoided at all costs when canoeing or kayaking. They can never withstand the abuse and are guaranteed to become a magnet for nuisance bears in the area.

Never dig trenches around your tent or cut down standing trees. Tents should be placed on bare rock devoid of any plant life, if possible. If not, then choose fauna such as meadow grass that can withstand being slept on much better than blueberry bushes. And when you're leaving your site, make sure you depart with everything you came with. Nothing should be left behind.

Some campers believe that brightly colored tents and other gear take away the natural look of the forest. It might be a good idea, especially for large, organized groups, to keep to natural tones when purchasing your next bit of camp gear so your neighbors don't think the circus has come to town.

GROUP SIZE

Most regulated parks have a limit on group sizes allowed in the interior. For example, in popular paddling parks only nine canoeists are permitted to camp on each designated site. The number seems odd, since canoeists usually travel in pairs. Traditionally, however, local camps would have three children per canoe, and it was the camps that made most of the heavy impact on the park's campsites. The same problem is now occurring in some non-regulated areas. Group sizes are not limited, which means large organized groups will choose to use these areas rather than operating parks. It's not that they are actually being malicious. In fact, most of them are far more environmentally conscious than other users. They have even gone out of their way in the last few years to clean up the areas that are no longer being maintained by the government. However, the problem still remains: if you have too many people making use of a campsite, it will definitely be detrimental to the natural surroundings. Therefore, large groups should split up to make camp, having one leader per seven kids.

CAT-HOLES AND TREASURE CHESTS

Toilet-paper mounds have to be one of the worst things to find littering a campsite — it can ruin the entire trip. If there isn't a treasure chest (makeshift outhouse) made available on the site, go back at least 150 feet (50 m) from camp, turn up 1 to 2 inches (3–4 cm) of topsoil and, when finished, cover up the waste and toilet paper with a mound of dirt, just like a cat does in a litter box. In two weeks or less the waste matter will become perfect potting soil.

TP Substitutes

According to the National Outdoor Leadership School (NOLS), the best alternatives for toilet paper are pinecones, snow, sticks, and weathered rocks. The Roman army used a sponge attached to a stick, soaked in salt water. Natives in coastal areas used mussel shells. The Cree preferred sphagnum moss. And the Ojibwa liked the soft and fragrant leaf from the wild ginger plant.

▲ *Dishes should be washed well away from the shoreline.*

Poop in the Sea

Sea water can degrade human waste far faster than topsoil. Some ocean-side campers wade out into the surf to poop. Do this only in lesser used areas. Better to carry a small marine toilet or baggie with cat litter and burn TP, if needed, in the fire.

Feminine Hygiene

Feminine hygiene products should either be burned in a hot fire or carried out in a plastic bag. Do not dispose of them by burying them. Wild animals, especially squirrels and bears, will be attracted to the strong scent of the pheromones and dig them up, decorating the camp with them.

COMPOST TOILETS

Some parks are now experimenting with compost toilets placed at campgrounds and interior campsites. Rather than being the traditional hole-in-the-ground outhouses or water-based disposal units, these ecological toilets use layers of sawdust and the microorganisms already present in human waste to break everything down. Each spring the toilets are emptied and their natural fertilizer is spread out over the forest floor.

WASHING UP

The days of washing dishes at the water's edge are gone. Even if you are using biodegradable soap, the bacteria from greasy pots and pans create a major problem. It's also a very ineffective way to do dishes. It's far better to fill a pot with warm water, walk back from the shoreline at least 100 feet (30 m) and, using pine needles and sand as a scrub brush, wash up and then deposit the gray water in a small cat-hole.

Washing yourself away from the shoreline is extremely important. Many campers become ill after getting their drinking water in the same area where others have cleaned up. Wash with a pot of warm water a good distance behind camp and dispose the waste water in a small cat-hole.

> *"Going to the woods is going home, for I suppose we came from the woods originally."*
>
> JOHN MUIR

▲ *A homemade eco-fire can be easily constructed out of a couple of tin cans.*

▲ *The intrinsic value of a wild area is in its wildness. It is priceless and worth protecting.*

FIRES VERSUS STOVES

Campfires are an important part of the camping experience. However, with so many places now becoming void of dead wood, sites are being stripped of living trees as well as essential cover for fauna and flora. So, as a rule, campfires should be thought of as a luxury, not a necessity. A stove is much faster for cooking meals than a fire and creates less of an impact on a site. When choosing a stove to purchase, make sure that it runs on white gas rather than butane or propane. This takes away any chance of someone leaving an empty gas cylinder behind, which is quickly becoming a major problem in the interior.

The Environmental Fireplace, or firebox, was an idea of canoeists and film maker Bill Mason, who then had Ric Driediger at Horizons Unlimited mass produce it for environmentally conscious campers. The basic idea is to contain the campfire rather than build a traditional campfire ring, which will inevitably scar the rock surface. It also requires half the wood to cook up dinner or boil up a pot of tea. A homemade version can easily be made from a large tin can and metal cutters.

LOTUS

BRINGING THE KIDS ALONG

At three months, she gurgled and squirmed, a gummy grin peeking out of her lifejacket cocoon. The bow was her universe. Nothing existed beyond the bond of our smiles; and as though she soaked up our tranquil mood, she fell asleep to the gentle rock of each stroke.

LIZ LUNDELL, *STORIES FROM THE BOW SEAT*

THE MOMENT MY wife and I told our friends and family our great news about being pregnant with our first child, I was amazed at how quickly everyone informed us how drastically life would suddenly change for us. It was almost as if they were more pleased that we also had to suffer along with them than that we were finally having a child. It's not as if they didn't congratulate us first. But soon after came the warnings about how our days of spending the summer season paddling remote rivers in the far North would now and forever be a thing of the past. Obviously we knew that having a child would alter our day-to-day life, and we weren't so naïve as to think that our canoe trips would be the same as before. But come on. I was finally pleased that I would soon have a young adult to carry my canoe for once!

It seems that camping with kids, especially in the interior, is a mixed experience. We've seen friends of ours give up on their former outdoor lifestyle altogether the moment they had children. It's depressing visiting them, actually, as every time I meet them the parents constantly complain about how having a family has taken away their love of the outdoors and how they'd get back out there in a second if it wasn't for their newfound responsibilities. Other friends, however, claim that sharing their love of camping with children is a magical experience that adds a priceless component, not only to their trips, but to the relationship they have developed with their children.

◀ *"I'm having the time of my life." Ian Bush.*

Be sure to read the book *Cradle to Canoe: Camping and Canoeing with Children,* written by Rolf and Debra Kraiker and published by Boston Mills Press. It's got everything you need for a family outing.

I guess both have valid points. Let's face it, kids require a lot of patience, especially on a camping trip. They slow you down and reduce the time you spend in the interior. Definitely, the experiences you once had will be far different. But what exactly is wrong with that? Sometimes I think we want more quantity rather than quality out of our time spent in the outdoors, and I think it's great how a child can show you how wrong that really is.

A Few Pointers Learned by Trial and Error

- A positive attitude can mean the difference between a terrible nightmare and an unforgettable holiday.
- The secret is to adapt to the level of your children; don't try to force them to meet yours. It is much easier for you to adjust to a shorter, less strenuous trip than it is to push the child all day without a break.
- Make sure to start early — they will adapt much more quickly at a younger age.
- Make sure the kid's first trip is a good one. Start out by camping in the backyard or take a number of easy daytrips. Then try a weekend and slowly graduate to a week-long trip into a semi-wilderness park.
- Frequent rest stops, long lunch breaks, late starts and early finishes are a must when camping with kids.
- Invite friends along who have children the same age as your own.
- If you choose a canoe trip, paddle for only two hours and then make base camp, hopefully where there's a nice sandy beach for the kids to play on.

MORE ADVICE

- Pack plenty of Band-Aids and a good collection of soothing words to help heal all the little cuts and bruises that are sure to appear.
- Choose safe campsites. Stay away from steep dropoffs and slippery rocks. Have them wear their PFD along the shoreline and watch for those nasty patches of poison ivy.
- Give them some camp chores to do. It gives them a routine and keeps them out of trouble.
- Don't pack along a huge toy box. Allow only one of their favorites. Once out there they will soon create their own toys from pine cones, rocks, and weird-shaped pieces of driftwood.

- For canoe trips that require extra-long portaging, make sure to pack a favorite book and have one parent read to the children after the first carry-over while the other heads back for the rest of the gear.
- Have lots of games prepared for those rainy days at camp and a good collection of stories for the campfire, along with a large supply of marshmallows.
- Have them keep a journal while on the trip. It's a great way to share the adventures of the day and will become a priceless treasure for years to come.

▲ *Lily Dipper Sarah Hicks.*

Keep to the Basics

Don't try new food recipes with the kids while out camping. It's best to just stick to the foods they like at home. And always make sure to have a constant supply of snacks for them to munch on and juice to drink.

KID-PROOF GEAR

- Finding a PFD to fit a fifteen-month-old is a little tough and, just like buying shoes for your child, it will end up not fitting for the next trip. So it's much less expensive to rent one if you can. Make sure it fits snugly but that they also feel comfortable wearing it. There's nothing worse than having them hate putting the thing on. And it should go without saying, if you want them to wear a PFD, make sure you wear one yourself.
- A baby jogger (a stroller with three large wheels and a sling seat) is designed for heavy off-road use and is good for almost any type of hiking trail.
- Consider a playpen on a canoe trip or campground camping; it's a great way to keep them out of mischief.
- Give each child his or her own small daypack to carry personal items such as snacks, rain gear, water bottle, and a teddy bear.
- Each child should have their own flashlight. It gives a great sense of security, as well as a way to play shadow puppets before bedtime.
- Each child should have a whistle clipped to their belt and know to use it if they happen to wander off the campsite or trail.
- A sunhat should be worn at all times.
- Children dislike being cold and wet just as much as you do. Make sure to dress them as well or even better than you dress yourself. This is no time to make good use of those hand-me-downs your friends and family have pawned off on you.
- Forget those cheap sleeping bags decorated with Barbie or Star Wars figures. They may be okay for sleeping over at the grandparent's house, but aren't close to being warm enough for the bush.
- Pack sneakers or sandals for use in a canoe and good old rubber boots for kicking around camp.

THE DIAPER DEBATE

One of the biggest concerns parents usually have when traveling with the two-and-under crowd is what to do about the diaper dilemma. First, there's the cloth versus disposable debate; both have their drawbacks. Cloth diapers can be washed and dried at camp, but this means doing a serious laundry every day. And don't rinse them in the lake; bring a portable basin and make sure to dispose of the contents of diaper and rinse water in the outhouse or at least 100 feet (30 m) away from camp. Many parents find it much easier to carry disposable diapers, carrying out the used ones in a double-lined garbage bag. I have seen some campers try to burn disposables in the fire pit before leaving their site; however, the diapers definitely don't burn, they just

▲ *The younger they are, the easier to transport. Mom and Kyla on a day hike.*

look like big crusty globs of charred plastic goop, making the campsite a complete eyesore for the next camper who comes along.

One parent I know recommends the stoop and scoop method. He packs disposables when camping with his one-year-old but lets the child go without diapers or pants most days at the campsite. Another idea is to pack along cloth and disposable diapers, cleaning the cloth diapers on sunny days at camp and saving the disposables for rainy days on the trail.

How to Deal with the Bugs

Be sure to use a mosquito repellent that doesn't harm sensitive skin. A bug jacket might be a good idea, even a bug tarp. Or better yet, plan your holidays late in the summer when bugs aren't as much an issue. Those After-Bite pens can also help relieve the nasty itch of insect bites.

CAMPFIRE CLASSICS

I've never really felt comfortable telling ghost stories to a group of young campers around the evening fire. The problem is, when the moment comes to douse the flames and call it a night, the terrified kids curl up in their tents and stay awake all night, jumping at every little sound.

On the other hand, it is also very difficult to disappoint a group of enthusiastic kids who have been brainwashed into thinking that spooky stories (and marshmallows) are a part of any true camping trip. So, when I'm asked to spin a tale of horror around the campfire, I make everyone happy by telling "harmless" hair-raising tales. Here are two classics.

The Purple Gorilla

I had a friend once, a shy, unusual fellow named Myron. He was unlike any of the other kids on the block, especially when it came to owning a pet. You see, Myron didn't own a dog, cat, or even a hamster. Instead, he kept his very own pet gorilla. Not just an everyday gorilla, but a huge, purple gorilla.

One night Myron asked me for a favor. He was going out of town and wanted me to take care of his purple gorilla for him. I hesitated at first. After all, I've never taken care of someone's gorilla before. But Myron assured me his pet was quite tame. So I agreed, and Myron handed me a list of important instructions to follow as he headed out the door.

As I read the list, noting what to feed the gorilla and such, I noticed a special note Myron had placed in bold at the bottom of the page. It read "Whatever you do, don't touch the purple gorilla."

I thought the strict notation was a little harsh. After all, the gorilla looked innocent enough. But I made sure to follow Myron's wishes and didn't touch the beast while I scooped out his dinner and placed water in his dish. But then he gave me this sweet little grin and motioned for me to touch him on his shoulder. I just couldn't resist. I squeezed my hand through the iron bars of his cage and touched him.

The gorilla suddenly went nuts, bending the bars apart with his big purple hairy hands, and bellowing out a tremendous roar. Then he chased me, across the living room, over the couch and under the kitchen table. I knew the only way to escape was to run outside and get to my car. So I did. But the car wouldn't start. The gorilla wasn't far behind, so I jumped out of the car and started running down the road, screaming "Help Me! Help Me!"

Then, just as I built up a good lead over the hairy beast, I tripped and fell. Seconds later the gorilla caught up with me. I lay there, shaking with fear, as he crept closer and closer, purple sweat dripping from his stinking armpits and his foul-smelling breath rushing down the back of my neck. I new the jig was up! I knew the end was near!

As I lay helpless on the roadside, the beast slowly lowered his sharp claws toward my exposed throat. I screamed out, "Why? Why didn't I listen to Myron? Why did I touch his pet purple gorilla?"

It was obviously too late for regrets, for the beast's paw was inches from my limp and quivering body. Death seemed only seconds away. Then, with a slap of his massive paw, the ugly purple gorilla touched me and yelled out . . .

"You're it!"

Land of the Silver Birch

Land of the silver birch,
Home of the beaver,
Where still the mighty moose
Wanders at will.

(Refrain)
Blue lake and rocky shores
I will return once more.
Boom di de ada
Boom di de ada
Boom di de ada boom

High on a rocky ledge,
I'll build my wigwam
Close by the water's edge
Silent and still.

(Refrain)
Down in the forest glade,
Deep in the low-lands
My heart cries out for thee,
Hills of the North.

(Refrain)

One group sings the verses while the other keeps repeating the chorus.

The Haunted Cabin

Late one afternoon, I became windbound on a small, dark lake deep in the bush. I could make no headway, and decided to camp for the night. Going ashore, I noticed a decrepit but usable trapper's cabin a short distance into the gloomy woods. I opened the door and was amazed to find a clean, but obviously quite old cabin with kindling, a table, and even a bed. The layers of dust made it obvious that no one had been here for many years.

I ate a quick supper and went to bed, exhausted. Later that night, a noise made me sit straight up in alarm. Rap! Rap! Rap! Looking wildly around, I could see nothing in the gloom. Mice, I figured, so I lay back down and tried to go back to sleep.

There it was again! This time I distinctly heard three sharp raps on the wall. Rap! Rap! Rap! I also noticed that the room was growing lighter. Jumping out of bed, I saw a back door that had escaped my notice when I first entered the cabin. Underneath I could see a soft, orange glow that grew brighter as I watched. I stood paralyzed in fear.

Rap! Rap! Rap! The noise came again! Something gave me the courage to approach the door. Reaching out slowly, I tugged it open. There, inside was . . . Are you ready? Wait for it. A huge old box of — wrapping paper!

Alice the Camel

Alice the camel has – ten humps,
Alice the camel has – ten humps,
Alice the camel has – ten humps,
So go, Alice, go!
(Ba Boom-boom-boom-boom)

Alice the camel has – nine humps,
Alice the camel has – nine humps,
Alice the camel has – nine humps,
So go, Alice, go!
(Ba Boom-boom-boom-boom)

Continue to sing, decreasing the number of humps with each verse.
Last verse:
Alice the camel has – no humps,
Alice the camel has – no humps,
Alice the camel has – no humps,
So Alice is a horse!

The Old Lady Who Swallowed a Fly

There was an old lady who swallowed a fly
I don't know why she swallowed a fly
I guess she'll die

There was an old lady who swallowed a spider
That wiggled and jiggled and tickled inside her
She swallowed the spider to catch the fly
I don't know why she swallowed a fly
I guess she'll die

There was an old lady who swallowed a bird
How absurd! To swallow a bird!
She swallowed the bird to catch the spider
That wiggled and jiggled and tickled inside her
She swallowed the spider to catch the fly
I don't know why she swallowed a fly
I guess she'll die

More verses:
Cat . . . Imagine that! She swallowed a cat
Dog . . . What a hog! She swallowed a dog
Goat . . . She opened her throat and in walked a goat
Cow . . . I don't know how she swallowed that cow

Last verse:
There was an old lady, she swallowed a horse
She died of course!

"For the five year old, the mossy trunks hid super heroes; our tent was shelter from monsters he'd conjure up excitedly. How proud the little guy was of making a difference with his paddle, even though the spurts were interrupted by lily pad harvest and waterplay, streams pulsing through his fingers as he leaned over the gunwale. "When can we roast the marshmallows? How much farther? Can I go swimming now? When will we see a bear? Why is the moon out in the day?" When, how, why, why, why? It was all new again."

LIZ LUNDELL, *STORIES FROM THE BOW SEAT*

"RUFFING" IT: CAMPING WITH DOGS

To me, Cooper brought the same joy as seeing a beautiful lady, or a soaring falcon, or a little baby saying "Da da" for the first time. I loved Cooper, my forever friend, and he loved me.

PETER JENKINS, *A WALK ACROSS AMERICA* (1979)

DOGS ARE A strange breed. Some are well-behaved and considerate, while others are just a plain nuisance, which is why the question of having them join you on a camping trip is not all that cut-and-dried. Much of it depends on the actions of the owners themselves. I witnessed someone's beagle harass a cow moose by leaping out of the canoe and swimming after the poor beast. Half my food pack was once consumed by a golden retriever at the take-out of a portage. At a public campground I saw a poodle, which was leashed to a tree during the night, torn apart by a pack of coyotes. I had the displeasure of mistaking an overly friendly and unleashed black Lab for a marauding black bear. And more than once I've set my tent on top of a mound of fresh dog doo-doo and didn't realize it until I packed up the next day. I blame these incidents not on the dogs, but on the owners themselves. Quite honestly they have no business having a pet in the first place, let alone bringing them along on a camping trip.

My wife and I have been tripping with our springer spaniel, Bailey, for six years now, and believe that the golden rule is to take responsibility for the dog's actions. Things like chasing animals or leaving feces behind on a campsite are normal dog behaviors; but owners who allow them to

◀ *It just doesn't seem right. Bailey gets treated royally on all canoe trips but never once paddles a single stroke.*

▲ *I like to slip some of my gear into Bailey's pack when she's not looking.*

conduct themselves in such a way are inexcusable. When we first took Bailey camping, Alana and I made sure she was always with us and was never allowed to wander off. We even leashed her while on busy portages or hiking trails. It wasn't easy training her — Bailey simply loves being off the lead. But by using stern commands (and a few treats) our dog learned never to leave our side. Now she's better trained while on a canoe or hiking trip than she is at home. It's all a routine for her now — staying still while in the canoe, heeling the moment we spot an animal or bird, heading off the trail to relieve herself, not complaining about having her PFD put on before we run a dangerous set of rapids, and waiting for her dog pack to be strapped on before heading down the portage.

We've also built up a routine of watching over Bailey, generally because she doesn't always look after herself. A trip to the vet is always planned before we head out to make sure her shots are up-to-date and she's in good overall health. Ask your veterinarian if extra shots for diseases such as leptospirosis or Lyme disease are necessary. We pack a first-aid kit specifically designed for dogs. Bailey's regular choke collar is replaced with a glow-in-the-dark nylon collar. And I've glued a slab of foam padding on the bottom of the canoe for her to sit on (this gives her a place to call her own and helps to control her while in the boat). I've even attached an umbrella holder on the gunwale to give Bailey some shade while we paddle across a large lake. And rather than put bug repellent directly on her skin, which she'll definitely lick off and make herself sick with later on, I'll spray it on a bandana that we tie around her neck. The bandana also helps other campers identify her as a dog and not a bear if they accidentally run into her on the trail.

Speaking of bears, we also don't assume Bailey will keep us safe from them. I know a lot of people who have brought dogs out with them for that specific reason. It's true the bear will most likely think twice about coming into a camp with a dog barking. However, a bear once wandered into our campsite because of Bailey's constant whimpering. It thought she would be an easy meal, I guess. I guarantee that if the bear ever went for Bailey, our dog's instant reaction would be to run right toward us, bringing the bear along with her!

FIRST-AID KIT FOR DOGS

Be sure to check with your veterinarian as to whether the listed medications are appropriate for your dog in an emergency.

- Ace self-adhering athletic bandages
- cotton balls or Q-tips
- Vetrap bandage — your vet will have it
- adhesive tape
- sock — great for keeping a foot bandage on
- gauze sponges
- liquid bandage — works well on patching mild cuts on pads
- antiseptic towelettes
- hydrocortisone cream, 1 percent
- rubbing alcohol
- eye rinsing solution
- small container of Vaseline
- hydrogen peroxide — a good way to induce vomiting (1–3 tsp. every ten minutes until dog vomits)
- Benadryl
- Pepto-Bismol tablets
- Aspirin
- Kaopectate tablets
- emergency ice pack
- ear syringe
- antibiotic ointment such as Polysporin
- bandage scissors
- tweezers
- rectal thermometer (a dog's temperature is generally 37.5 to 39.3 degrees C)
- blanket
- dog's health record and phone number of regular vet

▲ *Dog paddling.*

De-Skunking Your Pet

Forget the tomato juice – it's messy and turns your dog orange. Mouthwash mixed with beer and then rubbed down with toothpaste actually works, but it's expensive. The best way to rid your dog of skunk spray is a concoction of the following:

- 1 quart (1L) of 3 percent hydrogen peroxide (make sure container is unopened)
- ¼ cup baking soda
- 1 teaspoon of liquid dish soap

Make sure to wear a pair of rubber or latex gloves and watch that the ingredients don't get into the dog's eyes. Also, use the mixture immediately. Hydrogen peroxide, when combined with baking soda, churns out oxygen and quickly turns to water. You may have to repeat the procedure two or three times and even finish off by wiping your dog down with a sheet of Febreze.

De-Quilling Your Dog

Porcupine quills can be extremely dangerous to your dog. Whenever possible, have them removed by a veterinarian. The tip of each quill is covered in tiny backward-facing barbs, and once it imbeds itself into your dog's flesh it's like trying to remove hundreds of fish hooks. The quills are often inside the nose and down the throat, and can only be effectively removed under anesthetic. If you have to remove them on the trail, pliers can be used, but make sure to grab the quill as close to the skin as possible. Always follow up with your vet when you return home.

"Near this spot are deposited the remains of one who possessed Beauty without Vanity, Strength without Insolence, Courage without Ferocity, and all the Virtues of Man, without his Vices. This Praise, which would be unmeaning Flattery if inscribed over human ashes, is but a just tribute to the Memory of Boatswain, a Dog."

GEORGE GORDON, LORD BYRON,
"INSCRIPTION ON THE MONUMENT OF A NEWFOUNDLAND DOG"

SWIFT
WANAPITEI
c·a·n·o·e

DARKNESS AND SOLITUDE

To travel alone is risky business, especially into a wilderness; equally risky is to have dreams and not follow them.

ROBERT PERKINS, *INTO THE GREAT SOLITUDE* (1991)

Canada's guru of canoeing, the late Bill Mason, once remarked about solo tripping, "All of my life people have been telling me you should never travel alone. But it's interesting; I've never been told that by anybody who's ever done it." After all I have read and written about the benefits of venturing alone, Mason's simplicity says it best.

Many cultures have used solitude as a type of initiation into the meaning of life. Natives regarded aloneness as a way for shamans to conjure up magic. They looked at wilderness solitude with reverence, considering it a place for them to discover their own individual identity and to build character. After fasting alone, they believed a vision would grant each brave his guardian angel. For the individual, this "vision quest" was a time for regeneration, a cleansing of the body and mind, and a realization of nature's powerful magic.

My first big solo trip was years ago on a hiking trip north of Lake Superior. I battled loneliness for the first few days, spending each night curled up in the fetal position, wide awake and jumping at the night sounds. But every time I felt spooked, I reminded myself how many others had traveled alone before me and gained insight from solitude. The realization marked a turning point in my emotions. Complete loneliness was suddenly transformed into a sense of freedom, an invigorating and exciting awareness of the life around as well as within me. It didn't take long before the little noises that had kept me awake were lulling me to sleep.

◀ *Feelin' free.*

▲ *One of the biggest advantages of traveling alone is having no set schedule.*

Apart from the insight aspects of solo travel there are many other positive points: you can camp where and when you want, prepare food pleasing to your taste buds, travel when you think it's necessary, and relax when you believe it to be appropriate.

After an extended solo adventure I think back to my fears. Amazingly enough, what unsettles me most is not the loneliness that at times creeps up, the moment when complete darkness blankets the campsite, or the times when you are forced to deal with foul weather all on your own. It is when the trip is over and I am driving away from my place of vision and have to prepare myself mentally for the jam-packed expressway, crowded with thousands of people. More than once I have turned tail on one of the cutoffs, phoned home to let someone know of my altered plans, and then headed back into the wilds for a few extra days, alone and content.

Things to Consider before Going it Alone

- Intermediate to advanced wilderness skills are required.
- Being physically fit and, more important, mentally fit, is crucial.
- Your route and trip itinerary must be well laid out and given to the proper authorities.
- You must stick to your trip plan from beginning to end.
- You must consider taking on potential hazards (for example, running rapids on a canoe trip) logically, not haphazardly.
- You should spend at least five days alone; only then will you feel comfortable with your surroundings.

TRAVELING AT NIGHT

Traveling alone at night has to be one of the best experiences. The mood that the bush at night generates gives you an unforgettable feeling of worth. Not only is it one of the most peaceful times, but it can also be the only time a winter camper can escape the coldest temperatures or a paddler can escape becoming windbound. On one particular trip paddling across a huge northern lake, I had been kept in camp for two solid days due to heavy winds. So, with only a skin of clouds blanketing the light of the full moon, I packed up at midnight and took advantage of the evening calm.

It was an unforgettable experience. I kept close to the shoreline by constantly keeping an ear out for the sound of the water gurgling and sucking against the bank. Now and then I heard other noises break the silence. Around 2 A.M. I stopped paddling and coasted for a while, letting the cool night air descend on me. It was then that I turned and saw a timber wolf watching me from shore. What an incredible moment! At first I was absolutely terrified of the beast (I read a lot of Jack London tales when I was young) and I questioned my sanity (and the safety), being all alone on the expanse of Georgian Bay, surrounded by a blackened landscape, not another human for miles. Then I thrust my blade into the water and hastily made my escape.

A few minutes later, however, the light of the moon, now undraped by the band of clouds, illuminated the dark figure once again. The wolf was definitely following me.

I then did the unthinkable. To break the silence, and probably to relieve my fear somewhat, I gave out a loud yelp. The wolf howled back, then again and again. There was a pack of five in total. I was so moved by the experience that I decided to venture off every night of that trip, never once feeling afraid or alone.

EIGHT ESSENTIAL KNOTS

A sailor takes a turn he belays; he claps on a stopper, he slacks away, and casts off a line. He clears a tangle, he opens a jammed knot, and he works a Turk's head or a sinnet. But the only time he actually ties is when his voyage is over and he ties up to a wharf.

CLIFFORD W. ASHLEY, *THE ASHLEY BOOK OF KNOTS* (1993)

KNOWING HOW TO tie a perfect knot may come as second nature to some people. But to most, the ability seems elusive. I'm with the majority. I never got it back in the days of Boy Scouts and I doubt I ever will. And it's not that I haven't tried. I've bought knot books, sat on the front porch for hours practising things like the sheet bend, monkey's fist, Turk's head and hangman's noose. When it comes down to actually using them in the field, however, I seem to panic and tie things down with half-a-dozen granny knots and hope for the best. The day I watched my canoe drift off down some rapids because of a poorly tied bowline was the day I committed to learning at least eight of the four thousand knots out there. Here's a breakdown of what I think are the essential ones, or at least the ones that are easy to remember in a pinch.

◀ *Ashley McBride and the art of knot tying.*

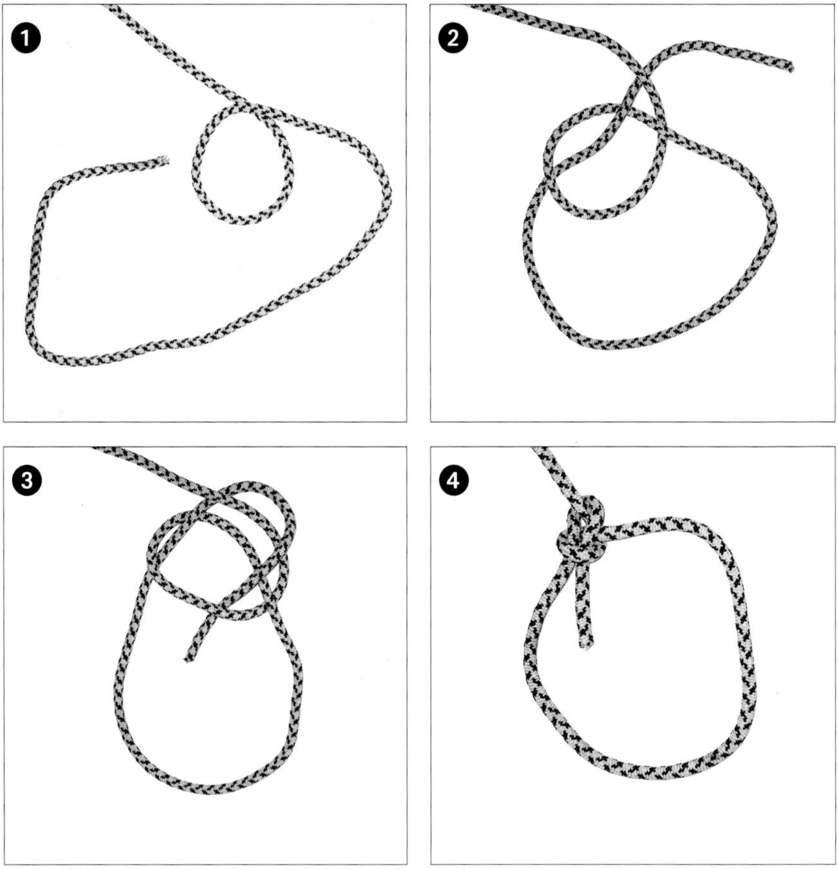

Bowline

This is the best method to form a non-slip loop. It's considered to be the "king of knots," and has the advantage of having that catchy "rabbit and the hole" chant to help you remember how to tie it. The rabbit comes out of the hole, round the tree, and back down the hole again. The hole is a small loop formed by twisting the rope, the rabbit is the free end of the rope, and the tree is the other standing part of the rope. For added security end the knot with a figure eight or two half hitches.

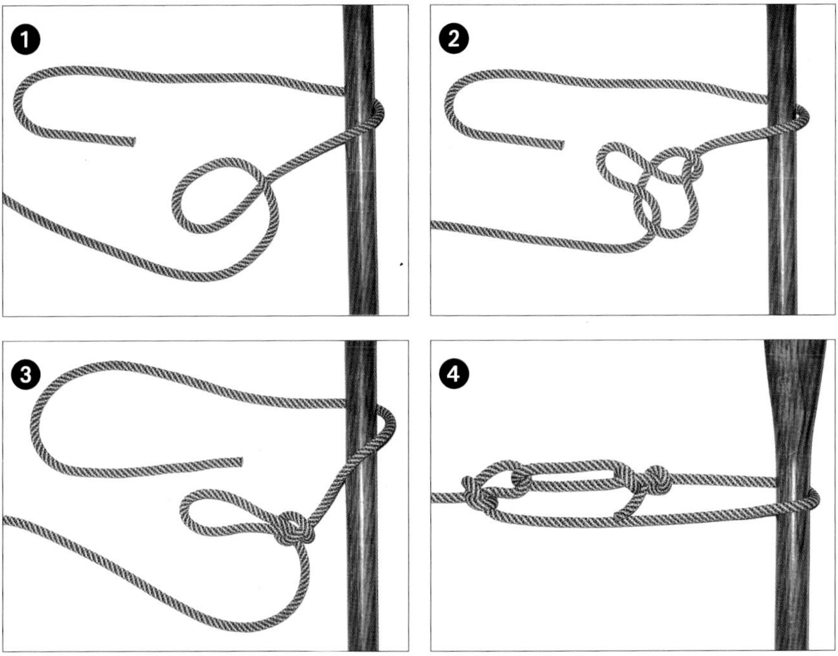

Trucker's Hitch

This is the ultimate combination of a knot-and-pulley system. It's a great way to rig rain tarps and tent guy ropes or just tighten up a clothesline. The best use, however, is for cinching down your canoe or kayak on top of your vehicle. First, tie off the rope onto the roof rack on one side of the load. Then, about three quarters along, twist the rope to form a loop and bring the loose end of the rope through the loop to form a second loop. Take note that the higher up you make the loop, the more powerful the hitch will be. Now, pass the rope around the other side of the roof rack and bring it back through the loop. Pull and hold down the grip by finishing off with a half hitch.

For the Record

According to the *Guinness Book of World Records*, the record for tying the seven basic knots described in the *Boy Scout Handbook* (square knot, sheet bend, sheep shank, clove hitch, round turn and half hitches, and bowline) on an individual piece of rope is 8.1 seconds, held by Clinton R. Bailey Sr. of Pacific City, Oregon, on April 13, 1977.

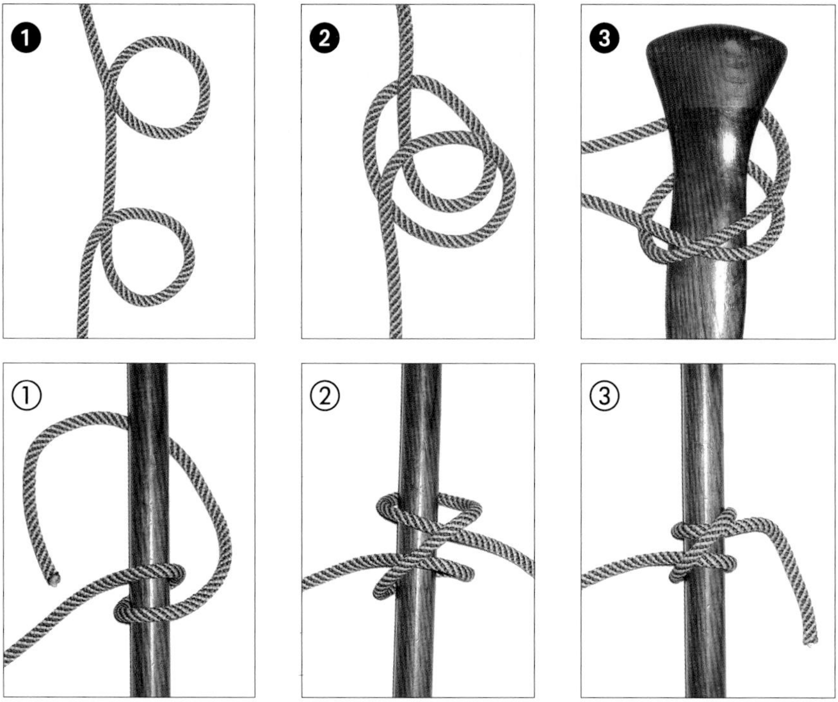

Clove Hitch

The clove hitch is a quick and easy knot to use for tying things up, and the best part is that it's easy to adjust and even easier to untie, even after a heavy load has been applied to the rope. There are two general methods to tie it. The first is to make two loops by twisting the rope in opposite directions. Now, place the left loop under the left side of the right loop. This forms the hole, which you then place over the object you want to tie on to. To finish, pull both ends of the rope to tighten. The second method is to wrap the rope around the object. Then wrap the running end around a second time and pass it under the first wrap. Pull both ends to secure the hitch. Either method works, but the first method can only be used when the rope can be placed over the object you're tying on to.

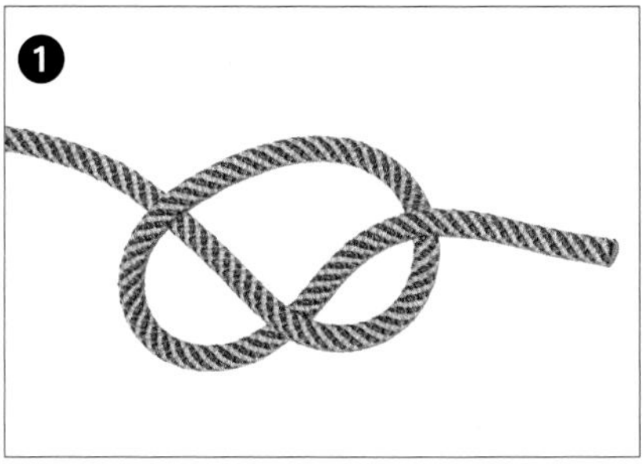

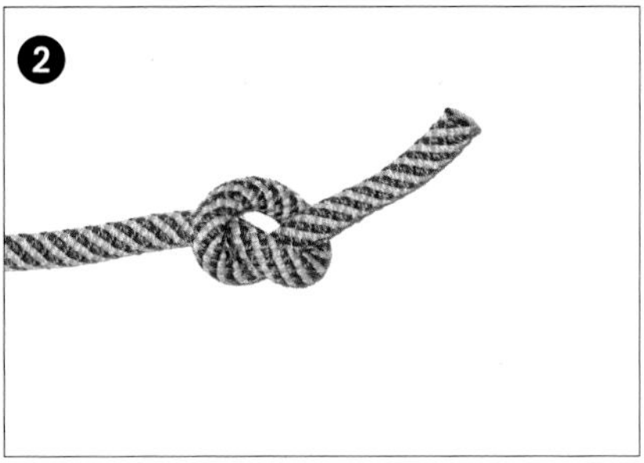

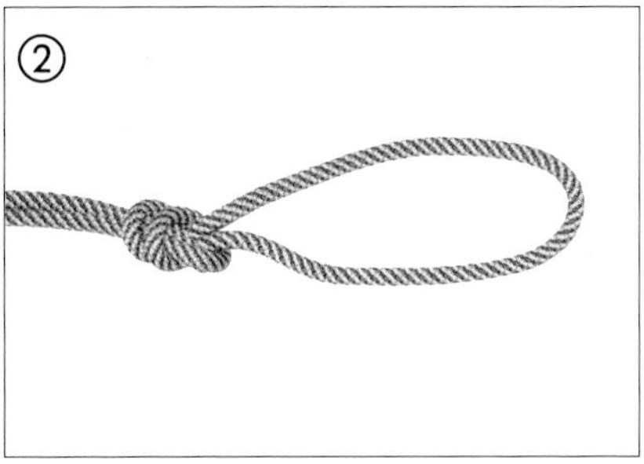

Overhand Knot

The overhand serves two purposes. The initial step creates a great stopper knot at the end of a rope to prevent it from slipping through another knot or just to tie off a loose end of rope. Just pass the end of the rope over itself and then back through the loop formed. Pull and tighten. If you do the same procedure but with a loop formed at the end of the rope, you can create a makeshift bowline. It's not as strong as the bowline, but it has the advantage of having a loop anywhere along a length of rope.

Knot, Knot Joke

Three pieces of string walk into a bar. The first string goes up to the bartender and asks for a drink. The bartender looks at him and says, "Sorry, buddy – we don't serve drinks to strings in here."

The second string then gives it a try but he too is turned down. The bartender says, "Listen, fella – I told your buddy, we don't serve strings here."

The two strings go off in a huff and tell their third friend the bad news.

The third piece of string insists on giving it a try anyway, but first he decides to disguise himself by tying himself up in a knot and fraying the top of his head to make it look like hair. Walking into the bar, the third piece of string firmly asks for a drink.

The bartender casts a suspicious look and asks, "Hey... Aren't you a piece of string?

The third piece of string then replies – "Nope, I'm a frayed knot!"

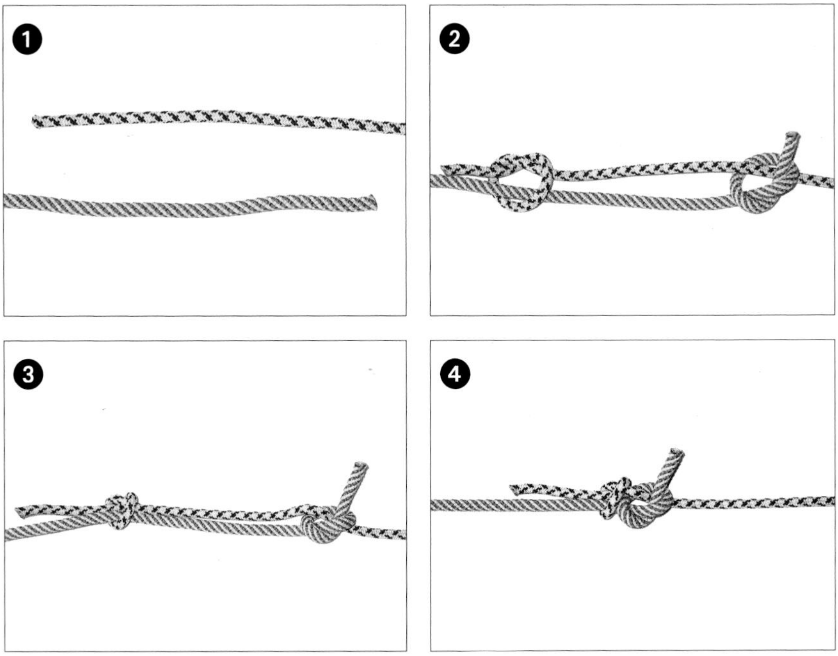

Fisherman's Knot

This is the best and quickest way to tie to ropes together. Start by placing the two ropes parallel to one another. Then tie one rope on to the other by wrapping it over and around the other, forming an overhand knot on the second piece of rope. Then repeat with the other two ends. Tighten and pull. It's an easy procedure but not as effective as a double fisherman's knot, which is a little more complicated.

The Knack of Untying Knots

To help untie jammed-up knots, quickly and firmly twist the sections of the rope outside of the knot back and forth while pushing in slack at the same time. This system is based on "compound sliding," the same process that makes it easier to insert the bathtub plug when twisting and pushing at the same time.

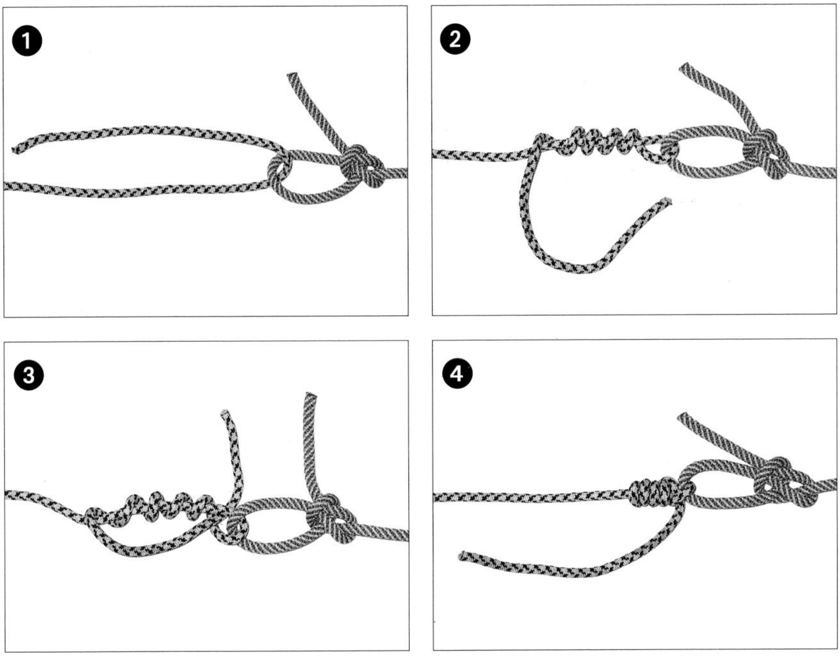

The Other Fisherman's Knot

This knot, known by some as the "improved clinch knot," is used to secure fishing line to a fish hook (it can also be used for tying down anything else around camp). Run the end of the line through the eye of the hook. Then, wrap the free end around the line five or six times. This forms another loop between the first wrap and the eye of the hook. Feed the free end through that loop and pull to tighten. Clip the end of the line that remains (a standard nail clipper works well for this part). The experts say it's the only knot that won't let the fish get off, unless it breaks the line, of course.

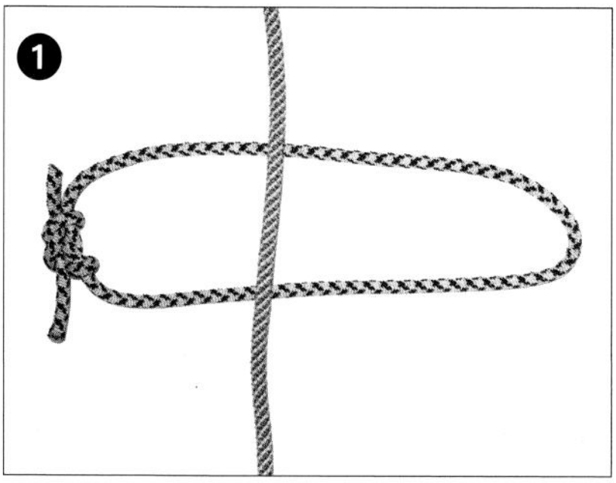

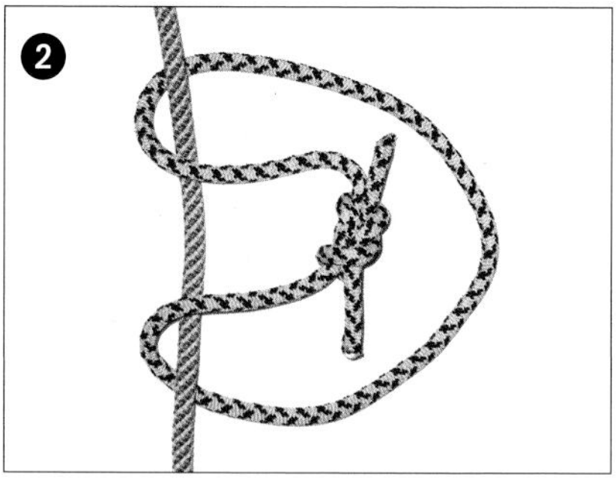

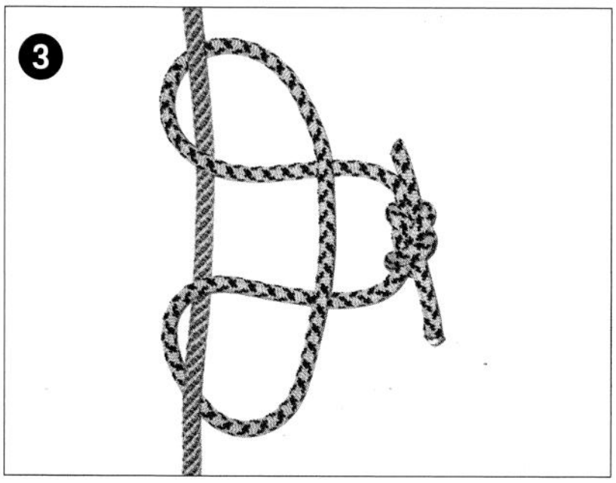

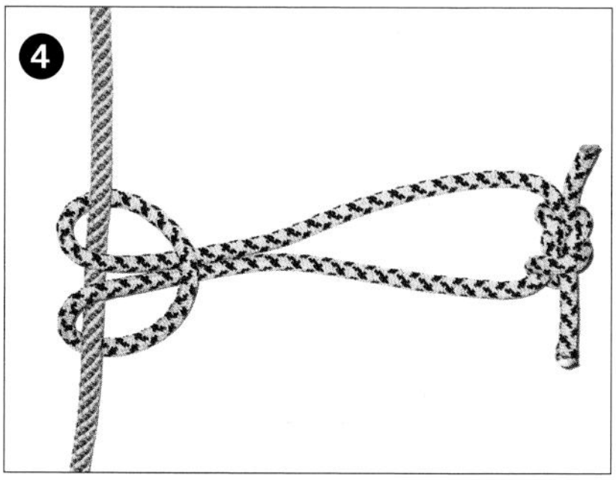

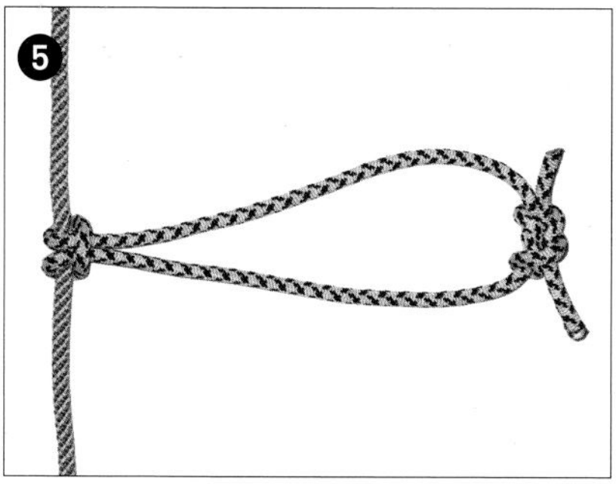

Prusik Knot

The Prusik knot, or Prusik hitch, has the great advantage creating a loop (which is usually tied onto another length of rope) that won't slip when weight is added but will slide easily when the weight is removed. It was invented over a century ago by Dr. Karl Prusik, and has been used extensively for climbers to move up or down a vertical rope. First, create a small loop or circle of rope by using the fisherman's knot (see page 138). Place the small loop on the far side of the larger diameter of rope. Wrap one free end around to the other side and tuck it under the loop formed. One wrap and tuck will do. But the more you repeat the process, the greater the friction of the knot.

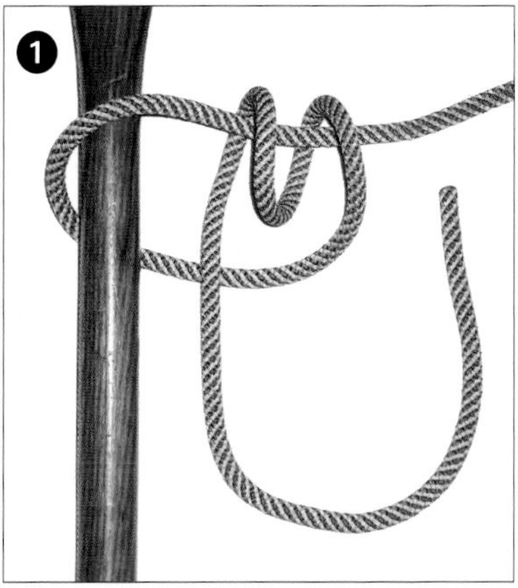

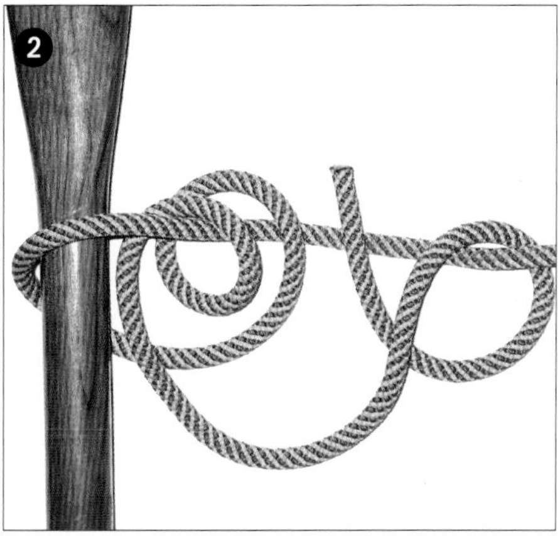

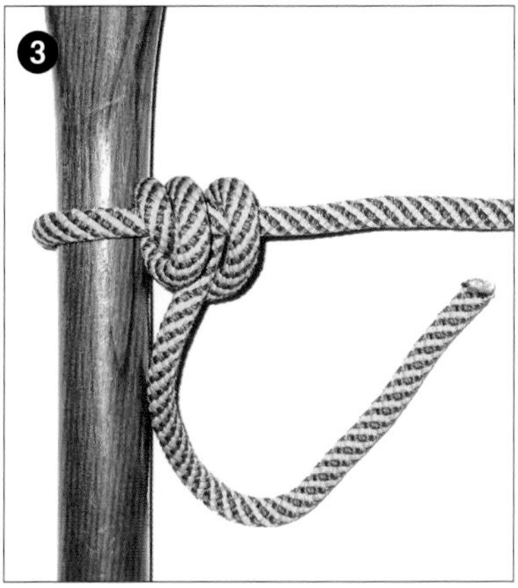

Taut-Line Hitch

This hitch knot is generally used to tie down and adjust the tension on a tent rope when attached to a tent peg. The knot forms a loop that can be easily adjusted by sliding up and down the main line. Start by pulling the free end around the object and placing it under the standing end. Now, wrap the free end around the standing end. Wrap it a second time. To cinch it off, bring the free end back to the standing line, placing it on top of the rope and just in front of the first wrap. Now, make a half hitch by tucking the free end under the loop you formed and pull to tighten.

50 70 105

SNAPSHOT MEMORIES

The finest images — the images that stir our souls — combine documentation of natural things with a sense of what they mean to us.

FREEMAN PATTERSON, *PHOTOGRAPHY OF NATURAL THINGS* (1982)

I ONCE DID THE unthinkable. While hiking I came upon a painter who was in the midst of trying to capture a moment on canvas. I stood beside him, snapped a photo of the same scene he was attempting to paint, and then commented, "You know, it's much quicker to take a picture." I meant it as a joke, of course. But the artist took my comment quite seriously and snarled back at me, firmly declaring, "It may be quicker, but you can't call it art!"

The artist was obviously right in thinking that my photo could not compare to a painting of the same scene. But I strongly disagree that photography is not art and that the mechanics of a camera cannot capture certain memories of a trip in the woods as effectively as a painter with a brush.

To record my favorite and not-so-favorite moments spent in the wilds, I use a 35 mm camera (also known as an SLR — single lens reflex camera), equipped with a regular 50 mm, 28 mm wide angle, and 80–200 zoom lens. Any other lenses carried along are for pleasure, not necessity. The worst thing a photographer can do is get hooked into purchasing and packing a pile of expensive equipment they'll probably never use. When I first started out, I spent a small fortune on all those extras. Then I was robbed and had to resort to taking pictures with just the essentials. It was the best thing that could have happened to me.

My wife is happy enough just to bring along her point-and-shoot camera. It's compact and has auto focus, auto exposure, and auto flash. And at times it takes just as good or even better photos than my fancy 35 mm camera. She's

◀ *When it comes to good photography, getting close to your subject matter is essential.*

Why Go Digital?

A digital camera allows you to view what you're shooting and then immediately delete any shots you're not happy with, saving you an incredible amount of money in the long run. Many models are also far more compact than a regular 35 mm camera and fit perfectly into a small waterproof container. The video option can also be a great source of entertainment each and every night of the trip. When you get home the images can easily be viewed, stored on disk, sent to trip mates, and turned into prints using your computer.

The only real problem with using a digital camera rather than a 35 mm camera, other than the fact that a 35 mm takes better photographs, is packing enough batteries to keep the darn things charged and to have enough file space for lengthy trips. These disadvantages can be solved, however, by bringing along a lightweight solar panel to boost your batteries and an extra memory chip for more photos. Definitely, the advantages far outweigh the shortcomings.

even brought along one of those waterproof throw-away cameras and taken some great photos. You do, however, lose your creative control, and the lens quality can't even come close to that of a professional camera.

A good tripod is a must, to compensate for my unsteady hands (I drink way too much coffee). I also bring along extra batteries (make sure they're the right ones for the camera), at least one roll of slide or print film for each day I'm out, a skylight filter to protect the lens from being scratched, and a release shutter for those long exposures of the evening sky or tumbling waterfalls.

A variety of waterproof bags can be used to store your gear if you're canoeing or kayaking. These can range from ammunition boxes purchased at the army surplus to an expensive Pelican case. I prefer the Pelican case. They are expensive, but I've owned mine for years and it's floated down seven rapids so far and never leaked once. If you're tight for money, though, it's possible to just use a large resealable bag. Just make sure to release the seal at night or the camera lens will fog up.

FILM SPEEDS

Film speed is recorded under a system called ASA (American Standard Association) or ISO (International Standard Organization). Slow film speed (ISO 50) works wonders for outdoor photography because more color is saturated in the photograph; however, a lot of light is needed and the subject will easily blur if it moves. Medium speed film (ISO 100–200) is the best overall film to use but limits your creativity. Fast speed film (ISO 400 and up) is fantastic for capturing fast-moving subjects and for low-light conditions. But it has a grainy look, poor color quality and is terrible for enlargements.

▲ *Above: Pink lady slippers (with a shallow depth of field). Below: Getting the shot.*

Equipment List for a Serious Photographer

- two camera bodies
- lenses: regular 50 mm, 28 mm, 80–200 mm zoom, and a close-up macro lens
- tripod (a bean bag placed on a rock makes a good lightweight substitute)
- a waterproof housing unit or one of those silly hats with a mini umbrella on top for shooting in the rain
- flash unit
- at least one roll of 36-exposure film per day, ranging from 50 to 400 ASA speed
- skylight filters
- spare batteries
- cable release
- lens cleaner
- large square piece of tinfoil to make a makeshift reflector

Film Types

As a general rule, Fuji film is great for showing off greens and blues and Kodak is best for showing reds and yellows.

Photo terms that can boggle the mind

F-stop The aperture setting of a lens is called the f-stop or f-number, and determines the amount of light the lens opening will allow in. The numbers (size of lens opening) are indicated on the lens itself (22, 16, 11, 8, 5.6, 4, 2.8, 1.8) and are derived by the focal length of the lens divided by the size of the lens. For example, a 50 mm lens divided by a focal length of 6.25 mm diameter aperture will have a setting of f/8. To make any sense of this, just keep in mind that the value of the f-stop is relative to the focal length; and to make sense of this, just remove your lens from the camera, turn the aperture dial back and forth, and watch as the curtain inside the lens gets bigger and smaller. A large opening will let a lot of light into the camera and a small hole will allow less light. To confuse you even more, the large hole will be a small number (1.8) and the small hole will be a large number (22). Forget trying to understand this one; just accept it.

Depth of Field This is the most confusing photo term. It's used to define the distance range of acceptable focus in front of your lens. But what does that mean? In simple terms, if you want everything in focus then you want a deep depth of field, and if you want just what's in front of you in focus then you want a shallow depth of field. But still, what does that mean? Depth of field is determined by how wide your lens is opened. The wider the lens opening (small f-number) the more "shallow" your depth of field and the smaller the lens opening (large f-number) the "deeper" the depth of field. This is because a lens has a curved shape to it. If you look through the entire lens the backdrop will be blurred. If you look through a pinhole in the center everything will be in focus. (It's like squinting when you forget to wear your glasses.)

Shutter Speed The shutter setting is on the camera body, usually on the upper right, and determines the amount of time the light going through the lens is allowed to hit the film inside the camera. In most cameras it ranges from 1/2000th of a second (really fast) to 4 seconds (really slow). For example, to take a photo of a moose running past you, without having it blur, you must have a fast shutter speed (i.e., 1/400th of a second). If you want to do one of those fancy blurred waterfall shots (you're basically capturing the motion of the water) then you need a slow shutter speed (i.e., 1 second).

▲ *Blur moving water in your photographs by slowing down the shutter speed to 1/15th of a second or less.*

▲ *"Freeze frame" a running moose to create a sense of movement by increasing the shutter speed to 1/250th of a second or more.*

Light Metering If you need a fast shutter speed because the moose is running past you, then not much light is going to have a chance to enter the camera. The photo will end up being underexposed. So you must compensate with a large lens opening (small f-number). If you want a deep depth of field to make everything in the photo in focus, then you need a small lens opening (large f-number). This will also let a small amount of light in the camera and your photo will end up underexposed. To compensate for this, you must let the shutter open up for a longer period. To keep it simple, think of it as a teeter-totter. If you increase the aperture by one, you must decrease the shutter by one. If you increase the shutter by one, you must decrease the aperture by one.

Freeze Frame

In cold temperatures keep camera batteries in your pocket to keep them warm and the camera as close to your body heat as possible.

For Better Photographs Always Remember

- Red is more attractive than yellow.
- Large draws more attention than small.
- Difference draws more attention than conformity.
- Jagged lines are more attractive than vertical ones.
- Sharpness is more attractive than blur.
- Rough is more attractive than smooth.
- Light is more attractive than dark.
- Never place your main subject in the center of the picture (rule of thirds).
- Isolate your subject by using a zoom lens.
- Use a wide-angle lens for landscape.
- Use a 500 mm lens for portraits.
- Eliminate clutter to keep the viewer's eye on the main subject.
- Don't be afraid to get as close as possible to your subject.
- Dark backgrounds (especially for close-ups) are better than light backgrounds.
- Shoot the same subject both vertically and horizontally.
- On average, one picture out of twenty ends up to be any good.
- Take photographs during the "magic hours," early morning and late afternoon.

And remember, photography is an art form and the camera is only a piece of technology that helps produce that art form.

ORAGE

MAP AND COMPASS

There's only a slight difference between being lost and confused.
ROBERT PERKINS, *INTO THE GREAT SOLITUDE* (1991)

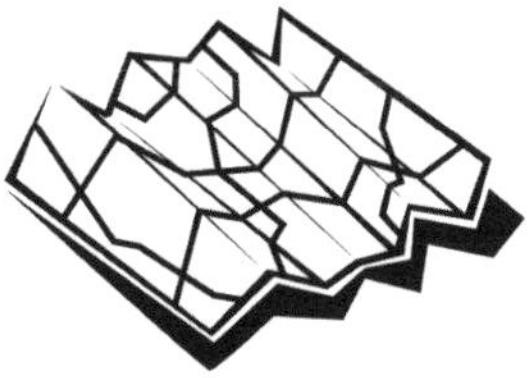

I failed my first practical exam in college. Embarrassingly, it was on using a map and compass. A bunch of us were dropped off on a county road, given a compass heading and detailed map of the area, and then told to meet at the next county road over. By noon our group was completely lost, and our instructor had to send out a search party to locate us. Not only did we flunk, we were also teased mercilessly throughout the rest of the semester by our other classmates. It wasn't that we didn't know how to use a map and compass — in fact, all of us aced the written portion of the test — the problem was that all of us believed we had some sort of supernatural ability to find our own way through the woods. We really thought that the quickest way to find the next county road, which was just over a mile (2 km) away, was to just trust in our built-in sense of direction. So we headed off in a straight line and were found later only a few hundred yards from our starting point. The entire group had spent the day wandering in circles.

Believe me. There is no such thing as an inherited sense of direction. Before heading off on any trip in the outdoors, learn how to use a map, compass and Global Positioning System (GPS), and make sure to use it while you're out there.

◀ *Noel Hudson conducts the reed section.*

▲ *Map reading is one of the most essential skills for any outdoors enthusiast.*

MAPS

The map, along with the ability to read it, is the crucial part of traveling in the outdoors. Even though I pack along a compass and GPS, I rarely make use of them. But I'm constantly gawking over a map to help get from point A to point B. Not only are they critical in helping you to navigate while you're out there, they also act as an excellent resource while planning your trip back home. I've spent countless hours during the long winter months looking over maps. I'll trace out a possible route and then unfold the same map a week later and inevitably discover another trip idea.

Topo maps are absolute dreamscapes, each one having all kinds of adventures hidden among its contour lines, river bends and island-cluttered lakes. Looking at them is simply addictive. A few of my canoe mates have even formed a local club, the "Map and Flap" (we meet on the same evening our wives gather for their "Stitch and Bitch" group).

Choosing which map to pack along depends entirely on where you're headed. If tripping in well-known parks, a detailed map produced by the park itself is usually good enough. It's more up-to-date, and designed specifically for your purpose. However, in non-regulated parks or other less traveled areas you need to bring along topographic maps.

The detail of each topo map is judged by its scale. The smaller the scale, the less detail that is shown. They range from 1:10,000 to 1:100,000. For back-country use the most common scale is 1:50,000, meaning 3/8 inches (1 cm) on the map is equivalent to 1,600 feet (500 m) on the ground. This scale size covers the most ground per map and still has enough suitable information, saving you a lot of money in the long run. However, if you require more detail on a specific area (a long series of rapids or cliff face), then use the 1:25,000 scale.

Apart from marking the location of lakes, rivers, rapids, falls, roads, trails, and so on, the most useful information that can be obtained from a topographic map is the topography of the land you are traveling on. The wavy brown lines on the map, labeled "contour lines," do just that. Each line marks where the position of the land is above sea level. Every fifth contour line, called an "index contour," has the elevation marked somewhere along its length. Each type of map may vary, but the vertical height between each

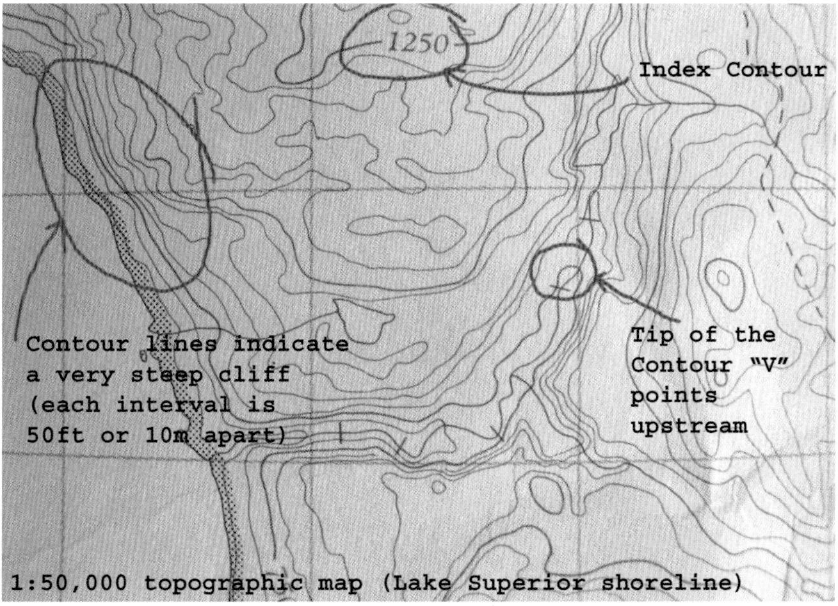

▲ *Understanding contours.*

interval is usually about 50 feet (10 m). So the closer the lines are together the steeper the grade. Also, the direction a creek or river is flowing is determined by having the closed ends of the contour lines (the tip of the V) point upstream.

To order maps in Canada you can order through the Canada Map Office (800-661-6277 or www.maps.nrcan.gc.ca) or one of their official distributors (800-465-6277, 613-723-6366, or www.fedmaps.com). For the United States, order through the United States Geological Survey Information Services (888-275-8747 or www.ask.usgs.gov). Most outfitting stores also carry most of the major map sections. It may be best to first order an updated index map. You can then locate the area in which you wish to travel and order it by referencing the grid number (for example, map number 31 G/5).

Map Scale

Map Scale	1 inch equals	1 centimeter equals
1:10,000	833.33 feet or 254 meters	328.1 feet or 100 meters
1:50,000	4,166.7 feet or 1,270 meters	1640.4 feet or 500 meters
1:250,000	20,833 feet or 6,350 meters	8,202 feet or 2,500 meters

Map Care

One of the major disadvantages of regular topographic maps is that they are made out of flimsy paper. This means, of course, that the moment you unpack your entire collection to second-guess your whereabouts, a steady rain will begin to fall, which is why some type of a waterproof system becomes quite critical. Some people do go overboard waterproofing their maps. They'll invest in expensive Velcro map cases or laminate each topographic sheet separately. They'll even use color-coded markers to signify route choices, hiking trails, portages and campsites. I simply stuff the maps into one large resealable bag, maybe glob on a bit of Thompson Water Seal for early spring outings, and use a pencil to jot down a few remarks beside an especially grueling portage or overly scenic campsite. At the end of the trip the map is guaranteed to be weathered, stained with spilled coffee and squashed mosquitoes, and ready to be placed on my office wall to gawk at all winter long.

Estimating Distance on a Map

To judge distance on a map, simply count the number of quadrants (squares formed by grid lines). Each one is equivalent to 3,280 feet or 0.6 miles (1,000 m or 1 km) in length.

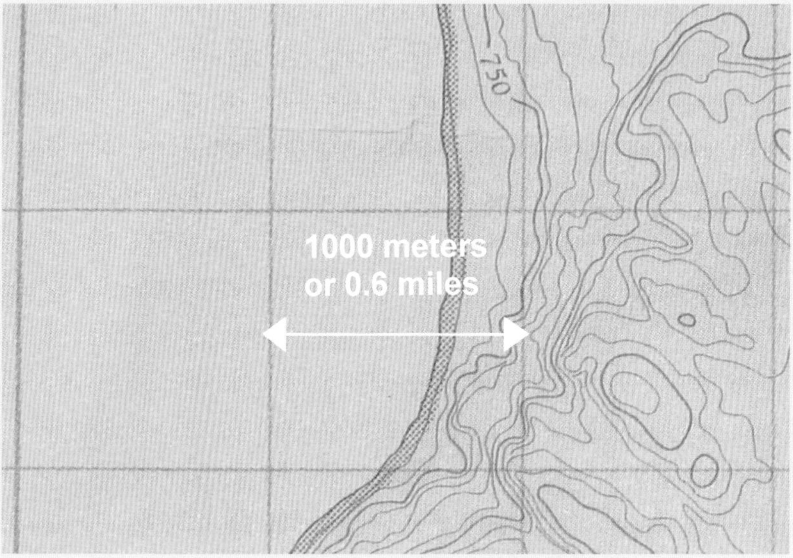

Estimating Distance on Land and Water

Calculating distance and time required while you're out there can be a difficult task. There are way too many variables. For example, it may be possible for a canoeist to paddle up to 15 miles (24 km) a day. Add a portage or two to the trip, however, and the distance can be cut in half. It's also possible for a backpacker to cover up to 20 miles (30 km) a day on a well-marked trail. But off trail they're lucky to get up to 10 miles (16 km). Here's a general guide that may help:

- Walking half a mile (1 km) on a flat trail, with a heavy backpack, would take approximately fifteen minutes or 2.5 mph (4 km/h).
- Walking half a mile (1 km) through thick bush, with a heavy backpack, would take approximately thirty minutes or 1.2 mph (2 km/h).
- Portaging a canoe for half a mile (1 km) on an even trail would take approximately twenty minutes or 1.8 mph (3 km/h).
- Portaging canoe for half a mile (1 km) on an extremely rough trail would take approximately forty minutes or almost 1 mph (1.5 km/h).
- Paddling a canoe (tandem) for half a mile (1 km) across a calm lake would take approximately ten minutes or 3.5 mph (6 km/h).
- Paddling a canoe (tandem) for half a mile (1 km) across a windy lake would take fifteen minutes or 2.5 mph (4 km/h).

How to Determine Pacing Factor

A single pace, or one's natural step, is equal to 30 inches (76 cm). A pace is defined by two natural steps, or what's called a "double step." This means when you touch down with your left foot, then you touch down with your right foot, that's one pace. The average person walks 5 feet (1.5 meters) per pace, but to figure out your own follow pacing factor, complete these steps:

- Measure out a given distance (for example, 66 feet, or 20 meters) in your backyard.
- Count how many "paces" it takes to go from one end to the other.
- Divide the distance (meters or feet) by the number of paces.
- This means every time you take a double step, you have gone that distance (i.e., 5 feet, or 1.5 meters).

Adjustments to Pacing Factor

- Slope can create an error in measurement. Your pace gets longer when you go downhill, and when going uphill your pace gets shorter.
- A poor surface or dangerous footing will reduce your pace.
- Your pace will shorten when you are unsure of your surroundings, feeling insecure or being cautious.
- Fatigue will also greatly reduce your pace.

Trying to keep track of each pace over a long distance can be overwhelming. Use a piece of knotted string or a handful of pebbles to help keep track. Each knot or pebble can be worth "ten Mississippis," or something like that.

COMPASS SKILLS

I made good use of my compass while working as a forest technician in Northern Ontario. The model itself was a regular orienteering compass, complete with a magnetic-tipped needle, a compass housing marked with an orienteering arrow and orienteering lines, a graduated dial, a base plate that doubled as a ruler (measuring in inches and centimeters), and an index line. However, it also had a few extra gizmos, like a preset declination (a must-have in my opinion) and a mirror with a "bull's eye" on top so you can read a bearing while holding the compass at eye level. (I also used the mirror to help out with my morning shave!)

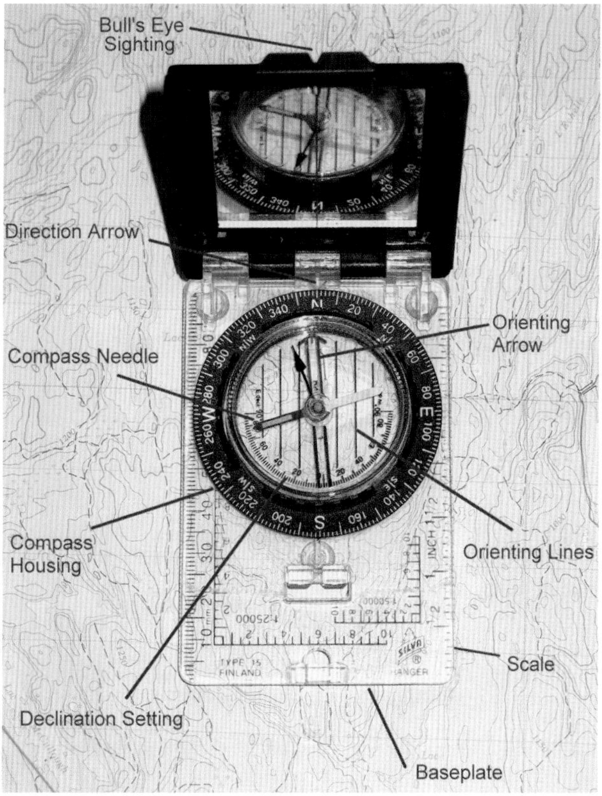

▶ *Parts of a compass.*

Declination

The first thing to note with an orienteering compass is that the red end of the floating arrow always points to magnetic north, not true north. Since the needle is magnetized, it will always point toward the Earth's magnetic field (made up of molten iron). To help confuse the issue, however, this is a different place than true north, or what's better known as the geographical North Pole. The difference in degrees between these two northern points is called "declination." To confuse the issue even more, the amount of compass error (declination) is not only dependent on where you are on the Earth, it also changes on a yearly basis. This variance is usually only a few degrees (30 degrees is the largest), but the further you follow it the more you're going to head off in the wrong direction.

To compensate for declination you must first check what the declination is in the area you are traveling in. The easiest way to do this is to contact the government agency for that area (Ministry of Natural Resources, Department of Mines, Department of the Interior) and just ask what the declination is. Then make sure you own a compass with a declination screw, preset the declination by turning the screw (west or east) to the proper degree, and never have to worry about it the entire trip. However, you can also do it the hard way by following these instructions:

- Search the margins of the topographic map (usually the upper right-hand corner) for a sketch of three arrows: True North (TN), Grid North (GN), and Magnetic North (MN). True North marks 360 degrees (0 degrees). Grid North represents parallel vertical lines as seen on the topo map. Magnetic North is marked to either the left (west) or right (east) of the True North arrow, with the variation of degrees shown between TN and GN. You actually want the variation between TN and MN, so either use what's given, since the amount between TN and GN is never that much to worry about, or add or subtract the difference.
- The declination will be marked in degrees and minutes (10° 45', which is where I live in Peterborough, Ontario). Take note that to round it off to the nearest degree you only increase it by one if it's thirty minutes or more (there are sixty minutes in a degree). So 10° 45' would round up to 11 degrees. 10° 27' would be 10 degrees.
- If the MN is to the left of TN, then the declination would be west. If the MN is to the right of TN then it would be east.

Here's a quick and easy way to find out a specific declination in Canada. Go to www.geolab.nrcan.gc.ca/geomag/cgrf_e.shtml.

- If the declination is to the east, then you would subtract the amount of degrees to your bearing. If the declination is to the west, then you would add it to your bearing. It helps to remember the rhyme "east is least and west is best." So if the declination was 10 degrees W, and your bearing was 42 degrees, you would then follow 52 degrees. If the declination was 10 degrees E, and your bearing was 42 degrees, then you would follow 32 degrees. This is where having a declination screw comes in handy. With the declination already adjusted on your compass you never have to add or subtract each time you take a separate bearing.

Problems with Old Maps

If the topographic map was produced more than a couple of years ago, which it most likely was, then you also have to compensate for the annual change in declination. You determine the change by following these instructions:

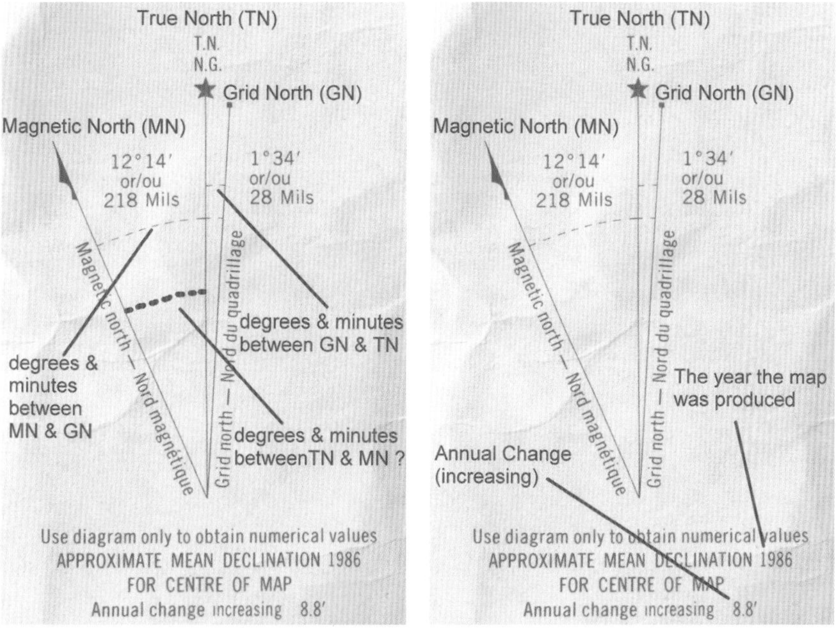

▲ *1. Declination is the variation between True North (TN) and Magnetic North (MN). Here you would have to subtract the variation from True North and Grid North (GN) from Magnetic North to Grid North to get the proper amount. 2. It's important to use the most up-to-date map available. The annual change corrections given on maps cannot be applied reliably if the maps are more than a few years old since the intensity of the Earth's magnetic field also changes with time in an unpredictable manner.*

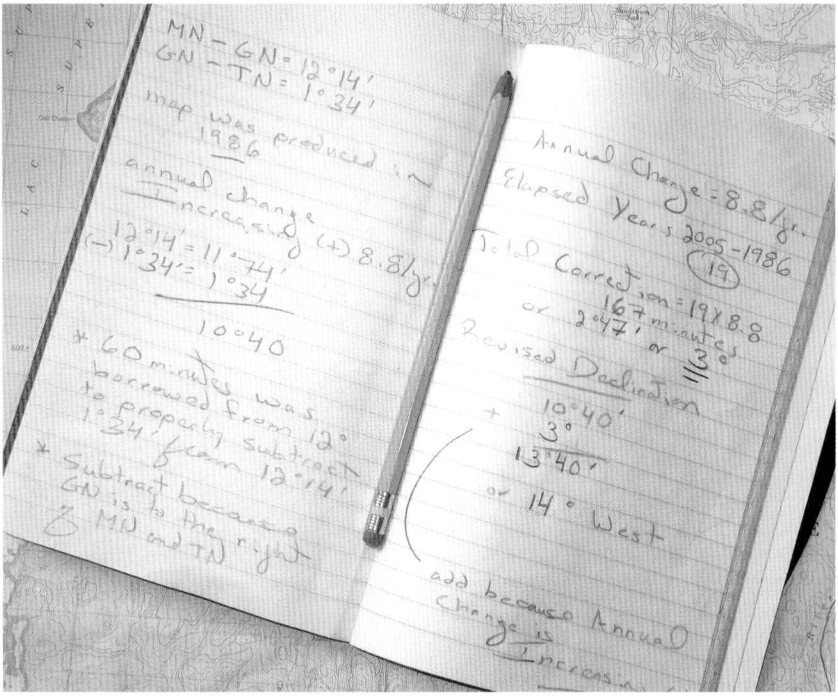

▲ *Calculations for the annual change in declination.*

- Record the degrees and minutes between MN and GN (here, 12° 14')
- Record degrees and minutes between GN and TN (1° 34')
- Record the year the map was produced (1986) and the annual change (annual change "increasing" at 8.8'/year). This information is usually found directly below the three arrows on the topographic map.
- Again, to get the exact degrees and minutes between TN and MN (declination) you can just use TN and GN (they're very close). But to be more exact you should either add or subtract the answers for instructions two (1° 34') from one (12° 14'), depending on the position of GN. With the example given, GN is to the right of MN and TN, so you would subtract 1° 34' from 12° 14'. But if it was to the left you would have to add.
- Take the total correction, rounding off the minutes to the nearest degree (10° 40').
- Multiply the elapsed years (2004-1986 =19 years) and the annual change (8.8'/year) to give you the correction (167' or 2° 47' or rounded off to 3°).
- Now add the correction if the annual change is "increasing" or subtract if the annual change is "decreasing" to the degrees and minutes between TN and MN. In the example given it was "increasing 8.8'/year and would therefore change the declination to 13° 40' (rounded off to 14°).

- If MN was right of TN then record the declination to be east. If MN was to the left of TN, as is the case of the example given, then record the declination to be west (14 W).

Taking a Field Bearing

A field bearing, properly known as an azimuth, is a degree (heading) calculated without the aid of a topographic map. This technique isn't used that often out there. Mostly you keep an eye on the map and use obvious landforms (islands, large hills, creek mouths) to keep on track. But let's say you find yourself "confused" while canoeing across a big lake and you want to stay in the correct direction. Or maybe you want to take a day hike up a ridge you've spotted from your campsite. Here's how you do it:

- Hold your compass level, at chest height.
- Point the direction-of-travel arrow (the top of the compass) at the point you want to go to (for example, a particular ridge top).
- Rotate the compass housing (the round dial with all the degrees marked on it) until the orienteering arrow (the one that doesn't float) is perfectly lined up with the compass needle (the red pointed arrow that floats).
- Read off the bearing (set in degrees) that is lined up with the direction-of-travel arrow.
- Keep following that bearing by constantly aiming off on an object ahead; put the compass away, walk to the object, take the compass back out, and aim off another object.

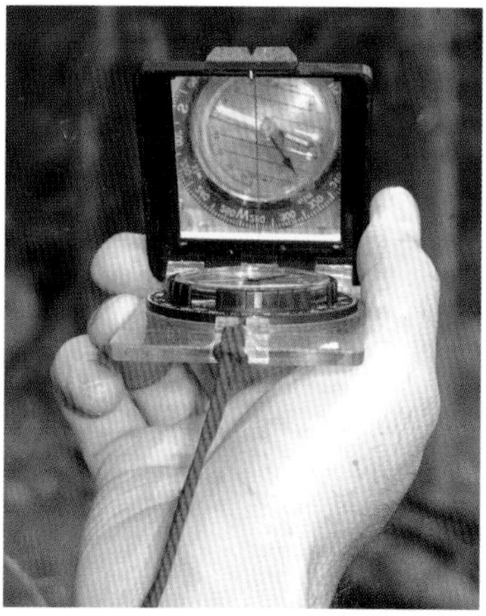

▲ *Left: A mirror plate and a "bulls-eye" on your compass can greatly improve your accuracy when taking a field bearing. Right: The heading is correct once the red floating arrow is lined up with the orienteering arrow (the arrow that doesn't float).*

- To get back to where you once were, just figure out the reciprocal (the opposite bearing). This can be found by either subtracting or adding 180 degrees from your previous heading or by just looking where the other end of the red needle is pointing to.

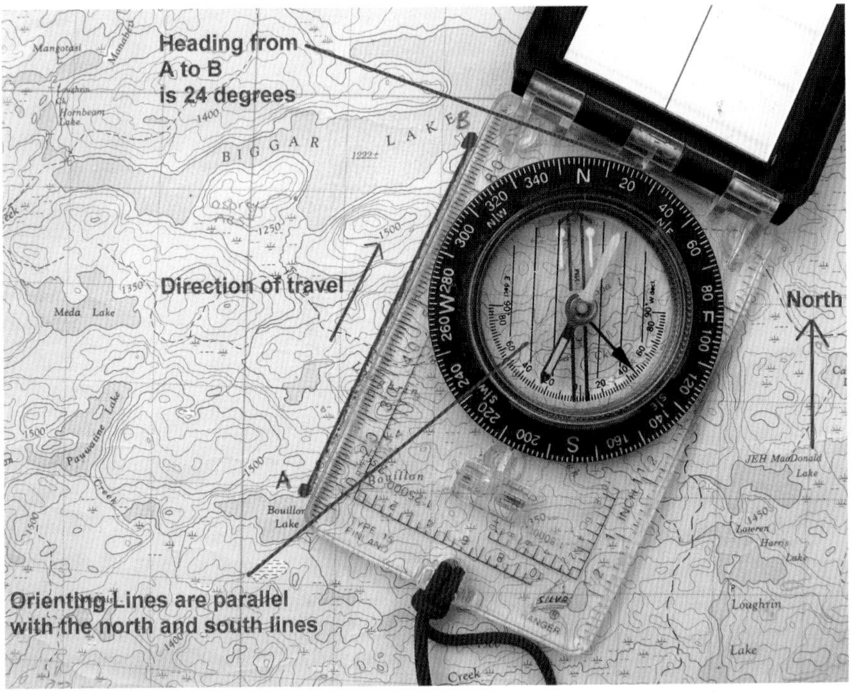

▲ *When using the map and compass technique to figure out a heading, the compass is used in the same way as a protractor.*

Top Five Errors Using a Map and Compass

- Magnetic needles can be greatly affected by nearby magnetic materials such as belt buckles, hydro lines, wire fences, and lead pencils.
- A large air bubble can form in the compass housing and will definitely cause a considerable amount of error.
- Don't take a reading off the wrong end of the magnetic needle. Remember, the red arrow is north.
- When placing the compass on the map to get a heading, don't place the compass housing so that north is pointing to the bottom end (south) of the map rather than the top (north). It should be the other way around.
- Having your compass point from B to A (finish to start) rather than A to B (start to finish). This is the most common error made.

Map and Compass Skills

Using a map and compass together is the technique used to figure out how to get from point A to point B. The compass, used in the same way as a protractor, gives you a reassuring line to follow on your map, and is the main reason why anyone traveling in the outdoors would unpack their compass in the first place. Just follow these basic steps:

- Place the map on a relatively flat surface.
- Mark the letter A on the map to indicate where you already are and then mark B where you want to go on the map.
- Line up the side of the compass's base plate from A to B (route of travel), making sure the direction-of-travel arrow (top of the compass) is pointing to B.
- Without moving the compass itself, rotate the compass housing (the round dial with all the degrees marked on it) until the orienteering arrow points north and the orienteering lines (inside the housing) run parallel with the north and south lines on the map.
- Read out the bearing marked at the direction-of-travel arrow. (Take note that since you are using the compass like a protractor, you can ignore the compass needle during the entire procedure).
- Lift the compass off the map and make the correction for declination to the bearing (if you don't have the compass already adjusted by a declination screw).
- Hold the compass at chest height and rotate your body until the floating magnetic needle lines up with the orienteering arrow. The compass is now pointing to B.
- To calculate the distance between A and B make use of the bar scale given at the bottom of the map. You can also get a quicker estimate by just counting the number of quadrants (square boxes) en route. Each quadrant measures 0.6 miles (1 km).

Offsets for Obstacles

An offset is a technique used to detour around an obstacle while staying on course. After all, how possible would it be to follow a heading without running into some type of barrier, like a swamp, while hiking through the woods or on a large island while paddling across a lake?

A deliberate offset is done by moving at right angles for a given distance. For example, if you are following a heading of 360 degrees (due north) and you come across a small pond, you would then follow a right angle (90 degrees) for 20 paces (or whatever distance would allow you to get around the pond). Then, you would again follow your previous heading (360 degrees), until you got to the other side of the pond. To get yourself back on track you then take the opposite right angle (270 degrees) for 20 paces.

But What If You Don't Know Where You Are?

Each bit of information I have given you so far tells you how not to get lost. But what if you are lost? What if you're even just a little confused as to your whereabouts? What if you're on a small island on a huge lake, but you have no idea which one? The method is called "triangulation." It's not as easy as the other steps, both in theory and in practice, but here's how it's done:

- Look around you and try to recognize at least two prominent landmarks (a high rocky ledge, a large bay or inlet, a fire tower).
- Search out those landmarks on your topographic map.
- Take a field bearing for both landmarks.
- Correct for declination.
- Calculate the reciprocal (back bearing) by either subtracting or adding 180 degrees or just looking at the degree marked on the opposite end of the orienteering arrow.
- Using your compass as a protractor (see Map and Compass skills), consider the two landmarks on your topographic map as A, draw a line out from each, and where they meet is where you are standing.

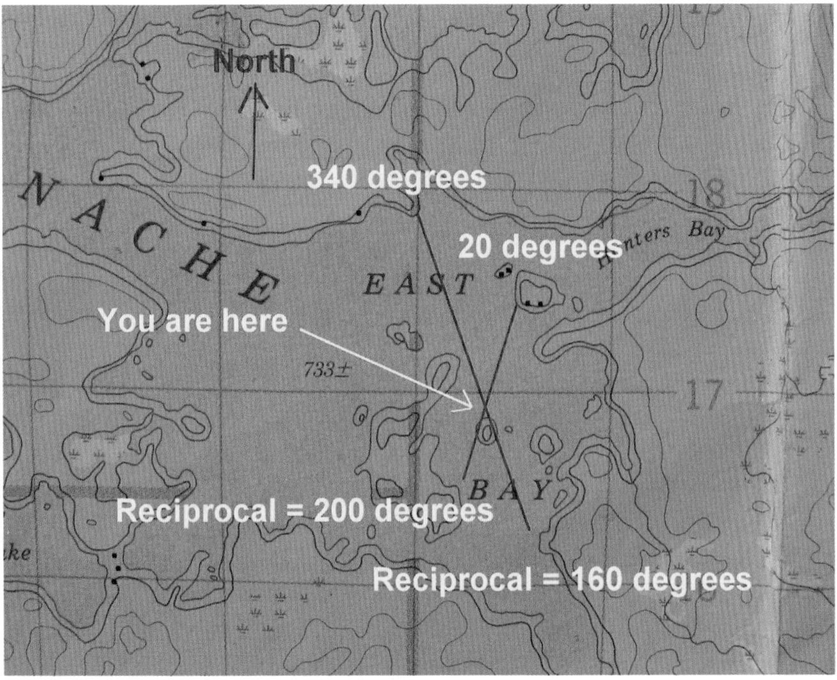

The reciprocal (back bearing) is the exact opposite of the given heading and is calculated by either adding or subtracting 180 degrees.

GPS: IT IS ROCKET SCIENCE

Global Positioning Systems are based on three separate parts: a network of satellites orbiting the Earth that send out electromagnetic frequencies (radio waves), a number of control stations that track and control the satellites, and the GPS unit itself, which receives the satellite signal and calculates your position by using latitude and longitude coordinates.

This navigation system has come a long way in recent years. First, the cost has dropped by half; you can pick up a half-decent model for between $100 and $200. The receiver itself is more accurate and can now determine your position between 33 and 333 feet (10 to 100 m). Problems with correcting for declination become a thing of the past. You can also enter map coordinates (latitude and longitude) and the receiver will provide a compass bearing, distance and time required to get to the desired location. And its best feature is your ability to punch in your present position, save it as a waypoint, and allow you to easily find your way back home, record a favorite campsite, or even mark a productive fishing hole.

A GPS becomes an excellent tool to have along when you want to quickly find a bearing to a given point, or the act of triangulation is next to impossible to complete with just a map and compass due to the lack of obvious landmarks. I finally bought one after guiding a family on a canoe trip in Ontario's French River delta system. Low water levels had dramatically altered what the topographical map showed, and what we actually paddled past. I was desperately looking for an inlet called Dead Island Channel and had to resort to asking a commercial fishing boat captain its position. I was embarrassed to discover we were drifting right through it at the time.

▲ *Remember; if you don't understand map and compass techniques, you will never understand how to properly use a GPS.*

That said, a GPS does not replace a good map and compass. First, if you do not know how to navigate with a map and compass, not only does it become impossible to use a GPS properly, you also won't have a clue how to follow the instruction manual when you buy one. Basically, if you don't know how to navigate without a GPS, you'll be just as hopeless with one. They are not the "Salvation for Lost Souls," that some manufacturers have claimed in their ad campaigns.

Understanding the Universal Transverse Mercator

The Universal Transverse Mercator (UTM) is a grid system developed by the military that is a much easier system for locating areas on a map than the traditional longitude and latitude system, especially when using a GPS. The GPS actually gives coordinates using UTM. The UTM system divides the Earth into sixty zones (numbered 1 to 60), each zone being 6 degrees wide and going from 80 degrees south latitude to 84 degrees north latitude. The lines don't converge like longitude and latitude lines. UTM lines remain as a rectangle, which is the main reason that they are far more user friendly.

Understanding the complex-looking UTM numbers seems a little overwhelming at first. After a few tries at it, though, you'll get the hang of it. The large numbers represent the "northing" coordinates and "easting" coordinates, the northing denoting how many meters the position is from the equator and the easting denoting how many meters the position is away from the zone's longitudinal origin. Remember, when naming coordinates, the easting comes first and the northing comes second.

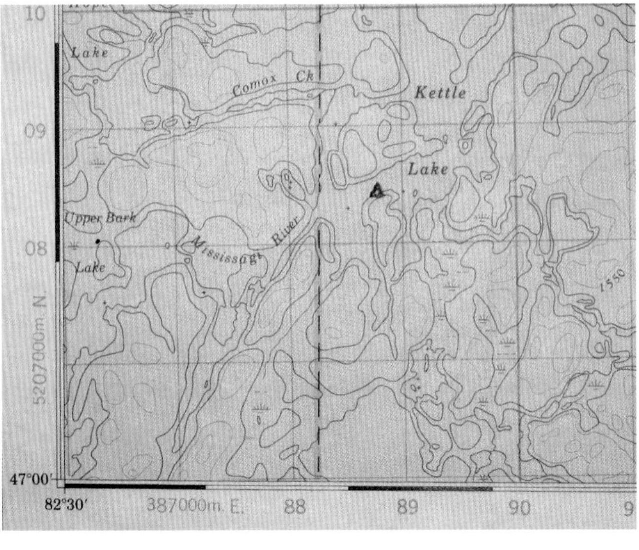

You have to understand the Universal Transverse Mercator (UTM) grid system if you plan to use a GPS unit.

Find the Campsite

- Let's practise. Find the campsite by following these steps:
- Locate the grid (square) that the campsite is in.
- Locate the closest up and down (north and south) grid line that is to the left of the campsite.
- Follow that line to either the top or bottom of the map and read off the number in the margin (the number is the same on the top and bottom). The answer is 88. Now you have the first two numbers of the UTM.
- Next, estimate the distance (in meters) east (to the right) the campsite is from the next up and down (north and south) grid line. Remember, every grid line on the map is 1,000 meters apart. The answer is 800 meters (if it was halfway the number would be 500 or if it was just under a quarter of the way it would be 2). Now, place the distance in tenths. The answer is 8. Now you have the third number and the "easting" for the UTM.
- The last three numbers are "northing" and work the same way, except you use the grid lines running west to east and the numbers on the left or right margin. The answer would be 084.
- The UTM reference point for the campsite on Kettle Lake is 888084.
- The important point to remember out in the field is which numbers are first, the easting or northing. A good way to commit it to memory is that it's like going up the stairs – you start from the bottom up.

Does This Make Any Sense?

387000m. E. (lower margin) is the easting number, meaning that the easting line is 387,000 meters east of the zone's western edge. 5207000m. N. is the northern number and means that the northern line is 5,207,000 meters north of the equator. Take note that two of the numbers on the easting number (87) and the northern number (07) are larger than the other numbers. These represent the main coordinates along the margin.

NATURE'S DIRECTION INDICATORS

First of all, forget what your Scout or Girl Guide leaders told you; moss does not grow on the north side of the tree. It's true that moss likes shade, and that sun rarely shines on the north-facing slope. But there are definitely way too many variables to bet your life on this. In fact, the only accurate direction indicators to use in the outdoors are the sun and stars.

Sun Time

Using the sun should be your first choice. It's no more accurate than using the stars, but it's obviously much easier to travel during the daytime. Morning and evening are the easiest times to get a fix on direction since the sun always rises in the east and sets in the west. At high noon the sun is due south, but this can seem a little confusing. So, it's possible to locate south by using an analog watch equipped with an hour hand. With the watch in a horizontal position, point the hour hand toward the sun. The halfway mark between the hour hand and 12:00 is approximately south. If you have a digital watch, just draw a clock on a piece of paper, marking the correct time, and follow the previous instructions.

Reading the Stars

At one time reading the stars in the night sky was the best way to get yourself around out there, and it's still possible, as long as you know how to separate them from all the blinking satellites, aircraft lights, and the odd UFO. The trick is not to try to identify the individual constellations. That's next to impossible. Keep to the simple ones — the Big Dipper and Little Dipper. These constellations not only look a little like the character they're named after, but also circle closest to Polaris (North Star) and don't change their position in the sky throughout the year.

The easiest of the bunch has to be the Big Dipper, which is the rump and tail of Ursa Major (the Great Bear). It's made up of seven bright stars, four in the shape of the bowl and three the ladle. The brightest star out from the lip of the bowl is the North Star, shining almost directly over true north. To use it for navigation it's best not to travel at night, for obvious reasons. Instead, mark the direction with a stick and wait until morning.

Many stories are told about Ursa Major. Native tribes of North America saw the ladle of the Big Dipper not as a bear's tail, but as hunters with dogs chasing the bear in circles around the northern heavens. Some tribes even connected the leaves changing color in the fall with the bear being wounded by the hunters and dripping its blood from the sky onto the trees.

Another common tale is from Greek mythology. The constellation is said to be Callisto, a paramour of Zeus. It is said that Callisto swore a vow of chastity when she became a favorite hunting partner of Artemis, goddess of hunting. But one afternoon, while she was resting under a tree, Zeus caught a glimpse of her and was entranced by her beauty. He changed into the form of Artemis and approached Callisto. When she reached out to embrace her friend, Zeus showed his true form and had his way with her.

Zeus returned to Olympus and left poor Callisto pregnant. She later gave birth to a son, Arcas. Eventually Hera, the wife of Zeus, found out about her husband being unfaithful and took revenge on Callisto by transforming her into a bear, now making the hunter the hunted.

Homemade Sundial

It's possible to use the old "stick in the ground" method to tell time. Plunge a stick into a flat piece of earth, away from any obstacles. Then, mark the point of the stick's shadow. Wait for ten minutes and mark the tip of the shadow again. Remembering that the sun travels from east to west, and taking note that you are in the northern hemisphere, you know that north has to be between the two shadows, south is completely opposite, east has to be to the right of the original shadow, and west is to the left.

Bootes, Guardian of the Bear

Despite what you may have been told, the North Star is not the brightest star in the sky. During the summer the star Arcturus, part of the Bootes constellation, burns 120 times more radiant and is 24 times larger than our sun.

To locate Arcturus and the Bootes constellation, follow the curve of the Big Dipper's ladle to the next brightest star. The group of stars, including Arcturus, is in the shape of a kite or ice-cream cone and is thought to be the guardian of the Big Bear.

Callisto supposedly wandered through the woods for years, until one day she met up with her son, Arcas. When she went to him, however, he mistook her for a real bear and went to spear her. Zeus quickly intervened by changing Arcas into the same form as his mother. He grabbed them both by the tail and hurled them into heaven, stretching out their tails in the process.

When Hera found out that Zeus had saved Callisto, she once again showed her rage by demanding Tethys and Oceanus, gods of the sea and Hera's foster parents, never to allow the Great Bear to bathe. And to this day poor Callisto has yet to set below the horizon into the waters of the northern hemisphere.

The Little Dipper, more commonly known as Ursa Minor (Little Bear) is also an easy one to locate. After you've identified the North Star (using your compass might be easier than looking out from the lip of the Big Dipper) you'll soon realize that it's actually the last star on the Little Dipper's ladle. This constellation was always thought to be the most important because it actually contained Polaris. The Arabs called it the "Guiding One." The Chinese named it "Tou Mu," a goddess who saved shipwrecked sailors with her supernatural powers and was later transported up into the sky. Ancient Norsemen labeled it the "Hill of Heaven," home of the guardian of the rainbow bridge joining heaven and earth. Native North Americans believed it to be a young girl who appeared to a group of lost braves and showed them the way home. And according to Greek mythology (and the story of Callisto), the Little Bear is obviously Arcas, the Big Bear's son.

Let Nature Be Your Guide

The key to using nature to find direction is that you should always keep everything in perspective. You'll most likely never use the sun or stars to help navigate, or even bother to look at how moss grows on a tree; however, it's crucial to realize that nature does have a way of helping you out there, as long as you're willing to listen.

I clearly remember the day this advice held true for me. When I was in my early twenties my Uncle Jim, who had lived and worked in the bush for years, had invited me up north for a bear hunt. I wasn't all that keen on the hunting part, but I couldn't pass up a chance to wander the woods all day with my uncle.

Problems arose almost immediately. Since I was under the impression that I would be with my uncle all day, I figured there was no need to pack anything important, like a map or compass. Walking together was not what my uncle had in mind, though, and I literally had a panic attack when I heard him command, "Time to split up." Embarrassingly, I informed him that I wasn't prepared to head out alone. He just laughed, told me to head

▲ *"Hey, Kevin, which way is north if moss grows on all sides of the tree?"*

east for a few hours until I reached the next township road, and then wandered off into the woods.

I was young at the time. At least that's my excuse. So, rather than do the smart thing and tell my uncle I had neither a map nor a compass, I blindly headed off into the forest. At first I tried to follow the sun, knowing that I would at least head east throughout the morning. However, by 9 A.M. it was pouring down rain, making it impossible to spot the sun. I then tried the moss trick, but quickly became frustrated when I noticed that the moss was growing all over the entire tree. By midafternoon I was totally confused as to my whereabouts. Not lost, just extremely confused — the difference is that I never panicked, I kept my cool through the entire event. I didn't even freak out when a bear and her cub wandered close by (honestly, they did). I just sat down on an outcrop of rock, let the bruins pass (I couldn't even think about shooting them), and began pondering over my next strategy. That's when nature gave me a helping hand. I looked up and noticed a large flock of gulls circling in the sky just ahead. I thought, where there are gulls there's garbage, and in ten minutes I wandered into the municipal dump, safe and sound.

BRUISES, BLISTERS AND BAND-AIDS

What if I fell in a forest: Would a tree hear?

ANNIE DILLARD

A first-aid kit is one of those necessary evils. Rarely do you ever take it out of your pack to use (at least I hope that's the case). But the moment you need it, the kit quickly becomes one of the most important items to have brought along. What's even more crucial is that it contains the proper items to do the job.

On a group canoe trip down a river north of Lake Superior, our designated member assigned to pack the first-aid kit for all of us never bothered to check the contents inside before our departure. On day three of a five-day trip each member was suffering various ailments. Four of us had poisoned ourselves by eating a bad can of oysters. (I was the one who served the oysters and took the blame.) Another member sliced his arm wide open on a sharp rock. And one more partner had a severe reaction to a wasp sting. Not one item in the first-aid kit proved useful for any of the medical ailments. The kit was armed with splints, safety pins, tick tweezers, a stethoscope, and oddly enough, a large quantity of anti-fungal cream. But not one decent-sized bandage could be found. No bee-sting kit was packed. We didn't even have a supply of laxative or nausea pills to help with the effects of the food poisoning.

We all managed to survive the ordeal. But it was a hellish trip, one that could have easily been avoided if our canoe mate had only brought a proper first-aid kit.

◀ *Breaking a leg on day 18 of a 21-day canoe trip – now that's just bad luck.*

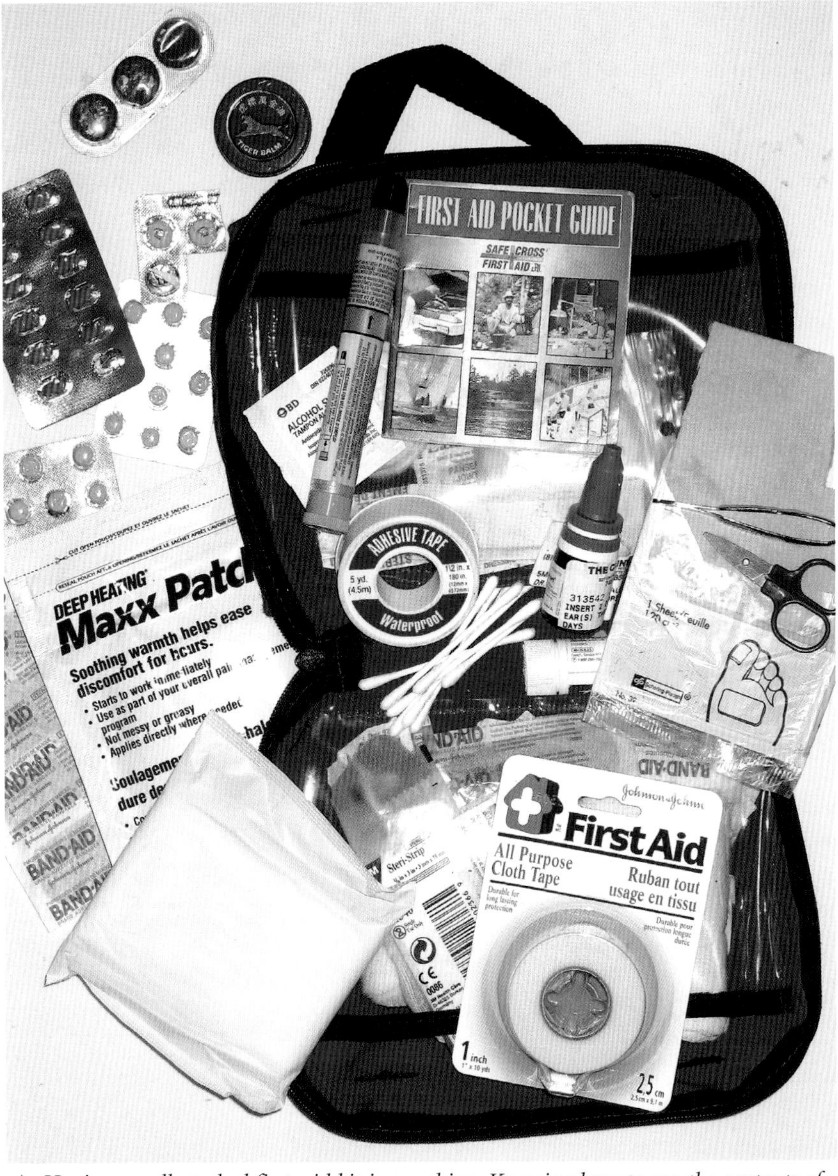

▲ *Having a well-stocked first-aid kit is one thing. Knowing how to use the contents of your kit is another. Take a first-aid course before you go out there.*

Since then I've always packed along my own personal first-aid kit. I also sign up for a wilderness first-aid course at least every two years. That way I know exactly what's in the kit and have a good idea of how to use what's inside.

First-Aid Kit

- Band-Aids (various shapes and sizes)
- Ace bandages (for sprained ankles or swollen knees)
- butterfly bandages
- gauze pads (various sizes)
- feminine napkins (for soaking up blood from cuts and scrapes)
- moleskin (for blisters)
- ice pack
- hot water bottle
- iodine
- alcohol swabs
- safety pins
- scissors (small)
- eye patch
- antiseptic cream
- sunscreen
- hand lotion (your dry hands will thank me)
- lip balm
- water-purification tablets
- throat lozenges
- antacid tablets
- antidiarrheal
- laxative
- Extra Strength Tylenol or its equivalent
- small pack of anti-inflammatory such as ibuprofen
- Caladryl (for bee stings and bug bites)
- an antihistamine such as Benadryl
- tweezers
- small mirror (for inspecting eye injuries, or giving yourself a clean shave)
- adhesive tape
- first-aid manual (explaining everything from splints to treatment of shock and CPR)

BACKCOUNTRY HYGIENE

I've guided people on remote canoe trips for years now, and the one thing I've never understood is the lack of hygiene they have the moment they're out there. It's commonplace to see people stop brushing their teeth, cleaning behind the ears, or even washing their hands after a bowel movement. I even caught one individual on a trip using my dishtowel to wipe his hands after going to the washroom. I absolutely freaked on him!

The results of not keeping clean can be a real bother. For example, 25 to 40 percent of all illnesses can be traced back to not washing your hands properly before eating (or having someone touch the communal dishtowel after relieving himself). The obvious way to eliminate this hazard is to use hot water and soap when washing up. The problem is that hot water is a rarity when you're camping. On past guided trips I solved this issue by providing a container of water mixed with bleach hanging from a tree near the outhouse. It was always a pain to set up, though, and I never knew if everyone was using it. So I've switched to handing out a container of germicidal soap (Betadine Scrub, Hibiclens or Klenz-Blu Gel). It's lightweight, easy to apply, and sure cuts down on yelling at the clients who misuse my dishtowel.

Waterproof First-Aid Kit

An inexpensive way to make your own waterproof first-aid kit is to store items in an old, large-mouthed Nalgene water bottle. Everything seems to fit.

I also make good use of antibacterial moist towelettes for cleaning up private parts. My wife and I started packing them along after leaving our soap supply behind on a campsite halfway along a ten-day canoe trip and then running out of toilet paper soon after. It was hot and humid but far too early in the year to go for a dip in the river every night. To keep us clean and free of infection we resorted to using up all our alcohol swabs from the first-aid kit. A fresh moist towelette would have been far better.

ALLERGIC REACTIONS

My wife and I were portaging in the far North when our dog, Bailey, disturbed a nest of wasps and brought them directly back to us. Alana was stung three times, I was stung twice, and Bailey had a total of five nasty stings, all on the tip of her nose. None of us had ever been stung before, and I was quite concerned we would suffer the severe effects of an allergic reaction. Luckily the stings just hurt a lot and Bailey's nose became slightly swollen. Now we just had to worry about getting stung again, since the more often you get stung the greater your chances of having a reaction. But what's the chance of being stung again, right? How about the next portage. Bailey disturbed yet another nest and we all got covered in welts. We were lucky. A few antihistamines and we were fine.

The safest way to deal with allergic reactions is to prepare for their occurrence and then pray they don't. People who know they are highly allergic to things like food items are usually quite prepared and are ready to deal with it when it happens. It's the victims who don't discover their allergies until out on a trip that could be in trouble. The most dangerous reaction to have in a remote area is anaphylactic shock, which can become fatal in a matter of minutes. The reaction affects the entire body, especially the cardiovascular and respiratory systems, and if left untreated may soon lead to respiratory failure and death.

The first step in treating anaphylactic shock is to know how to recognize it. Pain from a wasp sting or even slight swelling isn't a huge issue, but when a rash or swelling occurs in areas other than where you got stung, then you've got problems. The reaction usually occurs between five to fifteen minutes after being exposed to the allergy, and if the patient shows any sign of difficulty in breathing you must act quickly and administer a drug called epinephrine. This is a prescription drug that can be injected by way of an Epi-Pen. It's not difficult, but you must be trained by a physician before using it, as improper use of epinephrine can be dangerous. And once you have given the patient epinephrine you should also follow up with a dose of antihistamine and find the nearest hospital.

FOOT CARE

With all the various modes of travel, it is your feet that mainly get you around out there. So you can imagine how easily an outing can turn disastrous when something as simple as a blister disables you. To avoid blisters forming on your feet make sure your footwear is well broken in before your trip. I once met a canoeist who had just finished traveling the Steel River Loop, an extremely difficult route north of Lake Superior, who had worn a brand-new pair of hiking boots. He had lost most of his toenails (which he'd oddly stored in an empty tin can to display on his fire mantel back home), and produced enough blisters on both feet to make him crippled for weeks after the ordeal.

If you happen to have a blister starting to form while on a trip, make sure to place a piece of moleskin on it right away. It can literally save the trip. Moleskin is a felt-like material that comes with a very adherent backing and

▲ *A clean and dry pair of socks a day helps keep the doctor away.*

Pack a Pair Per Day

A pair of socks per day is not excessive. It's also good to have some thick woollies to wear around the camp with your sneakers or sandals.

is supplied in sheets that can be cut to the exact size and shape of the blister. Just make sure to clean and dry the skin before you apply it.

Another helpful product to toss in your first-aid kit is Second Skin. It's available in strips and is conveniently packed in a resealable foil envelope. Cut off a strip and peel the plastic backing off with gel film placed on the skin. It can be held in place by a larger piece of moleskin.

Clean, well-fitting socks are also essential on any trip if you want to keep your feet free of blisters, not to mention to rid your tent of foot odor (which always seems to linger even after your tent partner has tossed your boots out the front flap of the tent). This pattern of changing your socks daily will also keep you safe from getting "trench foot." The ailment, which got its name from soldiers constantly standing in wet trenches during the First World War, is similar to frostbite in theory. Prolonged exposure to moisture or cold will create nerve and muscle damage. The results vary from just having a slightly swollen, discolored and tender foot to excessive swelling and blisters, which later form ulcers, potentially leading to gangrene.

KNEE PROBLEMS

Some years back I was part of a rescue team that helped an injured hiker out of the interior. It took us two solid days of trudging through 3 feet of soft snow to get him to the highway, and as a result of putting so much stress on my knee joints I ended up with severe arthritis, a condition I've suffered from ever since.

The main problem with receiving such damage to the joints is that it's next to impossible to return them to normal, which, as I have stressed, is why prevention is the best advice when it comes to first aid.

Walking downhill is the first thing to watch, especially if you have a heavy pack strapped to your back. You're actually falling forward, and what keeps you upright, and your knees from sagging, is the action of the big muscle in the front of the thigh, the quadriceps (the one that feels like jelly after a long day on the trail). The kneecap, since it's the center of rotation for the knee and is highly vulnerable to stress, can be easily damaged by weak quadriceps.

So, the best way to reduce stress on the knee and prevent damage is to keep the proper muscles in condition. The better the muscles work, the better they guide the kneecap along the front of the knee. In return, the knee can withstand more pressure. The muscle knows what to do, but without the right conditioning, it does it haphazardly.

To properly condition your knees for hiking, it's important to choose the proper sport. To tune up the quadriceps in an aerobic way, cycling, running, and cross-country skiing work well. Don't choose stop-and-go sports such as tennis, racquetball, or weightlifting. In these sports, the quadriceps work in a sporadic way.

It is important to warm up properly before starting out, as well as to warm down at the end of the day. If damage does occur, remember the acronym RICE (rest, ice, compression, and elevation). This will sooth the tendon and muscle unit. Stretching also helps a damaged muscle, and a good heel-to-butt stretch helps an inflamed unit.

As the pain subsides, try an isometric exercise. Lie down and extend your legs straight out, then hold them at about 45 degrees, and then 90 degrees. Whenever possible do at least fifty of these, holding each for the count of three. I know all this sounds like a lot of work. But believe me, after my unforgettable mishap in Killarney Park, an ounce of prevention would have saved me a lifetime of pain.

ORTHOPEDIC PROBLEMS FOR PADDLERS

Paddling all day against a headwind or constantly maneuvering through long stretches of whitewater can really push your muscles beyond their limit, especially the wrist and forearm. The pain in these two areas comes directly from gripping your paddle too tightly, which then stresses the muscles and tendons.

Again, prevention is the best medicine. It's highly recommended that you ease up on the paddle on every stroke. But is that really realistic? It's probably easier to try to practise keeping proper form. Even if you simply

Prevention is the Key

Apart from having a complete first-aid kit packed, not to mention completing a wilderness first-aid course, prevention is a camper's best medicine. This makes total sense when you see the studies showing that serious problems, like fractures, allergic reactions or lacerations, only account for 5 percent of camping injuries. The rest are common ailments such as sprains, strains, blisters, sunburn, wounds to soft tissue, or diarrhea. All of these can be easily avoided rather than treated.

keep your wrist straight during the pull phase of the paddle stroke, the discomfort will be greatly reduced.

Shoulder injuries are also a common problem for canoeists and kayakers. I once strained both my of shoulder muscles by pushing myself way too hard on a long solo trip, forcing me to lay idle for three full days. Once the injury has happened, all you can do is rest and apply ice and heat alternately to the injured muscle (I always carry cold packs and a hot water bottle for this type of treatment). To forestall stress on your muscles and joints, however, stretching exercises before heading out on the water, proper paddle strokes while on the move, or doing a few bench presses prior to the trip may help.

FRACTURES

Treatment of a fracture is critical out there, and whether the injury is to the bone, joint or muscle, it's important that the area is quickly immobilized. Using some type of splint is ideal, whether it is made from a broken paddle, tree branch, walking stick, or blanket. I was told by my neighborhood doctor that a perfect way to set a broken leg is to wrap a Therm-a-Rest sleeping pad around the leg, hold it in place by wrapping it in duct tape, and then inflate the pad. Also, a good rule mentioned in most first-aid manuals for treating for any fracture is to splint them where they lie. Don't move the victim before immobilizing the injury. If it happens to be a broken bone, moving them will only increase the chances of the broken bone tearing away at tissue or blood vessels. It also hurts the victim a great deal and may put them into shock.

For a broken bone, fix the splint above and below the joints at either end of the bone if possible (as well as to the bone itself). If it's an injured joint, fix the splint above and below the joint (as well as to the joint itself).

Types of Fractures

CLOSED FRACTURE • This is a break to the bone without an opening in the skin, although there still may be tissue damage below the skin. Dislocations and sprains should be treated as closed fractures. One true sign of a closed fracture is if the injured area is in an unnatural position. Also look for tenderness to the area when touched and swelling and discoloration of the skin.

OPEN FRACTURE • This is when the bone has broken through the skin. The bleeding, if there is any, should be dealt with first. Then it's treated the same way as a closed fracture, with a splint. The major concern with an open fracture is the high risk of infection.

Personal Needs

Along with the essentials of the average first-aid kit, each camper will need to bring extra items for their own individual needs; items such as ear drops for sensitive ears, cream for athlete's feet, an epinephrine shot kit, and personal medications.

Assessment of the Injury Is Key

If the patient is conscious, calmly talk to them to determine the type and extent of the injury. Check them out thoroughly, looking especially for arterial bleeding and fractures. If they are unconscious, check for a pulse; the carotid (at the side of the neck) is best. Check for breathing by a rise and fall of the chest area or feel for an exchange of air at the mouth or nose. Examine, from head to foot, for obvious injuries and fluid exiting ears or nose. Before moving the victim, look for any signs of a spinal injury.

▲ *A Camp Wabun leader splints a bad leg fracture .*

Also, add some padding, like an extra shirt or jacket, between the splint and the victim to give them some extra comfort, especially over bony areas. The splint should be snug but not tight — you don't want to cut off the circulation and cause complications. The best way to check for proper circulation is to push down on a fingernail or toenail and make sure the pink color returns immediately. And remember, the injury will begin to swell inside the splint, so make sure to check continually for proper circulation.

Types of Bleeding

GENTLE OOZE • This is like when you nick yourself shaving and the blood seeps slowly from the wound. It's known as capillary bleeding and will usually stop on its own or when you place a bandage on it. The only thing you should be concerned about is the risk of infection.

SLOW-BUT-STEADY STREAM • A sharp camp saw will do the trick for this one. The blood comes from a number of blood vessels, building up below the skin and then exiting the wound at a steady and sometimes alarming rate. Direct pressure at the exact source of the bleeding will work – it's usually not as bad as it looks. Take note that cuts to the head or face will usually produce a lot more blood. Use a sterile gauze pad, and if bleeding continues, place another gauze pad onto the blood-soaked one. Peeling off the first gauze will interrupt the clotting process.

SPURTING AND SQUIRTING • This isn't good. If the blood is streaming and pulsating out of the wound then expect that an artery has been severed. Bleeding can be severe, and must be stopped immediately. Place direct pressure on it even before getting a proper dressing out of the first-aid kit. It will eventually clot, as long as the area is not moved about too much. In major cases a tourniquet must be used, but this is extremely rare, and if applied to a leg or arm you must assume that amputation of the area later on is pretty much a given.

Pain Relief for Stings

Bees and wasps inject venom under the skin using a stinger. The bee's stinger is barbed, like a fish hook, and remains in your skin, whereas the wasp stinger is smooth and can be used numerous times. They both really hurt, producing a burning sensation, followed by redness of the area and possible swelling. Here are a few things you can do to relieve the pain:

- Remove the bee stinger with a scraping motion of the fingernail.
- Wash the area with soap and water.
- Wash with antiseptic.
- Place a cold compress or calamine lotion on the area (baking soda or even mud is a good substitute).
- Rub an Aspirin tablet on the sting area.

Check Your Pee

A well-hydrated camper pees frequently and has clear urine. Deep yellow urine, with a strong odor, is a true sign that not enough fluids are being consumed.

DEHYDRATION

Not drinking enough water is the number one reason campers get nauseous, have headaches, lose their appetite, become constipated or have constant diarrhea, and generally feel irritable. You need to drink at least 3 to 4 quarts (3–4 L) of water per day, replenishing it slowly throughout the day (about a quart an hour is good). Swallowing a huge amount in the morning makes it impossible for your body to process it all, and gulping it down at night doesn't help one little bit. The moment your mouth becomes dry or you crave a drink, it's too late; your body's fluids are too low. A cup of coffee or tea doesn't help either. Caffeine is a diuretic and will actually increase the loss of body fluids. Alcohol will do the same.

HEAT STROKE

When your body temperature (averaging at 98.6 degrees F, or 37 C) rises, the brain tells your heart to pump faster and peripheral blood vessels to dilate, forcing the blood to flow closer to the surface of the skin. By doing this the extra heat is lost into the air and you cool off. To help out, your body also starts to sweat, and with each droplet, heat is evaporated into the air. Sounds great, but if you don't drink enough fluids you can't sweat enough to get rid of the extra heat. If this happens you need to cool your body down as quickly as possible. Drink fluids, get out of the sun, allow a breeze to blow across your bare skin, and place a wet bandanna around your neck or groin area (the two main places where your blood flows closest to the skin).

Things really get serious when you stop sweating; then you quickly become dizzy, confused and even irrational. Your body has now gone beyond overheated and is starting to shut down. This is heat stroke. The remedy is the same as above, but it needs to be treated far more seriously. Place the victim directly in the water and fan them constantly to increase heat evaporation. Then seek medical help if possible. Many cases of heat stroke have led to death.

TREATING THE BIG CHILL

Only once did I suffer the ill effects of hypothermia. That was enough, however, to make me realize how easy it is to die from it. I foolishly paddled through some difficult rapids in early spring, without proper clothing and safety equipment, and I flipped over. In less than three minutes my body went numb and I had to be quickly rescued by my fellow canoeists.

Luckily I survived the ordeal and counted my blessings by enrolling in a safety course a week later. Who would have guessed that before the end of the season I would use the training and the experience from my mishap to save someone else.

It was mid-October and my wife, Alana, and I were spending the weekend at a local campground. Just as we were about to leave, I happened to spot an overturned canoe floating in the middle of the lake. We immediately formed a rescue crew with some other campers and quickly paddled out to save the two occupants, neither of whom were wearing a PFD.

By the time we reached them, the swimmers were in a state of panic and showing the first signs of hypothermia: awkward motor control, minor mental confusion, uncontrollable shivering, and worst of all, a constant denial that they were in trouble. Their refusal to let us help, not to mention the state of panic they were in, made saving them all the more difficult, and by the time we completed a canoe-over-canoe rescue and got them to shore, the victims were dangerously hypothermic. Their body temperature had dropped below 90 degrees F (32 C), shivering had stopped, one canoeist had lost consciousness and the other's mental status was severely limited, forcing him to convulse uncontrollably.

At this stage we had only one choice of action. We immediately removed all their wet clothing, since this is what conducts heat away from the body almost thirty times more quickly than usual, and got them into sleeping bags. Then Alana and I disrobed, crawled into the bags with them, and attempted to warm their bodies with our own body heat. Trust me, it was not a time to be self-conscious; this was life or death.

Thankfully the incident happened at a local campground and we had the luxury of being able to call an ambulance. If it had been on a remote trip, however, we would have had to continue warming their bodies up with hot (non-caffeinated and non-alcoholic) drinks, high-calorie snacks, a warm fire, and a hot pack placed over the major blood vessels in the neck, armpit and groin.

For extreme cases the medical treatment would have been even more invasive. Cardiopulmonary resuscitation and cardiac massage must be given to a patient whose heart has stopped. This must be maintained until

▲ *Bailey suffering the ill-effects of hypothermia.*

the patient is re-warmed and shows a pulse. In the hospital, hypothermic people have survived after hours of resuscitation efforts.

Of course, thinking back to this incident, prevention again should have been the key. They should have never been out paddling across the middle of a large lake in the month of October in the first place. Just like I should have never been paddling down dangerous rapids in early spring without the proper equipment and skills. Experience, practised rescue and first-aid techniques, preparation for trips (especially those during the off season), and basic common sense are the most essential life-saving ingredients to pack away to avoid the "Big Chill."

FROSTBITE

For all the cold camping I've done in the past I'm darn lucky to have gotten frostbite only once. It wasn't a severe case, just damage done to the outer skin of my baby finger. But every time the temperature drops the throbbing pain in my finger gives me a harsh reminder of how vulnerable our bodies are to the cold.

Frostbite can occur when temperatures reach below 32 degrees F (zero Celsius), and in most cases the cause is extreme wind chill against exposed skin (nose, cheeks, ear lobes) or lack of blood circulation in fingers and toes. The area of damaged tissue is similar to a burn. A mild case, known as frostnip, is more common and can be easily treated in the field by sharing body heat (skin-to-skin) with someone else. I placed my fingers in my trip partner's armpit. Immersing the area in warm (not hot) water is also effective. Don't rub or massage the area — you will just damage the skin.

Frostnip is more recognizable than frostbite — the skin becomes white or waxy looking — and it's important you keep watch for these early signs. Once you get frostbite the treatment isn't that easy. The skin tissue is frozen, and the victim needs professional medical care before permanent damage occurs. Severe blistering is common, as well as potential amputation of the damaged area.

Wind Chill

The moment a cold wind hits exposed skin it quickly begins robbing your body of heat. This is known wind chill. The more the wind increases the more dramatically the wind chill decreases. For example, -20 degrees F (-30 C) drops to -71 degrees F (-61 C) with a wind speed of 25 mph (40 km/h). At this point skin will freeze in less than thirty seconds.

If immediate evacuation of the victim is impossible then it's best not to attempt warming up the frozen area, only to have it exposed to the cold again and potentially making things worse. Just isolate the injury the best you can.

EVACUATION

Taking an injured person out of the wilderness is definitely not an easy task. My wife and I once assisted an evacuation on a remote river, and it had to be one of the most stressful events ever to happen to us. A camp group, who we had just come across on a portage, had a member fall on a steep portage and instantly complain about a very sore leg. The two leaders and I looked at the injury but couldn't come up with a solid diagnosis. One thing was for sure, though, the victim was in a lot of pain. We assumed the worst and treated him for a broken leg. After immobilizing the leg as best we could — splinting it with half a paddle on either side of the leg, held together with duct tape — the leaders of the camp group had to decide whether to try to carry the camp kid out or to go for help.

Any injury or illness that prevents a person from walking makes any evacuation far more difficult, and the idea of carrying an injured person for two days down a remote river — well that would just be foolish. So the leaders decided to send two runners. Both were exceptional paddlers and competent with navigational skills. They headed off with food, water, shelter, and everything necessary to make the rescue a success (injured person's medical history, precise location of victim, who to contact once help was found). They even agreed to take every precaution to make their trip out a safe one, even if it meant slowing down the rescue.

In less than twenty-four hours a rescue helicopter arrived with paramedics. The boy was air lifted to the nearest hospital, where it was discovered he had a broken femur with danger of a blood clot. Moving him could have been fatal.

> "*Collapsing on the road, I lit a candle and peeled off my socks to assess the damage. The skin on my feet was white, puffy, and lifeless; the bruises on my ankles and lower shins had broken into open sores. Pain was returning to my feet — a good sign.*"
>
> DAVID HALSEY, *MAGNETIC NORTH* (1990)

WHAT ELSE CAN GO WRONG?

S.O.S. I need your help. I am injured, near death, and too weak to hike out of here. I am all alone. This is no joke. In the name of God, please remain to save me. I am out collecting berries close by and shall return this evening. Thank you. — Chris McCandless, August 1992

A NOTE FOUND DEEP IN THE ALASKA INTERIOR.
CHRIS JOHNSON MCCANDLESS EVENTUALLY STARVED TO DEATH.

THERE ARE TIMES when I think it's the misadventures on a trip we enjoy more than the moments of calm and serenity. After all, it's always the stories of bad trips rather than good ones that are told around the campfire at night. Who knows, maybe we all need some type of wild escapade to enhance our lives — a way to challenge ourselves physically and even spiritually. Or maybe it's that bizarre trips just seem more exciting to tell friends and family when you get home. It's obvious to anyone who has spent quality time out there that the pleasant times in the wilderness always outweigh the moments of horror. It's really not that unsafe an environment, and usually the things that could go wrong never do. But one good thing about all of us wanting to shock and terrify others is that by constantly telling stories about dealing with bears, bugs and bad weather, we're guaranteed it won't be crowded the next time we head out. Here are a few of the worst things that could go wrong, and a bit of knowledge to help reduce your fears.

◀ *Look on the bright side; half a canoe is better than no canoe at all.*

BATTLING BEAR PHOBIA

I've had some really bad luck dealing with bears. I'm not sure why. A bear biologist once suggested that it was due to my fear of the animal, explaining that if bears sense any anxiety, they will use it to their advantage. His theory actually makes sense. I had a bear scare me off my campsite and then steal a chocolate cake I was in the middle of baking. I had a bear bully me away from my camp gear while on a portage and then steal a tube of toothpaste from my pack. I had a bear harass me the moment I pulled into a park visitor center parking lot and then attempt to steal, oddly enough, my Thermos of coffee. And I must admit that each time I was absolutely horrified. Who wouldn't be?

▲ *"All bushes can't be bears." — Theodore Roethke*

Typical Bear Sign

Bear Tracks

Bear Poop

Out of pure desperation I soon learned to battle my bear phobia. The first time I stood my ground was at a public campground. A large male bear had bothered me to no end throughout the week. Finally, I couldn't stand the stress of having the bear intimidate me any longer. So the next time he wandered into my camp I stood my ground. First I banged some pots together. That didn't seem to work. Then I tossed some rocks his way, with one actually hitting him on the ass. So he charged me. The bear ran full tilt toward me, stopping dead only a few feet away to beat the ground in front of him with his front paws, while snapping and growling. It was a classic fake charge (of course, I didn't know that at the time). I responded by waving my arms up in the air and yelling obscenities at him. Surprisingly, the bear backed down. In fact, he ran away. Before leaving the site, however, he did manage to swat the bow of my canoe with his paw a few times (I have out-of-focus photos to prove it). He definitely was a bear with an attitude.

BEAR BAGGING

Food storage is a crucial element in keeping yourself safe from nuisance bears. Load all food, and anything else with strong odors (toothpaste, sunscreen, hand lotion, soap, bug repellent) in a separate pack. Then string it up either between two trees or over an outstretched limb. Make sure to set up the bear rope early in the evening so you just have to go and pull the food pack up before bed. There's nothing worse than looking for a proper tree to hang your food in when it's pitch dark. Also, make sure to choose a tree well away from camp, at least 90 feet (30 m) into the forest, and not on a well-used trail. A bear, especially in well-used parks, will quickly get to know each campsite's food cache if it's easy to locate.

▲ *The easiest way to hang your food pack is with a rope thrown over an solid tree branch. If the pack is too heavy to haul up on your own, use a homemade pulley system.*

▲ *Above: Guard your food pack from bears by hanging it between two tree limbs. Below: Just make sure the limbs are sturdy enough to hold the weight of the pack.*

It helps to tie a piece of fluorescent flagging tape onto the bear rope; it's not all that easy to relocate your bear rope hanging in the back bush when it comes to rigging the food bag up later in the evening.

Pulley System

For the first few days of a trip the food bag may be a little too heavy to lift. Try bringing two sections of rope, one with a small metal pulley (found at any hardware store) tied to one end. Throw the pulley rope over the branch, with the other rope passed through the pulley. Then tie the other end of the pulley rope to a tree and hoist up the heavy pack with the other rope.

Bear Barrels?

Some canoeists have opted to use barrels to keep their food safe. They're a great system to keep everything dry and relatively odor-free, and they can come in handy when traveling in the far North, where there are no tall trees from which to hang your food. But in no way should they be considered "bear barrels." In the last few years there have been numerous reports about campers who have placed their food barrel right beside their tent and been woken up to a bear smashing it to pieces. Remember, if a bear can break into an automobile with one swing of the paw, then a thin plastic barrel is no match for it.

Food Floating Technique

Another food storage alternative for canoeists is to load up your boat and then anchor it out in the lake for the night. Personally, I'd be far too paranoid about a storm blowing the canoe away to attempt this. If a storm blows in, however, you could be in for a surprise come morning. Bears have also become used to this technique in some parks and will swim out to fetch the food stored in the canoe.

Bear-Proof Campsites

- Never keep anything in your tent that will attract a bear. They have been known to come into tents to steal a bottle of water or munch on a container of deodorant.
- Always make sure to cook well away from your tent. Food odors are an important issue.
- Consider not cooking up strong-smelling foods (the main ingredient placed in bear traps is cooked bacon, sardines, and vanilla extract).

Bear Protection

There are items that have proven effective in protecting yourself against bear attacks. Bear bangers and pepper spray are the most commonly used. The bangers are considered the least harmful and safest deterrent. But they're obviously not as effective as pepper spray if the bear actually attacks. You'll probably never use the can of bear spray, but having it packed along gives you some sense of security. It can, however, make a bad situation worse. I've heard of people blasting at a bear and then having the spray blow right back into their face. There's also the story about the tripper in Jasper National Park who sprayed his tent with the pepper, thinking it would keep bears away. That night a grizzly wandered into his camp, and finding the actual spray tasty, he ate the tent and accidentally injured the occupant in the process.

Knowledge Is Power

- Seeing a bear in its own natural environment should be, and most likely will be, an extremely positive experience. They are, after all, the true spirit of wilderness.
- The chance of being attacked by a bear is so limited it makes little sense to spend your time worrying about it while you're out there.
- Apart from the rare predacious bear (the one that decides to hunt humans), the bear that wanders into camp is only there for your food. It has no interest in you whatsoever. Think of it as a raccoon coming into camp (the bear actually belongs to the raccoon family). If they can't get to your food then they will eventually move on, which is why keeping your camp clean is your best defence.

HANDLING A BEAR ENCOUNTER

This is the most-asked question I get when talking about camping. It's also the most difficult to answer, as there are just too many variables to consider. But in a perfect scenario, this is what you should do. First, never run. Running away may trigger a predator-prey response, and a bear can outrun the best Olympian athlete. You could climb a tree, that is if one is nearby and easy to climb, and it's not a black bear or a young grizzly, which can climb trees better than you can. It's best to stay put and assess the situation. If you stay put the bear may eventually move on and the encounter becomes an enjoyable experience.

But what if it charges you instead? Well, in most circumstances the bear is faking it. But you wouldn't know the difference between a real charge and a pretend one, so the next move is to decide if it's a male or female bear. If it's a male bear then a mild aggression technique may work (making lots of noise and standing erect, waving your arms in the air). It's rare, but male bears have been known to stalk and hunt humans for food, and the only way to protect yourself against a predacious bear is to fight back. Really fight back. However, if you try to be aggressive with a female, especially one with cubs, then she is most likely to attack in defence. You're best to play dead. Lie face down with your hands wrapped around your neck and spread your legs somewhat apart to help anchor yourself in case the bear attempts to flip you over.

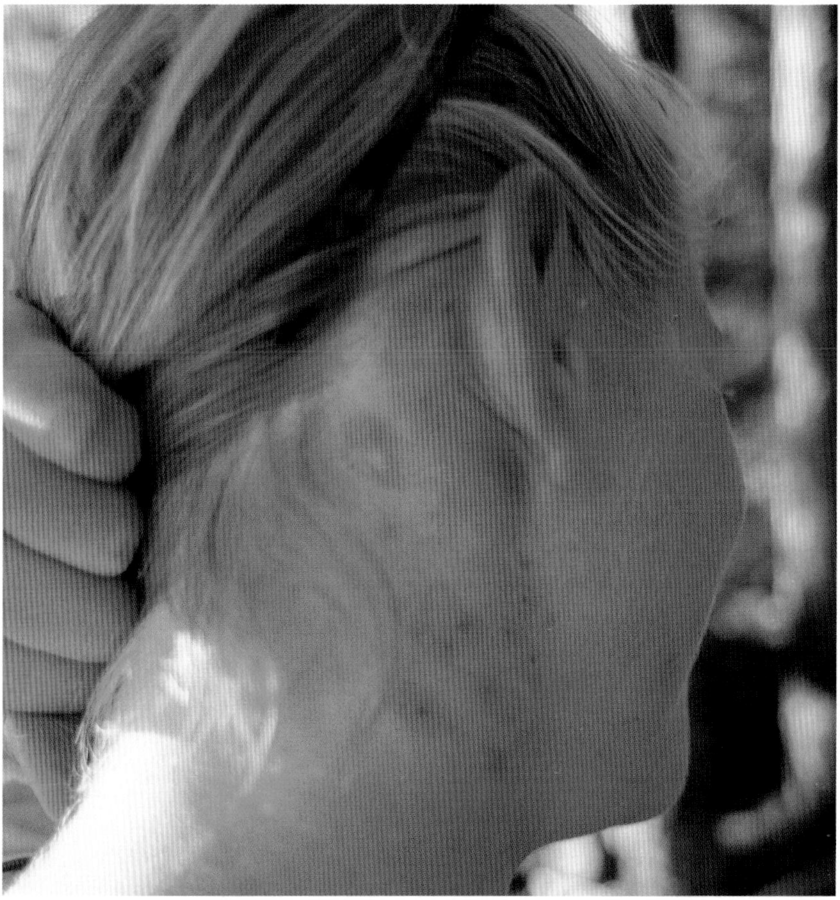

▲ *"It was the blackfly, blackfly, blackfly, everywhere, A-crawlin in your whiskers, a-crawlin in your hair; A-swimmin' in the soup and a-swimmin' in the tea Oh the Devil take the blackfly and leave me be."*

BUGS! BUGS! BUGS!

Expert entomologists have stated that a person in the northern woods, not wearing the proper protective clothing, could actually die of blood loss in less than two hours as a result of severe blackfly and mosquito bites.

Of course it's only a theory. None of these bug authorities has ever been crazy enough to stand naked in a forest and allow himself to be bitten alive. However, after spending a goodly amount of time in the outdoors during prime bug season, I can relate. There's only a slight weakness in their hypothesis, though. I think it would only take you an hour to drop dead.

Peeing on the Run

Women definitely have it worse when it comes to peeing in the woods during bug season. To help speed up the process and eliminate bites, try a product called the Travel Mate. It's a palm-sized plastic funnel that acts like an instant male appendage and does away with dropping your trousers and exposing your fanny to millions of bugs.

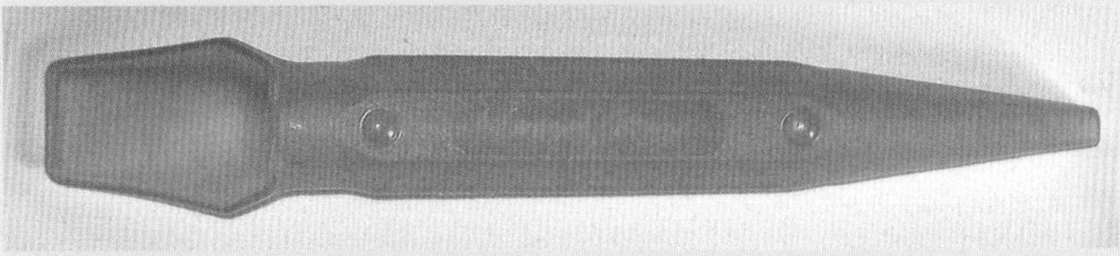

Blackfly

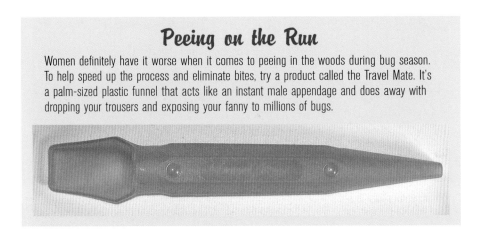

The first bothersome bug to hatch in early spring is the blackfly. Unlike the mosquito, which lays its eggs on the smooth surface of a pond, marsh or stagnant puddle, the blackfly lays its eggs in a running brook or river. After hatching, the baby blackfly (larvae) drifts downstream, holding on to a strand of silk like a spider to its web on a windy day. Once it finds a place to feed, the blackfly then spins a disk-shaped pad of silk on a rock or log, holds itself in place with its hooked rear end, and begins to snack on tiny bacteria, protozoa, diatoms, and even the odd brother or sister blackfly that drifts by.

When the blackfly grows into an adult, the bug pulls itself out of its skin, stretches out its wings, rises quickly to the surface in a tiny gas bubble, and pops itself free. The males fly off to munch on plant nectar. The females, however, search out victims for a meal of protein-rich blood, which they need to produce their eggs.

Mosquito

The female mosquito also feeds on blood. Mosquitoes hatch in a similar way to the blackfly, the only real difference being in the way they get their blood meal. Female blackflies feed by slicing your skin open with jagged mouthparts, like a pair of scissors. After the initial cut, other mouthparts (called stylets) hold back the skin with tiny hooks while the insect snips again and again until it eventually carves open your capillaries and tastes blood. It then fills up with half a teaspoon (2 ml) of enriched protein.

The victim usually doesn't feel the blackfly cutting away. It's after she finishes and then wrenches her head from side-to-side, trying to free the hooked mouth part that really hurts. Unlike the blackfly, mosquitoes don't

▲ *One way to deal with the bugs.*

actually bite. They suck your blood. Using a needle-like mouthpart, the bug pierces your skin, spits saliva into the wound to stop your blood from clotting, fills its blood bank, then quickly pulls out and flies away. Mosquitoes have become more of a concern in the past few years due to the fact that they spread West Nile virus.

Other Flies I Have Known

Horseflies and Deerflies Horseflies and deerflies have to be on top of the list. These bothersome insects are not only among the most fierce, painful biters, they're also excellent fliers, having the ability to chase you down the trail or portage (the record speed for a horsefly is 67 mph, or 112 km/h). They're well known for patiently buzzing around your head until they find a safe place to land, and are mostly attracted to shiny objects, which is why the shimmer of wet skin on swimmers draws them in for miles around. Their bites are also vicious, because they literally take a chunk of skin out of you, leaving behind a trail of blood and an open wound that can become infected.

Symptoms of West Nile

The symptoms of mild infection are flu-like. Those of severe infection (West Nile encephalitis or meningitis) include headache, high fever, neck stiffness, stupor, disorientation, coma, tremors, convulsions, muscle weakness, and paralysis. It is estimated that 1 in 150 persons infected with the West Nile virus will develop a more severe form of disease.

The deerfly usually hunts in groups of four to five and is the more common of the two pests, which is a good thing since horseflies are almost three times the size. The deerfly is slightly larger than a house fly, has a yellow to light brown abdomen with darker stripes, a darker pattern to the wings, and bright green or gold eyes.

Sandfly Another irritating insect is the sandfly, or what's more commonly known as the "no-see-um." I hate these miniature pests, especially because they have the ability to squeeze themselves through the fine bug mesh sewn to your tent door. There have been a few nights, especially in the province of Quebec, when I've camped on a scenic sandbar and quickly become overwhelmed by these tiny midges. They're almost impossible to see, and just as difficult to hear. But their bite is a nasty one — it feels like a hot ash from the campfire landing on your bare skin. In fact, a second nickname for them is "punkies," derived from the Native word *punk*, meaning "living ashes."

Stable Fly Stable flies are also quite annoying. Many people mistake these bugs for biting houseflies, and they do have some resemblance. But make no mistake, these things really hurt. They usually go for the ankles, and are equipped with a sharp, piercing mouthpart capable of penetrating the thickest of wool socks. Unlike other biting insects, which snip and slice, stable flies jab their slender proboscis into your skin. Then, miniature recurved spines at the tip of the proboscis grab hold while the mouthpart is moved from side-to-side, enabling the insect to get deeper and deeper. The worst part, however, is that both the male and female bite.

Ticks The very worst out there, in my opinion, is the tick. The very thought of having one of these parasites feeding on me is enough to make my skin crawl. It's not so much that they are known vectors of Lyme disease and that they feed by plunging their beaklike mouthpart deep inside you and then secrete a concrete-like saliva that literally glues them in place, it's the fact that they prefer dark and moist places on your body to which to attach themselves — places like armpits, bellybutton holes and, you guessed it, your crotch. These are all places I'd rather not have something nibbling at.

Performing regular tick checks is crucial in heavily tick-infested areas, and it's best to use the buddy system for this. Of course, this can get embarrassing at times. I'll never forget when my wife and I, while traveling through the Boundary Waters Canoe Area, began our nightly routine of stripping down and checking each other's private parts for embedded ticks, when a group of Boy Scouts paddled by. I tried to explain to them what we were doing, which, according to my wife, made the scenario even worse.

If you do find a tick lodged into your skin, make sure not to panic and start yanking away at it. You're just liable to pull the thing in half, leaving its head inside you and increasing the chances of infection. The best way is to first spray it with a good amount of bug repellent. This will definitely force it to relax its grip, since the tick actually breathes out of its backside while its head is lodged into your skin. Don't burn it with a cigarette or match like some older guidebooks recommend, as this will just make the tick hold on tighter and become more difficult to get out. After allowing some time for the repellent to take effect, place a pair of tweezers (tick pliers can also be purchased at most outdoor stores) and, without squeezing the tick, reach inside, beneath the body, and gently pull it out. Then disinfect the area with antiseptic or soap and water.

How to Repel the Little Buggers

All blood-feeding insects find their prey by body temperature, activated by lactic acid produced by muscle movement and the carbon dioxide emitted when you exhale. They absolutely love warm, sweaty skin on a cool day. Warm days, however, seem to confuse them. All species also dislike pouring rain, cold days when temperatures reach below 10 degrees C (50 F), and blowing winds. The blackfly in particular is not a strong flier and can only reach a top speed of 0.5 mph (1 km/h).

Dark colors attract much more than shiny, bright colors. Wearing blue jeans is just asking for it; lime green neither attracts them nor keeps them at bay; and hot pink works well for repelling.

Bug hats, or better yet, bug jackets, are an essential part of your equipment list from the first week in May until around the second week in July.

Symptoms of Lyme Disease

- a circular red rash forming around the bitten area
- flu-like symptoms
- painful joints
- insomnia
- local paralysis
- skin sensations
- hearing loss

Bug repellent is also a must. There are lots of formulas out there, but the best is anything that contains lots of DEET (diethyl toluamide). The chemical is mostly effective in keeping blackflies, mosquitoes, no-see-ums, and ticks away from exposed skin. I wouldn't squirt too much on, however — the stuff also works well stripping paint and melting plastic.

I remember back during my tree-planting days for the Ministry of Natural Resources in Northern Ontario we were told never to put DEET on our hard hats. One worker ignored our supervisor's rule one day and soaked his helmet. He got caught when the foreman saw thousands of dead blackflies stuck to his bright yellow hard hat. To show the reasoning behind the rule, the boss smacked the hard hat against a rock. The plastic headgear cracked right down the middle. After witnessing that, I've kept to only putting small amounts of DEET directly on my skin. Usually, I just spray the chemical on the bandana wrapped around my neck. I also make sure to keep my shirt sleeves and pant legs tight with elastic bands.

Repellents containing citron, such as Avon's Skin-So-Soft lotion, are more gentle to the skin and are almost as effective as DEET. They usually don't last as long, though. Taking vitamin B tablets for three months before your trip has also been proven effective. Eating lots of citrus fruit and garlic and avoiding bananas are other suggestions to think about. Even applying a combination of spices — cinnamon, rosemary, basil, thyme and allspice —

▲ *Eureka's VCS Parawing bug shelter – I wouldn't leave home without it.*

Ain't No Flies On Us

There ain't no flies on us.
There ain't no flies on us.
There may be flies on some of you guys,
but there ain't no flies on us.
(repeat)

Two groups sing the song back to one another, beginning as quietly as they can and building up louder and louder until the groups are yelling back at one another.

to your skin may work. But my all-time favorite weaponry against bugs is my Eureka bug tarp.

The bug shelter (called "VCS Parawing shelter system" in the Eureka catalogue) is a regular rain tarp with fine mesh netting attached to the four walls. The whole outfit weights about 5 pounds. It also uses no-see-um netting, which makes the price a little higher, but it's far more effective against punkies. The netting is attached to the four walls by plastic clips, making it possible to detach that section and just pack the tarp along during less buggy conditions.

My regular canoe mates teased me to no end the first time I brought the tarp along on our annual spring fishing trip. They said I was a sissy. However, when the bugs got really bad and I went inside my bug-proof shelter to cook up dinner in peace, they pleaded with me to be allowed in. Payment was a shot of brandy each and an immediate apology for calling me names.

BEAVER FEVER

If you think being in a remote wilderness area means that the water you find out there is safe to drink, then think again! There are so many pollutants and pathogens floating around in our lakes and streams that the days of dipping your cup directly into the water for a drink are long gone.

One of the worst bugs to pick up is *Giardia lamblia*. These microscopic, one-celled parasites enter the water cycle in the feces of an infected animal. The usual host is the beaver, which is how this waterborne pathogen got its nickname "beaver fever." But it can be deposited by any mammal, including humans. It only takes about ten giardia to infect your body. They hatch inside the small intestine after an incubation period of five days to several months (usually one or two weeks), reproduce like wildfire, establish a colony, and then have a little party in your gut, making you feel as if Montezuma has moved north to seek his revenge, for two to six weeks.

Symptoms can be severe or completely unnoticeable. They include: diarrhea, abdominal cramps, fatigue, weight loss, flatulence, and nausea — not a pleasant experience when you're away from flush toilets and a local pharmacy. Usually, however, you get it when back home, and then just assume it's the flu. But, if untreated it can cause severe problems. I've been affected three times, and each case took over a month to treat with antibiotics.

▲ *Water filtration is the best choice when it comes to water purification.*

Giardia is the most common pathogen to find swimming around in your water bottle. The good news, however, is that it's the least dangerous. Infection with the bacterium *Francisella tularensis,* known as tularemia, is more serious. It is found in many animals, particularly rabbits, rodents and hares, although it does not spread between humans. A very high number of trappers fall ill to this sickness due to their constant contact with the internal organs and body fluids of mammals.

The bacterium spreads via bites from infected insects, handling of infected animal carcasses, eating or drinking contaminated food or water, or breathing in the bacteria. Symptoms include a high fever, headaches, chills, muscle aches, diarrhea, joint pain, a dry cough, and weakness, and it may be fatal.

Giardia and tularemia are just two of the risks that you may expose yourself to by drinking untreated water. Bacteria such as E. coli and salmonella can give you a nasty case of food poisoning, and then there are surface-water pollutants such as fuel, pesticides, and heavy metals from old mine sites. All are good reasons to treat all water while you're out there.

WATER TREATMENT

Boiling

Boiling is probably the most common method of killing germs. Boiling water for five minutes will eliminate pretty much everything, and just bringing it to a rolling boil is sufficient enough to get rid of some protozoa, bacteria and even viruses. The problem with boiling all the water you'll need, however, is that it's quite simply a waste of stove fuel. What usually happens is that the water boiled the night before quickly runs out halfway through the day. So rather than stopping to boil up some more (which would be rather silly on a hot day), campers either don't drink at all, making them severally dehydrated, or they get lazy and just drink water directly from the lake (a big mistake).

Chemical Treatment

Iodine tablets are another option for cleaning water. The chemical works well in killing most of what's out there. It should be noted, however, that there's a strong odor, not to mention a bland taste, to the water. And there's also a warning "use only for emergencies" placed in fine print on the bottom of the label.

The other dilemma with using iodine is that it kills both the bad bacteria in the water and the good bacteria that are in your gut helping you digest.

After frequent use, this can cause a problem. For infrequent use, however, it can be a bonus. The treatment is one tablet for every quart (liter) of water and then wait fifteen minutes, or two tablets if the water is cloudy or colder than 50 degrees F (9 C) and then wait for one hour. To get rid of the bad taste of the treated water, simply disguise it by adding flavored drink crystals.

You can purify water by passing it through fine mesh filters containing iodine. The iodine is only released when there are micro-organisms present. The temperature of the water is irrelevant, and your water doesn't get spiked with iodine unless it needs it. The disadvantage is trying to figure out when to change the iodine-laced replacement filters.

There are other chemicals that are just as effective. Some campers trust in using a few drops of bleach added to their water bottle. Others have changed over to a new system called Aquamira. This chemical treatment, produced by McNett Company to directly kill the bacteria, works by releasing oxygen in a highly controlled form. It has no bad taste or odor and two 1-ounce (30 ml) containers can purify 30 gallons (114 L) of water.

Filters

The best purification system for drinking water is a filter. You just pump and drink. And by making water collection so quick and easy, there's less chance of becoming dehydrated.

There are a few disadvantages, though, starting with the high cost. The main body of the system itself is not that bad. But the price of the replacement filter is outrageous. If you only go on a one-week trip per year, then the filter should last you a couple of years. But if you're out all season, you're going to use up at least one or two filters, which cost close to $40 each. The only way to save money is to always wash the filter out after each trip. It's also a great idea to wrap a coffee filter around it to help extend the use.

Filters strain out microscopic contaminants but they don't necessarily eliminate bacteria or viruses. The purity of the water depends greatly on the size of the filter's pores. Any pore size of 2 microns or smaller will get rid of nasty pathogens such as giardia and surface pollutants. However, it takes a pore size of less than 0.4 microns to remove bacteria and viruses.

POISON IVY

Leaves of three, let it be. Unknowingly using poison ivy as a substitute for toilet paper has to be one of the biggest bloopers of my father's life; he was hospitalized for nearly a week. I've seen worse cases, though. The nastiest has to be when a fellow park worker cut grass containing a giant patch of poison ivy and then burned it in a giant pile while he stripped to just shorts

▲ *Top: Poison ivy. Bottom left: The juice of crushed jewelweed leaves and stems is a natural remedy for poison ivy. Bottom right: Fragrant sumac looks like poison ivy but the middle leaf is not separate.*

Poison Ivy Remedies

- If you think you've been exposed, make sure to wash with soap and water immediately.
- To relieve the itching, wash with soap and water and lather on calamine lotion.
- A wet compress with equal parts ice water and whole milk or baking soda added to cold water may help blistering.
- A natural remedy is to rub the juice of crushed jewelweed leaves and stems on the affected area.

and sunbathed. The poison was released in the smoke and covered him from head to toe, even affecting his lungs.

Urushiol oil is what causes that unsightly rash and unbearable itching and blistering. The poisonous substance is contained in the sap, which flows through the plant's stems, leaves, roots and fruit. Basically, the stuff is everywhere. The worst part, however, is that it can still be transmitted for up to five years after the plant is dead, which makes it impossible to eliminate the danger of catching it. And you will catch it. Nobody is immune to poison ivy. Some people are less affected by it during their first encounter, but the intensity will increase every time.

The oil is held inside the plant, so in theory you can't get poison ivy by just brushing up against it. But the plant is so fragile that the chances are extremely high that some plant in the patch has been broken by an animal walking by or even a slight breeze blowing across it. Even an insect chewing on the plant can release enough poison to cause irritation. It doesn't take much. Experts have stated that hundreds of people can be affected by the amount of urushiol oil covering the head of a pin. Humans alone suffer the curse of poison ivy, as it has no effect on animals. In fact, many of them eat it. Birds even consume the berries and spread its seeds in their droppings.

The three-leaf identification is not always the best; there are lots of other plants out there with clusters of three leaves. Poison ivy can also take on various forms, growing as a ground-cover plant, a low woody shrub, or as a vine up a tree trunk. However, there is always more than one plant, and the shiny, waxy green leaflets have a slight droop, with the two lower leaves meeting close together at the stem and the middle leaf separate.

POISONOUS SNAKES

Snakes really aren't a major problem out there — it's the phobia of them that's the problem. I once helped a snake biologist release three Massasauga rattlesnakes fixed with radio transmitters back into wild. When she opened the box to let them slither out I immediately backed away, and surprisingly came uncomfortably close to stepping on a fourth snake. The biologist was ecstatic that I had found another wild specimen, and she instantly grabbed it to fix on another radio transmitter. I reacted a little differently, screaming and running off into the woods, knocking my head on a low tree branch in the process. In retrospect, the low tree branch was far more dangerous. The snake had every opportunity to bite me, but didn't. Again, it was the phobia that was the problem, and that day the biologist proved to me that a little knowledge always reduces the fear.

North America has two families of poisonous snakes. The first is in the cobra family, its only member the coral snake. It's rare, living in Florida and the southwest United States. The snake has bright red, yellow and black bands circling its body. Remembering the phrase: "Red on yellow will kill a fellow but red on black, venom will lack," is important, since there are many other snakes with similar coloration that are not poisonous. The venom of the coral snake affects the nervous system, making it the most dangerous of all snakes.

The second family of snakes — pit vipers — includes rattlesnakes, moccasins (cottonmouths) and copperheads. The venom of these creatures affects

▲ *The rattle of the Massasauga rattlesnake sounds more like a muffled cicada bug than an actual rattle.*

the circulatory system. The one you're most likely to come across, due to its wide range across North America (everywhere except Alaska, Maine, Hawaii and northern Canada), is the rattlesnake. There are over thirty species of rattlesnake; all are poisonous, and all usually warn you before striking by shaking their tail (it sounds more like a muffled cicada bug than an actual rattle). They rarely strike, though. Most snake bites happen when people knowingly approach and even handle a rattlesnake. Even if you do get bitten, you have little chance of dying, especially if you are a healthy adult and seek help immediately. Your pet dog is probably the one you should watch out for; far more dogs have been injured or killed by bites than have humans.

Snake Handling

- Prevention is the best method for dealing with snake bites. Wear thick socks and boots and have pant legs hang over your boot.
- Watch where you place your hands and feet while doing activities such as gathering firewood or climbing rock ledges.
- Each morning, carefully check your boots and other gear that is stored outside at night, and check underneath your tent before packing it away.
- If you hear a rattle — freeze. Try to locate the snake and slowly walk away from the area.
- If bitten, don't panic! Get to a hospital immediately, calling ahead to make sure they have antivenom available. Also, properly identify the snake, killing it if you have to. Rattlesnake poison is totally different than that of a coral snake, and being treated with antivenom for what is actually a non-poisonous snake bite will make things a lot worse.
- If the hospital isn't an option for some time, the victim should remain still or walk out slowly. If you have a venom extractor (available at most outdoor stores), use it. If not, wash wound with antiseptic or soap and water and bandage it. Don't cut the wound open and suck out the poison with your mouth. This will only cause infection.
- Any bitten area on the body should be kept below the heart to decrease the spread of the poison.

Symptoms of a Rattlesnake Bite

- actual fang marks
- swelling, which occurs from a minute up to an hour after being bitten
- discolouring of the skin and a good amount of pain around the bitten area
- nausea
- numbness
- difficulty breathing
- temporary blindness (rare but possible)

POISONOUS SPIDERS

There's really not much to worry about when it comes to spiders in the backwoods. Most don't bite, they just look scary. And of the ones that do bite when handled or threatened, only two justify medical treatment: the black widow, found throughout North America except for the northern States and Canada; and the brown recluse, found only in the southern United States. Both spiders avoid people at all costs and are only a problem for small children or unhealthy adults.

Of the two, I would worry more about the brown recluse. Only the female black widow spider bites, and she's easy to recognize — jet black with a large, round abdomen decorated underneath with a red or orange marking. If you do get bitten, the effects range from nausea to muscle spasms for a day or two. Death only occurs from breathing paralysis, and if you're a healthy adult it's unlikely you'll suffer any serious complications.

The brown recluse, a small brown spider with long legs and a dark violin-shaped marking on the upper back, is a little different. It's harder to recognize, and beyond just making you sick and giving you a nasty blister at the bite area, it may cause long-term health problems if not treated. The problem is that medical treatment is very specific to this spider bite, and with identification of the spider not being easy, it's crucial you find the spider that bit you.

Spidey Sense

- Avoidance is the best advice. Shake your boots and gear out every morning and watch where you're putting your hands and feet.
- If bitten, don't panic!
- First aid for a venomous spider bite is like the treatment for a snake bite; use a venom extractor if you have one and wash and bandage the wound.
- Analgesics can help with the pain.
- Seek proper medical treatment immediately.

SCORPIONS

Scorpions span temperate North America and all have venom that affects their victim's nervous system. The good news, however, is that there's only one species in North America, *Centruroides exilicauda,* that is powerful enough to affect a human's long-term health. They are also found only in the southwestern states and Mexico. It's a good size at 2 to 4 inches (6–10 cm), and can easily be differentiated from all the other species by a solid yellow to yellowish-brown-colored body with irregular black stripes on its back.

The poison is injected by the scorpion thrusting its tail, tipped with a stinger, over its head and into the victim's skin. A sting from a "non-poisonous" species is still very painful and will cause swelling and discoloration. But a sting from a poisonous scorpion will create numbness, frothing at the mouth, facial distortion and quite possibly death due to cardiac or respiratory failure within a few hours of being stung.

Where is Thy Sting?

- Scorpions are nocturnal (more active at night) and stay inactive during the day under rocks and logs and in crevices. Watch where you put your hands, and shake your clothing and boots before putting them on in the morning.
- It's not easy to identify a sting mark from a scorpion. So, if you feel a painful sting make sure to look around for whatever did it and administer the proper first aid.
- If stung, stay calm and seek medical help immediately.
- Don't administer drugs for pain relief; it will increase the toxicity of the venom.

LEECHES

I've tried to like leeches. I really have. But the moment I see one wriggle past me while bathing in the water I start screaming uncontrollably and make a beeline for shore. It's as if the killer shark from *Jaws* has entered the beach area. I am embarrassed about my actions. After all, the leech is more or less harmless, especially when compared to a shark. But I'm not alone in my phobia. Humphrey Bogart absolutely loathed having them on him in the movie *The African Queen*, and the gang of youth in *Stand by Me* had similar feelings, especially when they found them inside their bathing trunks.

Over seven hundred species of leech can be found in the world, ranging from the usual fare found in northern swamps and ponds to tropical kinds

Leeches in Medicine

As far back as one thousand years ago the act of draining the blood with leeches to enable the body to make fresh blood was thought to be the cure for many ailments. The practice of bloodletting reached a peak in the early nineteenth century and was used extensively for various skin diseases, gout, obesity, and mental illness. Leeches are still used today in modern medicine. Their anticoagulant reduces blood clots after major surgery, and by applying them to reattached fingers the blood flow to the area, a potential problem leading to serious complications, is greatly reduced.

Get It Off!

To reduce the chance of having a leech attach itself onto your skin while wading in water, try lathering on a layer of dish soap, apply eucalyptus oil, or wear a pair of pantyhose. If you do manage to have one attach on, don't pull it off. This can leave a nasty open wound that could lead to secondary infection. Instead, either allow it to finish feeding and just drop off on its own or apply one of the following tried and true repellents:

- salt
- DEET
- vinegar
- lemon juice
- tobacco juice

that drop out of trees. They all have suckers at both ends, are hermaphroditic, and come complete with thirty-four body segments. They all have a number of ways to find you: heat sensors, motion detectors, chemical receptors, and at least one pair of primitive eyes. And they are all carnivores.

But not all are actual bloodsuckers. In fact most don't even have a taste for human blood. Leeches are host specific — some only prey on ducks, others prefer fish. Remarkably, there's only one in North America that actively seeks out humans. The North American medicinal leech, *Macrobdella decora*, identified by its black body and bright orange belly, desires mammalian blood for its high nutritional value (with frog blood being a good substitute).

The medicinal leech first secures its posterior sucker, making sure you're the proper host. It then sinks its teeth into you with its anterior sucker, flushes the wound with an anesthetic to numb the skin and an anticoagulant keep the blood flowing freely, and begins to suck over half its body weight in blood.

The whole idea of having one attached to you sounds rather disgusting, but they really are quite harmless. After all, there's only one out of the fifty known species in North America to worry about, the bite is painless, and the leech is not a carrier of any known transmittable disease. That said, however, I still would have to agree with Bogart's "If there's one thing I hate, it's leeches. Filthy little devils."

COUGAR ATTACKS

Until recently, the threat of being mauled by a cougar was not that much of an issue. For instance, look at California's statistics. From 1886 to 1986 there were no cougar attacks reported. Since then there has been at least one camper injury or death per year. And in 2001 Banff National Park recorded

Prime Targets

The majority of all cougar attacks in North America involved young children or people who brought their pet dog along for protection.

three separate incidents involving at least two separate cougars in just one day, one in which the victim was killed. This alarming increase in attacks is happening all over the cougar's range of the western United States and Canada, and it has everything to do with habitat displacement. Quite literally, we are taking away their home and forcing them to live with us, and dealing with the consequences of our actions.

The good news is that a cougar attack is still quite rare. The average may seem high — fourteen people per year with one out of fourteen a fatality — but it's nothing when compared to dog attacks. Over eight hundred thousand people are bitten annually and a dozen are killed. So it's safer wandering in the woods than on your neighbourhood street.

What If?

- Cougars are predators. It's important to convince them that you are not prey. Never crouch down low or run away.
- If you see a cougar feeding on an animal carcass, leave the area immediately.
- Never turn your back on an approaching cougar.
- Never look directly at a cougar.
- Take full control of the situation by standing your ground and then slowly walking away from the area.
- Keep a close watch over children (and pets). They are especially vulnerable due to their size and inability to defend themselves.
- Keep pets leashed.
- Travel in groups.
- Make noise to warn cougars of your approach.
- If attacked, be aggressive and fight the cougar off with everything you have (the majority of attacks are not fatal).
- Try not to panic.
- Report the attack to the proper authorities as soon as possible.

FOREST FIRES

One of the most stressful times I've ever had while in the outdoors is when my wife, Alana, and I came upon a forest fire during a remote canoe trip. It was the end of a very long day and we were finally at the lake we had chosen to camp on, only to find that at the far end a small forest fire had just ignited. The fire was probably brought on by the intense heat of the day. Or maybe it was even started by a lightning storm the night before. Whatever the reason, we knew it was unsafe to camp there. To play it safe we chose to continue on for another couple of hours. By then we would reach a much larger lake, one that also had a couple of outpost camps equipped with radio phones if the fire happened to get out of hand.

The trip to the lake wasn't easy. Two long portages blocked the route, and the trail was lined with tinder-dry trees. It wasn't until we caught a glimpse of a government spotter plane flying low overhead, followed by a helicopter with a load of water, that we eased up a bit. In retrospect, we had little to worry about. The circumstances could have been a lot worse. The important point here, however, is that we kept calm (relatively anyway) and planned an escape route.

▲ *There's nothing more devastating, and ecologically important, than a forest fire.*

Forest Fire Protection Tips

- Stay calm.
- Evacuate the area immediately; even if it seems to be a fair distance away (a fire can easily outrun you).
- If you're in a forested mountain area, head downhill. Fires travel four to five times faster uphill.
- Avoid narrow valleys, steep slopes or canyons. These areas act as natural chimneys for fire and smoke.
- Stay in open areas, fields when hiking, or the middle of open lakes if paddling.
- If you manage to be trapped, go to an open area and remove any flammable materials around you (including the camp stove and fuel container in your pack). Remove all clothing that is synthetic — it will melt to your skin in intense heat and cause severe burns. Cotton or wool is much better. Do not wet clothing or skin with water. Again, the intense heat will create steam and scald you. Cover your bare skin with sand if possible. Lie face down on the ground and filter out the smoke from your lungs by placing a dry bandana or cotton shirt over your mouth (a wet bandana or shirt will burn your lungs).
- If it's a large fire, expect a lack of oxygen for several minutes. Try not to panic.
- If you have left a detailed trip plan with officials, help will soon arrive.

LIGHTNING

I once agreed to write a short story for an outdoor magazine about the likelihood of a kayaker or canoeist ever getting hit by lightning. The editor of the periodical and I thought the chances were comparable to getting mauled by a nuisance bear — yes, it's possible, but the risk itself is so minimal it would be a waste of time worrying about it. We were wrong. After a few days of research, documenting several deaths in North America involving outdoor pursuits and lightning strikes, I discovered that it was one of the number

How to Calculate the Distance of the Storm

Count the number of seconds (one Mississippi . . . two Mississippi . . . three Mississippi . . .) between the flash of lightning and the thunder. Then divide by five. You now have the distance in miles. The reasoning behind this calculation is that sound travels approximately a fifth of a mile per second.

Lightning Lowdown

- A lightning bolt can travel up to 60,000 miles (100,000 km) per second.
- Intense heat from lightning striking a tree can produce steam inside the trunk and build up enough pressure to literally cause the tree to blow up.
- A single lightning flash is five times hotter than the sun (50,000 degrees F or 27,760 C).
- An average lightning strike lasts 1/1,000 of a second.
- A bolt of lightning can be 4 to 5 miles long (6–8 km).
- Thunder is actually the sound wave created by lightning heating up and then expanding the air around it.
- According to the National Lightning Safety Institute study on deaths due to lightning strikes between 1999 and 2003, the safest place to live in North America was Rhode Island (0 fatalities) and the most dangerous was Florida (126 fatalities).
- The National Oceanic and Atmospheric Administration has reported that after thirty-five years of lightning strikes (1959–1994) the victims were 84 percent male and 16 percent female.
- The Earth is hit by lightning about one hundred times per second.

one hazards out there. And of all the campers killed by lightning, over half were on or near open water.

So it's obvious that water and lightning are a natural combination. A lake represents a flat base, and you and your kayak or canoe are most likely the only thing out there that extends above that flat surface. Doing something to protect yourself isn't that easy, though. Getting to shore the moment you spot the buildup of cumulonimbus clouds that signal a thunderstorm is the obvious choice. In fact, you're more vulnerable as the storm approaches and departs (if you can hear thunder, you are in striking distance). But most storms are combined with high wind and waves, making a quick paddle to shore more difficult than it sounds.

And even when you do reach land, it doesn't necessarily mean that you're safe. In the majority of cases, victims were injured or killed right at their campsite. Some were hit while they stood on shore watching the storm. The majority, however, were struck by a corresponding ground charge while lying asleep in their tents. Lightning is formed as a negative charge from the base of the storm cloud passing over, inducing a positive charge where a negative charge usually is. The positive charge is pulled up and lightning is produced where there's an arc. If you're anywhere near the path of the lightning discharge, you can get zapped.

Weathering the electrical storm on land, however, is still far better than being out on the water. Some kayakers and canoeists claim that you can paddle safely on the water during a lightning storm as long as you keep close to the shoreline. A protective "umbrella" is formed, at about a 45-degree angle, from you and the treetops along the bank. This is just a theory, however, and I think I'd rather take my chances on shore. Just make sure you pitch you and your shelter far away from any mound of high rock or tall tree. Also, the deeper you go into the woods, the greater the chances of the lightning hitting another object. Keep as low as possible, but don't lie flat out. Sit on top of a pack or, if you happen to be in the tent when the storm hits, squat on top of your sleeping pad with both feet close together.

SUDDEN SQUALLS

On July 4, 1999, a massive storm swept through the Boundary Waters and Quetico Provincial Park, downing twelve million trees and endangering hundreds of canoeists. Surprisingly there were no deaths. But many were injured and search-and-rescue teams worked for days to extract people from the interior. Countless stories have been told by the survivors, all of whom indicated it was one of the worst sudden storms they've ever witnessed. One of the best descriptions, however, was recorded in the Quetico Foundation's quarterly newsletter by former park ranger, Art Madsen, who was ninety-four at the time, paddling with his daughter on Saganaga Lake when the squall hit:

> I could see it was coming fast and black clouds had a brown yellowish color under them. Lightning and thunder were flashing all around and wind was really getting up. After a few miles I was following along a rock wall as I know lightning will hit the highest part. Quick as a flash I did not see the lightning but one of the loudest thunder cracks I'd ever heard nearly knocked my ears off. Then I could see this grayish wall of cloud coming fast and knew it would really put down heavy rain. When I crossed by Powells' place the wind was so strong it was pushing rain horizontally. I was coming into the dock area very fast. My granddaughter rushed out and snubbed my bow rope to the dock. Within minutes the waves became 5 feet. This was the worst storm in memory.

Staying off the water during sudden squalls like this is obviously a smart choice. It's important to note, however, that it was the broken trees and flying debris that caused most of the injuries in the 1999 hurricane (forecasters only called it a "straight-line windstorm"). So your best bet is to weather such a severe storm out in the open, huddled down in a depression

▲ *The calm after the storm. Boundary Waters.*

or hollow. At Boundary Waters and Quetico, it was the campers who rushed inside their flimsy nylon tents, which were completely surrounded by falling and uprooting trees, who received the most severe injuries.

On a positive note, squalls rarely last more than fifteen minutes (even though it may be the longest fifteen minutes of your life). You can also be thankful that the chance of being caught in the worst of it is very limited. I'll never forget when my wife, Alana, and I weathered out a squall while on a northern Ontario canoe trip. It was brought on by the intense heat of the day, and along with the turbulent winds there was hail the size of ping-pong balls. It was a frightening experience. But when we paddled farther upriver the next morning, we realized the brunt of the storm had actually missed us. Half a mile or so upstream a wind burst had toppled over a couple of dozen trees, with the worst area affected being the actual campsite we had initially planned on staying at (the toilet seat from the outhouse had actually been catapulted across the river!).

HEAVY WINDS AND WAVES

Getting caught in heavy wind and high waves has to be the most dangerous and terrifying circumstance to ever find yourself in. You should obviously avoid paddling across the expanse of any lake, but it happens to the best of us.

You end up finding yourself deciding whether to head straight across an open stretch of water or to hug the shoreline, which would triple your time spent on the lake. Many people, without even thinking, will take the shortcut.

A regular canoe partner and I once succumbed to the temptation of paddling right across a gigantic lake in northern Ontario, and it was one of the stupidest decisions we've ever made. We had managed to get on the lake early. We were even lucky enough to have only a slight breeze coming out of the north at the time. Making a quick decision, we headed straight across rather than playing it safe and following close to the western shoreline. It's not that we didn't have a strong reverence for such a large lake, especially one that only has an average depth of 13 feet (4 m) and is well known for brewing up in high winds. But we knew that bad weather would soon be on us and there was absolutely no place to camp on the south end of the lake.

Facts about Wind

- Wind is produced by air moving from an area of high pressure to an area of low pressure. The greater the difference in pressure, the more powerful the wind will be.
- A quick change in wind direction means a rapid rise in air temperature, which is a good indicator of a long period of warm weather accompanied by lots of rain.
- Cold air is heavier than warm air and will lift up warm air while approaching, causing precipitation. The amount of wet weather depends on how quickly the wind brings the front in. A fast-approaching cold front will push the warm air up quickly, bringing on violent but short showers or squalls. A slowly approaching cold front will not cause the warm air to rise as fast, and the result is less severe but it will last much longer.

Comparing Waves to Swells

A wave is far more dangerous than a swell. The difference is that swells, usually formed far from your location, don't break very often and your vessel can ride along with them. A wave, especially one produced by sudden high winds and in shallow water, will break when its height reaches one seventh of its length (it no longer can support itself). A windswept wave less than 2 feet high can easily swamp a canoe or even a kayak.

It was the wrong decision, of course. There were no islands or small bays to act as windbreaks. We didn't bother to shift our load farther back to lighten our bow and minimize shipping water. We weren't even equipped with a spray skirt.

Everything seemed to be going well until we reached the halfway point. Suddenly the wind changed direction and hit us broadside. Before long, the waves had doubled in size, and we grew increasingly vulnerable. At least with a headwind you can tack the canoe like a sailboat, and even with a heavy tailwind you usually have time to bail the excess water while surfing the crests of the waves. With the wind hitting us directly broadside, however, it became impossible to have any great amount of control, and we could only push on and hope to reach the opposite shore before the waves tripled in size. We also knew that the moment we stopped paddling our paddles would no longer work as outriggers, and the boat would immediately start to wallow and take on water.

By digging in, arms aching with the strain of each and every paddle stroke, we eventually beached the canoe on the opposite shore, just in time to witness whitecaps form out in the center of the lake. In retrospect, taking the shortcut was definitely not worth it.

SOGGY SURVIVAL

Henri is using the word "bummer" at about double the rate he was using it an hour or so ago.

JOHN MCPHEE, *THE SURVIVAL OF THE BARK CANOE* (1975)

OVER THE YEARS I've become severely phobic of storms, and for good reason. I've endured far too many. I've had hurricane winds snap my tent poles and hail the size of ping-pong balls severely damage my canoe. I had a lightning bolt take a tree down directly in front of me while on a hiking trail. Not one but two tornadoes barely missed me in a public campground. The list goes on.

I've tried everything to relieve my fear of the elements, and the only thing that seems to help, apart from having the local weather reporter as my tripping partner, is to memorize some ancient proverbs and adages. It's still one of the best ways to guess the upcoming forecast out there. Not all of them hold true, mind you. Some are just products of ignorance and whimsical contradictions. Others, however, have survived the test of time and are based on long-term observation and scientific reasoning. The general rule to follow is that any weather lore relating to the appearance of the sky, movement of the clouds, wind change, or the reaction of flora and fauna with air pressure or humidity has some credibility. Everything else is just plain nonsense.

◀ *You're a true camper if you can smile during a downpour.*

NATURE'S WEATHER FORECASTERS

Campfire smoke descends, our nice weather ends.

Smoke from your campfire will hug the ground if a storm is close. If it rises straight up, clear weather can be predicted for at least the next twelve hours. The reason for this is quite simple. Smoke particles have a tendency to absorb moisture from the air. So the more moisture in the air, the lower the smoke from the campfire will be. Also, the heavier the smoke particles the longer they will disperse.

Red sky at night, sailors delight.
Red sky in the morning, sailors take warning.

This proverb is probably the most common as well as the most accurate. It's also been around the longest. It was Aristotle's pupil, Theophrastus of Eresus, who coined the actual phrase. But the first record of the aphorism is in the Bible (Matthew 16:2–3). Christ said, "When it is evening ye say, it will

▲ *Red sky in the morning, sailors take warning. An hour after this dramatic sunrise it started raining, and then rained for three solid days.*

be fair weather for the sky is red. And in the morning, it will be foul weather today for the sky is red and lowering." Shakespeare also wrote, "A red morn that ever yet betokened, wreck to the seaman, tempest to the field."

What it all means, basically, is that dry dust particles are in the atmosphere and can easily be seen during sunset and sunrise. Most storms move from west to east. So, with the sun setting in the west, the red sky at night usually indicates dry weather because dust particles are being pushed toward you. With the sun rising in the east, the red sky in the morning indicates that the dust particles are being pushed away by an approaching low-pressure front.

Rainbow in the morning, shepherds take warning.
Rainbows at night, shepherds delight.

Despite the fact that rainbows are usually seen after a rain shower, spotting one during sunrise and sunset is not uncommon and is a good forecaster. The reason a rainbow forms in the morning is that the light from the rising sun in the east is reflecting off water droplets in the west. And, again, since most storms travel from west to east, seeing the rainbow would mean that a storm is approaching. Seeing one in the evening would then mean that the storm is past.

When leaves show their undersides, be very sure that rain betides.

The old wives' tale of leaves flipping upside down, showing their light-colored bottoms flickering in the breeze, is based on actual biological fact. The air temperature and wind alters significantly before an approaching storm. So when leaves curl up, which is a direct reaction to the high level of humidity and a quick change in wind direction, rain is definitely not far away. Under the same principle of dropping air pressure, the lower the leaves turn on the tree the more severe the storm will be, meaning that if only the top of the tree is affected there's less chance of the rainfall being severe.

If birds fly low, expect rain and a blow.

All creatures in nature react to severe changes in weather. It's not known why they're so much more sensitive than humans. It's most likely due to the fact that they live in closer harmony with the environment than we do and can easily feel a drop in air pressure. Whatever the reason, they are among the best forecasters.

Everything from cows herding up in a farmer's field to leeches swimming to the top of a mason jar has been used. But birds seem to be the best, especially insect-eating birds such as swallows. They will chase their dinner closer to the ground just before a storm hits. They will also fly higher when rain is no threat. It's actually the insects that are being mostly affected by the fair-weather updrafts, but the birds are easier to watch. When the air pressure is high, the insects have no problem flying at a higher altitude. However, when the air pressure is low, which is a sign of an approaching storm, the insects have a difficult time flying high due to the lower density of the air.

Rain before seven, fine before eleven.
Weather patterns change more in early morning and evening. They are also generally in motion, never stagnant. So this statement, even though it's less valid than most, has some legitimacy.

When halo rings the moon or sun, rain's approaching on the run.
Sun halos ("sundogs") or rings around the moon give meaning to this phrase and are excellent indicators of upcoming precipitation. The halo is formed when light from the sun or moon refracts as it passes through ice crystals formed by high-level cirrus and cirrostratus clouds. The clouds themselves don't produce rain or snow, but often denote an approaching low front, which usually brings poor weather. This is the same reason that if a jet airplane's trail persists for several hours, rain could arrive within one day.

When the wind is in the north.
The skillful fisher goes not forth;
When the wind is in the east,
'Tis good for neither man nor beast;
When the wind is in the south,
It blows the flies in the fish's mouth;
But when the wind is in the west,
There it is the very best.
Even if you're not an avid angler this proverb is a good one. Strong winds coming from the west usually signify good weather. Anything else means that a change is on the way. However, relating all this to how the fish bite is just speculation. It is true that fishing seems to slow down especially when the wind blows in from the east or north (an indicator that the storm will be around for a while). But it's also true that a quick change in pressure will create bubbles that rise from the bottom of the lake, freeing lots of insect larva (fish food) from the mud and creating a feeding frenzy. I guess the only true way to see if they're biting is to head out and wet a line.

If your muscles all ache and itch, the weather fair will make a switch.
Again, low pressure usually foretells bad weather. Studies have shown that most people who suffer from muscle aches and pains can foretell the drop in pressure. Nobody really seems to know why, however.

Barometer Watch

If all else fails, it should also be noted that some new digital watches now come with a built-in barometer that works quite well.

CLOUD WATCHING

Clouds are also excellent weather forecasters. Low fronts include stratus, nimbostratus, and cumulonimbus. Stratus are gray clouds that have a uniform, flat base and may bring light rain. Nimbostratus are darker gray in color and usually bring moderate rainfall. Those dark, almost black clouds with flat bottoms and towering thunderheads (looking something like an upside-down anvil) are the cumulonimbus. They are the clear indicator of an approaching thunderstorm.

The middle groupings of clouds include altocumulus and altostratus. The altocumulus are made up of a sheet of white or gray cloudlets, sometimes formed in rows. The altostratus, striated and uniform in shape, spread across the sky in a thin gray layer. Both cloud formations tell of inclement weather, but with the altostratus you have at least twelve hours before it begins to rain.

Cirrus, cirrocumulus, and cirrostratus clouds form in high altitudes and are the least trustworthy forecasters. Cirrus are separate, scattered wisps and usually indicate fair weather unless they become bunched together, meaning rain may fall the next day. Cirrocumulus clouds form a thin rippled pattern in the sky. They may grow perpendicularly throughout the day, and if the vertical growth does not disperse, a quick shower may follow. And last, cirrostratus, a transparent veil that creates a halo around the sun, are a prime indicator of a warm front; if they lead an altostratus cloud formation, "refreshing" rain could come down in less than twenty-four hours.

▲ *1. Fair-weather cumulus clouds. 2. Cumulonimbus clouds typically have dark, flat bottoms. 3. Altocumulus sometimes resemble fish scales, thus a "mackerel sky." 4. Cirrus clouds are high-level scattered wisps. 5. A "whale's mouth" may appear in altostratus clouds during the first gusts of wind, before the storm front passes over. 6. A "sundog" or, in this case, "moon dog," may appear in a cirrostratus formation.*

▲ *Stratus clouds are usually associated with a long, drawn-out drizzle.*

RAIN SUITS THAT WORK

Like the majority of outdoor enthusiasts, when the new high-tech "breathable" rainwear came out on the market, I spent a small fortune in an attempt to keep dry. The first year the suit worked well. But after some wear and tear it began to leak like a sieve. Present-day Gore-Tex-style rain suits work much better, but I'm still apprehensive about paying a lot of money for something that may work for only a season or two.

For the price, a two-piece nylon rain suit coated with a thin layer of neoprene rubber or several layers of polyurethane will keep you just as dry. The problem is that your sweat will have a difficult time escaping. The cheap nylon rain suits also fail when the coating begins to peel off. But despite their shortcomings, I've gone back to the inexpensive nylon suits, and when the water starts finding its way in, I toss it and purchase another.

When buying a rain suit, make sure it doesn't fit too snugly. In colder weather you're going to be wearing lots of layers underneath. It should also have a tight collar and wrist closures. You don't want rain leaking in, especially down your back. The hood should also be wide enough to accommodate your hat underneath — you definitely need some type of hat to hold up the brim to help you see where you're going. Some people even pack along one of those

▲ *"Rain, rain go away and come back another day." Alana tests out her new Gore-Tex rain suit.*

silly looking sou'wester hats. They actually work well, but be prepared to take some teasing.

Rain pants should have wide ankle openings. You definitely don't want to take your boots off before putting your rubber trousers on, especially when you're sitting in a canoe during a downpour. Those pants with suspenders are also difficult to get on in a hurry, so buy the regular kind. Make sure though that they don't have those side pockets that split wide open the moment you sit down. I don't know how many times I've gotten soaked right through while sitting in the canoe in a downpour.

Your hands usually take the brunt of the cold when it rains, so you may consider packing a pair of neoprene gloves. You can purchase them at scuba-diving shops or fancy outdoor stores. But your best bet is to go to the ice-fishing aisle in one of those large chain stores and buy a much cheaper version.

Make sure to stay clear of ponchos. Not only do they provide inadequate protection, especially during a heavy wind-blown rain, they are extremely dangerous if you ever capsize in a canoe. I once met a group at the end of a river trip who had one of their members drown because he was wearing a poncho. It began to rain as they were running a long stretch of whitewater known as the Albany Rapids. A sudden drop took them by surprise and one boat managed to flip over. The man in the bow, who was wearing a rain poncho, was repeatedly pulled down in a souse hole. In less than a minute he was dead.

RAIN PROOFING YOUR GEAR

The best way to keep everything dry is to store items in a number of waterproof bags, and I don't mean garbage bags. Even if you're using heavy-duty plastic bags, they will eventually tear open. I'm talking about the solid dry bags you buy from high quality outdoor stores or, to save you money, heavy-duty plastic placed between two nylon sacks.

If I'm kayaking I just stuff individual waterproof bags inside the kayak. And if I'm backpacking or canoeing I start off by either placing my gear in a pack that's totally waterproof (for example, a Cascade Design Pro Pack) or using a waterproof liner inside my regular nylon or canvas pack. The liner should be oversized for the pack, giving plenty of length to roll up, and secured at the top. Then, in a number of separate color-coded stuff sacks I place my clothes, sleeping bag, first-aid kit, repair kit, and anything else that's important to keep dry.

When I'm canoeing, my food is either stored in a regular barrel pack or one or two of those smaller olive barrels slipped inside a Duluth-style pack.

▲ *During inclement weather, life can be much more pleasant with everyone sheltered under a rain tarp instead of crammed inside a stuffy tent.*

The large blue barrel is my wife's favorite, as long as she has a top-of-the-line harness for it. The smaller olive barrels stuffed in a regular pack, with a sleeping pad placed between the barrels and your back, are a much cheaper way, though. You can buy these barrels at some outdoor stores or find your own, free of charge. I visit any place that buys olives in bulk (large-chain grocery stores, delicatessens or restaurants) and either ask for them or wait until garbage day and pick them out of their recycle bin. Make sure to stay away from mushroom barrels. They look similar but will leak if submerged.

Cameras have to be the worst to keep dry on a trip. I've tried everything over the years, from ammunition boxes to roll-top rubber bags. I once even made my own out of a small plastic pail. Five years ago, however, I finally splurged and bought a Pelican case. It's the best solution, not only for keeping your camera dry, but to keep it from getting knocked about. I've had mine go down three major rapids, and everything inside was still dry and intact. The medium-sized box was perfect for one camera body, three lenses, and six rolls of film. It also makes a perfect solo seat for my canoe.

RAIN TARP

My tent is only used for sleeping, basically because it's smaller than a dog house. So when it rains I depend on a good tarp to shelter me. I started off with one of those big blue nylon reinforced plastic tarps. It actually worked quite well, but was a real pain to carry, as the material was extremely stiff and bulky. And the cheap corner grommets had a tendency to snap in heavy winds. Eventually I upgraded to a lightweight, polyurethane-coated, rip-stop polyester tarp (you can get them in even lighter nylon material). I love it. As soon as it rains, I erect the 10-foot-by-12-foot (3 m by 4 m) tarp, build a small fire under it, and sit, relax and cook up a pot of tea or hot soup. There's nothing like it.

There's no specific trick to putting up a tarp. It's just that some campsites have a better tree arrangement than others. The perfect scenario is a tree for each of the four corners. More than likely, however, you'll have to unpack an extra length of rope and extend one or two corners to a nearby exposed root or alder bush.

The most common position in which the tarp should be placed is a lean-to style. This consists of having two ends placed up high, preferably attached to a rope strung between two trees, and the other two placed low to the ground, toward the prevailing winds. Make sure it's snug, or the tarp will flop around in the wind and irritate you to no end throughout the night. I've attached small bungee cords on each corner grommet to help keep the ropes tight. A center pole also helps keep the tarp taut. However, rather than searching all over for a tree limb to place in the center of the tarp, purchase a paddle strap. This neat device was designed by Thomas Benian of Outdoor Solutions and works by lashing two paddles tightly together to act as a solid center pole.

> *"The trail everywhere became boggy and slick. Puddles filled every dip and trough. Mud became a feature of our lives. We trudged through it, stumbled and fell in it, knelt in it, set our packs down in it, left a streak of it on everything we touched. And always when we moved there was the maddening, monotonous sound of your nylon going wiss, wiss, wiss until you wanted to take a gun and shoot it."*
>
> BILL BRYSON, *A WALK IN THE WOODS*

QUEST FOR FIRE

Fire's burning, fire's burning,
Draw nearer, draw nearer,
In the gloaming, in the gloaming,
Come sing and be merry.

Sing as a round, in groups of three of four

THERE'S NOTHING LIKE gathering around the warmth of a campfire, especially if you've spent the day traveling out in a cold, miserable downpour. Your appreciation verges on primitive. To have a chance to dry one's clothes, or at least scald them a little, and then toast the insoles of your boots, is an absolute pleasure. That's if you can get the darn thing going, of course. Learning to light a fire during inclement weather is a real art form, and if you're able to master it, I can guarantee that everyone in your camp will treat you with high regard.

My regular camping companions and I have someone in our group, Peter Fraser, whom we cherish for his fire-starting abilities. We call him "Peter the Pyro," as he has the peerless ability to ignite a small flame in the worst conditions: wet wood, soaked matches, and a howling wind.

Peter's first trade secret is to never use store-bought waterproof matches. He claims that his homemade versions — regular wooden matches with their heads dipped in melted wax and then stored in a waterproof container (a recycled Tylenol container works well) is far less expensive and actually works. He also rarely uses matches to light the fire; Peter prefers butane lighters. And just in case both fail, he also brings along flint and steel as a backup.

Gathering the appropriate wood is Peter's next move. He claims the species of tree used is important. Conifers (softwoods) such as pine and cedar

◀ *Gathering around a cozy campfire is a great way to end a long day on the trail.*

▲ *Campfire essentials: birch bark or dried moss for fire starter, conifer twigs, and dry wood no larger than your forearm.*

Homemade Fire Starters

When thin strips of birch bark, dry pine needles, or globs of pitch squeezed from balsam blisters don't work as fire starters, try a few of these homemade substitutes: strips of wax paper, pieces of wax crayon, birthday candles, pieces of newspaper, sawdust or dryer lint dipped in paraffin and stored in an egg carton, cotton balls soaked in Vaseline, small squares of rubber tubing, steel wool, or small clumps of duct tape coated with a few squirts of bug repellent.

ignite better. When it comes to heat value, however, the flame is short-lived, creates dangerous sparks, and produces very few coals. Deciduous woods (hardwoods), such as maple, beech and oak, are the best for heat value. This dense, heavy wood keeps a long-burning flame with good hot coals left behind for cooking.

More important than the type of tree used, however, is how dead it is. The wood can't be green or punky. A perfect piece is a fallen tree or limb that has not touched the ground. The size of the deadfall that he gathers ranges from finger to arm size, along with a handful of dry twigs (no thicker than a pencil) collected from dead bows from under a conifer tree.

When a heap of fuel wood is piled beside the fire pit (if there's no designated area to build a fire, make sure to use a slab of bare rock or at least a place free of exposed roots), Peter's assistant (usually me) begins to cut the wood up while he works on starting the fire.

For wood cutting I never use an axe. I did pack a hatchet on a solo canoe trip once, and while hacking away it glanced off the wood and embedded itself into the top of my right hand. It took three changes of gauze and a whole role of surgical tape to stop the bleeding, along with several Tylenols to control the swelling while I paddled back out to my vehicle. Now all I use is a lightweight, fold-out saw for wood cutting.

While I'm occupied stacking wood, ranging from small kindling to large "all-nighters," Peter is meticulously building up the fire. His golden rule is to start small; claiming one of the biggest mistakes of first-time fire starters is to be too eager to start a roaring flame. Too much fuel too fast, especially wet fuel, robs a fire of valuable oxygen and will eventually smother the flames.

To start, Peter places a row of arm-sized hardwood in the fire ring to act as a base plate. Then he lays a handful of the dry tinder (or one of his own homemade fire-starters) on top of the hardwood with dry, pencil-sized kindling placed parallel over it, approximately 3 inches (7–8 cm) apart. In the opposite direction he then lays another row of twigs, finger-sized. Now, while shielding the well-constructed pile of wood from the strong winds, he lights the tinder at all four corners. Only when the kindling completely catches

▲ *A variety of lightweight, compact folding camp saws are available (above), as long as you know how to put them together (below).*

does he begin to place larger arm-sized pieces, making sure to always keep a gap between the sticks to allow the fire to breathe.

For his efforts Peter always gets a double shot of spirits or second cup of tea while we all gather around the warmth of the fire to tell a joke, spin a tall tale, chat about the meaning of life, and keep the night at bay.

BEST CAMPFIRE TREATS

Marshmallows

It's an age-old debate. Is the best toasted marshmallow one that is roasted to a golden brown or charred black on the outside with a glob of sweet gooey mess on the inside?

S'mores

Place a piece of chocolate on a graham cracker. Top it off with a toasted marshmallow and another graham cracker. This camp regular recipe first appeared in the 1927 Girl Scout's guide *Tramping and Trailing with the Girl Scouts*, and got its name from campers continually asking for "some more." The trick is to make sure the marshmallow is hot enough to melt the chocolate that's sandwiched between two graham crackers.

Popcorn

Popping popcorn around the fire has been a tradition for thousands of years. The original method, used by Natives in Mexico, was to throw the kernel of corn on a hot stone circling the fire. The popcorn eventually would pop, and the one who caught it was allowed to snack on it. New-age Jiffy Pop popcorn gets better results than a hot rock!

Banana Boats

This recipe is delicious. Peel back one section of the banana, leaving it attached at the end. Dig out some of the banana to make a trough for miniature marshmallows and chocolate chips. Put the peeled section back into position and wrap the banana in tinfoil. Place it on hot coals long enough for the chocolate and marshmallows to melt.

Hot Dogs on a Stick

To stop your toasted hot dog from falling into the fire, make sure to use a green stick. A dead, dried-up branch will burn up before the wiener is cooked. A forked stick also provides far better support than a single poker.

Safe Axe Handling

Some campers disagree with me, and do pack along an axe or hatchet, believing it the only way get at the drier heartwood inside a log. It's true that this is an effective way. But it's just not worth it. A much safer method is to pack along a plastic or aluminum felling wedge. By placing it along the grain of the wood and hammering away with another log, you can easily split a large chunk of wood without having to worry about making use of your first-aid kit.

FUEL FOR THE FIRE

Conifer, or what's commonly known as softwood, makes a terrible cooking fire. It has a tendency to spark a lot and burns quite rapidly. However, it's the best wood to get your fire going, and sometimes that's more important. Here are some of the best to try out.

White Pine The white pine's silhouette is probably the easiest way to distinguish from among the other pines. The branches are feathered out, with the upper portion of the tree's crown sculptured by the prevailing winds, looking as if it's giving you the finger.

If you look at the white pine close-up, you can also identify it by counting the number of needles growing in a cluster. White pine has five needles (remember the word "white" has five letters) and all other pines have two. The bark of a young pine is smooth gray-green. With age, it turns rough, deeply furrowed with broad scaly edges, and gray-brown in color.

Red Pine The red pine, a much hardier tree than the white pine, takes root in rocky outcrops and nutrient-deficient sandy soil. It is protected from extreme heat, cold, and bug infestations by its thick resin. The silhouette has an oval appearance, forming at the crown. When it grows in the open,

▲ *White pine needles in clusters of five; red pine needles in clusters of two; red pine bark has a reddish tinge (left to right).*

▲ *Jack pine cones resemble dried-up scat; black spruce prefer sphagnum bogs; white spruce grow in well-drained soil (left to right).*

branches cover most of the trunk. Unlike the soft white pine needles growing in clusters of five, the red pine has sharply pointed needles (great for using as pot scrubbers) in clusters of two. The bark has a reddish or pinkish brown tinge and becomes furrowed into long, contoured, flat ridges as it grows older.

Jack Pine Of all the conifer species, the jack pine is the most likely to sprout first after a forest fire, since its tightly sealed cones usually don't open up until the air temperature reaches 116 degrees F (47 C). It also grows on the poorest soil conditions possible (which is why early settlers cursed the tree so much), and is so ridden with knots that it's usually cut for pulp more than lumber. To identify it, look at how the needles, growing in clusters of two, are a lighter green and somewhat shorter than that of the red and white pine, and they come to a very sharp point. The bark of the jack pine is reddish brown to gray and changes to a darker brown or gray with age. It is flaky, and furrowed into irregular thick plates on older trees. Its most distinguishing feature, however, are its cones. They look similar to a piece of dried-up scat hanging on a dead branch.

Black and White Spruce The black and white spruce are from the single-needle conifer group. The sharp, stunted needles are attached completely around the twig, in the shape of a cigar. One of the main differences between white and black spruce is the tip of the bud. If the bud scale is shorter than the bud, then the tree is a white spruce. If the bud scale grows past the tip of the bud, then it is a black spruce. There's a difference between the silhouette of the two spruces as well. The white spruce is more cone-shaped, with its branches evenly concealing the trunk (this is why it's commonly used for Christmas trees). The black spruce has very few branches along most of its length, except at its crown, where they are bunched together. The easiest way to tell the spruces apart, however, is to look at the surrounding habitat. Black spruce root themselves around sphagnum bogs and white spruce grow in well-drained, silty soils. So, if your feet are wet, then the tree is a black spruce. If they're dry, then it's a white spruce.

White Cedar For centuries Natives worshiped the cedar as the giver of life and praised it for its ability to hold strong spiritual powers. Today, campers still have a tendency to treat it with high regard, but not for its mystical qualities — it's just a good fuel source when you're trying to get a fire going in the middle of a downpour. A few shavings from this tree and you're guaranteed to get a hot blaze going. Cedar can be found in both wetland swamps and rocky outcrops, due to its ability to be both rot and drought resistant. The bark is colored a light gray to reddish brown, and its needles are unlike those of any other conifer, with light green, flat, scale-like leaves.

Hemlock The hemlock's trunk is filled with knots, making lumberjacks hate it. Campers also distrust the searing sparks it lets loose when burned in the campfire. And forest plants are unable to grow anywhere near it, since the decomposed needles create such an acid-rich soil. But deer couldn't survive the winter without it: they gather under the tree's dense canopy and nibble on its low-lying branches. The hemlock tree may be most easily confused with the spruce; however, its needles are not attached completely around the twig. They're flat, and lack the cigar-shaped twig of the black and white spruce. It also has two distinct white lines running up and down on the back side of its needles. The bark of the young hemlock is scaly and orange-brown, becoming deeply furrowed and purplish gray-brown with age.

Balsam Fir Similar to hemlock, the balsam fir needles are flat, not rounded like the spruce. They also have white lines on the underside, but usually more than two. The bark of the balsam fir, especially when young, is its most distinguishing characteristic. The gray, smooth skin is pocked with

▲ *Cedar needles are unlike any other conifer's; hemlock needles are flat on the twig and have two whites lines underneath; balsam fire needles have white lines underneath but less obvious than hemlock (left to right).*

▲ *Cookin' buns over an open fire.*

horizontal specks and blisters filled with resin, which, when punctured, oozes out and sticks onto everything you own. Thick, gooey sap is the reason why most conifers, except for the tamarack (which loses its needles in the fall), hold their needles year-round. Hence the name "evergreen." Deciduous trees must store their sap in their root system so that the sugar-and-water mix (mostly water) will not freeze and expand inside the trunk. Without the sap the leaves die and fall to the ground every autumn. The sugar-rich sap of the evergreen, however, acts as an antifreeze and allows the conifer to hang on to its needles throughout the cold dormant season.

> *"An open fire appeal to all the senses. The crack of exploding resin, the enthusiastic whoop of flame sucking oxygen, the thump of a log settling into coals are sounds we learn to associate with contentment and well-being. A fire sounds good and looks good. It also smells good. If I didn't come home surrounded by a nimbus of campfire scent, I'd think the weekend has been wasted."*
>
> JERRY DENNIS, *FROM A WOODEN CANOE*

COLD CAMPING

As he turned to go on, he spat speculatively. There was a sharp, explosive crackle that startled him. He spat again. And again, in the air, before it could fall to the snow, the spittle crackled. He knew that at fifty below spittle crackled on the snow, but this spittle had crackled in the air. Undoubtedly it was colder than fifty below — how much colder he did not know.

JACK LONDON, *TO BUILD A FIRE* (1908)

I'LL ADMIT THAT sleeping out overnight in the wintertime is definitely not for everyone. I'll also admit that cold camping obviously has a number of hazards, or at least some major discomforts. It's understandable that the moment the sun sets and the temperature drops, you're going to want to escape to a warm place. It's human nature. I'll even confess that the older I get, the more excuses I seem to find not to head out for my annual winter trip. In fact, lately I've had to have my wife call me a sissy before convincing myself to once again sleep out in frigid temperatures.

The point, however, is that I still manage to do it and always end up loving every minute of it. So I guarantee that, as long as you develop the necessary skills and pack along the essential equipment, your first time sleeping out in the cold definitely won't be your last.

◀ *The moment the sun sets and the temperature drops, you're going to want to escape to a warmer place.*

FASHIONS YOU CAN'T FREEZE IN

Keeping in mind that your body heat is what actually keeps you from freezing, the type of clothing you wear is crucial. But before you go out and spend your life savings on high-tech fashion wear, remember that old-timers survived months on end in the cold without the aid of Gore-Tex or polypropylene.

Bedtime Warming Techniques

You will rarely have difficulty staying warm during the day on the trail, but the night air brings a bone-numbing chill. Here are a few ways to keep yourself more comfortable:

- Daylight is greatly shortened during the winter months and it usually takes much longer to set up camp, so be prepared to end the day early.
- Avoid making camp on designated summer sites; with the heavy use they receive throughout the prime season they are usually far too exposed and have limited wood for a fire. Choose a well-protected forested area, well away from the wind and blowing snow.
- Make sure to provide a lot of ventilation inside the tent. Condensation will quickly form from your breathing and cause the interior of the tent to become completely covered in a layer of fine ice particles, which will eventually melt and soak everything inside.
- For extra insulation, pile up snow around the sides of the tent with your snowshoes or a small plastic shovel.
- The moment you finish setting up camp, change into an extra, dry pair of long underwear and socks (keep a spare set in the front pouch of your parka so they are nice and warm to put on) and wear a wool toque to bed.
- Sleep on a thick foam pad or Therm-a-Rest (not an air mattress). Your body will definitely lose more heat to the cold ground than to the air.
- Fluff your sleeping bag (a top-of-the line, high quality winter design) before crawling in. The action creates more air space between the fibers or feathers.
- Use a liner to increase the efficiency of your sleeping bag. Or better yet, double up two sleeping bags and share your warmth with a partner.
- Munch on high-calorie snacks just before bedtime. The fuel your body has to burn off will help you stay warmer.
- If you find yourself shivering inside your sleeping bag, put on your rain gear to act as a vapor barrier and hold in your body heat.
- Keep an empty (well-labeled) water bottle inside the tent to pee in. A full bladder robs the body of more heat than an empty one; and besides, who wants to crawl out into the cold night air to relieve themselves at 2 A.M.?
- Store your water bottle inside your sleeping bag to keep it from freezing solid. Even a Nalgene container filled with hot tea doubles as a hot-water bottle. Also stuff the next day's clothes, and especially boot liners, inside the bag as well.

The trick is to dress in layers. Start off during the cold morning temperatures looking like a walking puffball if you like, but as you generate heat through exercise, peel off the layers to avoid having your sweat freeze to your skin. The outer layer should not be the main insulator; save that job for the bulky wool sweater or fleece and synthetic long underwear. The "breathable" outerwear (jacket and pants) should protect your body from the cool wind, and should come equipped with an assortment of zippers to allow quick ventilation.

A foot wrapped in ten pairs of socks and then squeezed into a tight-fitting boot will definitely freeze due to poor circulation. You also can lose up to one third of your body heat through your head, so make sure to wear a hat. The traditional woolen toques or the new, softer Polarplus beanies work, but in extreme cold temperatures a balaclava, made from the same material as your long underwear, is preferred. Neck gaiters made from Polarplus fabric help to seal the gap between collars and caps.

▲ *The trick to keeping warm in the winter is to never sweat, and the only way to do that is to always dress in layers.*

Stay Hydrated

It's important to drink at least 3 to 4 quarts (L) of water a day. Staying hydrated keeps your blood thin and decreases your chance of becoming hypothermic. But remember, even snow and ice contain gut-wrenching microbes, so it's best to boil up water in the morning and carry it around in a Thermos to consume throughout the day.

The Later the Better

Choose to camp in late February or early March when the cold temperatures aren't as extreme.

It's crucial to keep your feet dry. So when choosing footwear make sure to choose something waterproof (a lightweight, full-grain leather boot with a Gore-Tex liner should do the trick). Leg gaiters also help keep moisture away, especially by stopping loose snow from falling into the top of your boots and soaking your socks. Foot powder (with a dash of cayenne pepper) will help prevent your feet from sweating, and plastic bags can be used as waterproof liners in a pinch.

To keep your fingers from turning numb it's best to wear mittens instead of fingered gloves. Moose-hide mitts are alright until they get wet, but the new mittens composed of a Gore-Tex shell and fiberpile or Thinsulate insulation will keep your hands warm even when coated in ice.

GIVE ME SHELTER

Tarp

Construct a simple tarp in front of a warm fire, complete with a makeshift heat reflector. Make sure to raise the sleeping area well off the ground and line your bed with a plastic tarp or some carefully chosen hemlock boughs. Compact snow or forest debris around the shelter to maximize insulation. Keep in mind, though, that this method is definitely not foolproof. The heat is not all that well-contained, smoke will nauseate you, and you'll end up sleep deprived from waking up every couple of hours to feed the fire.

Four-Season Tent

There are some excellent four-season tents now available that are designed to provide adequate ventilation and extra space for gear, and are able to hold up to heavy snow loads. Purchase a tent with lots of vestibule space and as many gear lofts and interior pockets as you can get to hang wet clothes and stow equipment. Double doors vent better than one. It's also a good idea to stomp down a tent platform with your snowshoes or skis, keep the door perpendicular to the prevailing winds, make use of ski poles as tent pegs and tie guy ropes to "dead-man anchors" (stuff sacks filled with snow and then buried a foot deep into the snow).

Canvas Prospector Tent

Dragging a durable canvas prospector's tent and a portable pot-belly stove behind you on a wooden sled may be a burden during the day. But come nightfall this type of shelter can be downright cozy. It's the smartest choice in extreme winter conditions. However, using a wall tent with a wood stove is not exactly no-trace camping. It shouldn't be used in well-traveled areas where cutting poles for the tent and using up lots of wood for the stove would degrade the site.

▲ *When the temperature drops there's nothing more cozy than a canvas tent, heated by a wood stove.*

▲ *Quinzees are warmer than you think, averaging 10 degrees warmer than the outside temperature.*

Quinzee

There's also a quinzee, or snow cave. They're warmer than you think, averaging 10 degrees warmer than the outside temperature. It's easier to construct a quinzee when it's at least 14 degrees F (-10 degrees C); that way you're guaranteed perfect snow to build with. Start off by piling loose snow in a mound 10 feet (3 m) wide and 6 feet (2 m) high, using a plastic shovel or snowshoe. Make sure not to compact it. Let the snow settle on its own for an hour or two. This reduces the chance of it collapsing. Then start digging toward the center, keeping the thickness of the quinzee constant by poking a number of foot-long (30 cm) pencil-thick sticks into the walls and roof. You know to stop digging when you expose the end of a stick. Finally, make sure to leave a small hole in the ceiling for ventilation and place a plastic tarp down on the floor. A platform can be built to raise the sleeping area, away from the colder air, and a candle can provide some warmth. The candle also acts as an excellent warning device for a build-up of carbon monoxide. If it begins to sputter or go out entirely, then clear out your ventilation hole.

Snow Types

SAND SNOW • Produced during extremely cold temperatures, and has such a sharp, granular texture it becomes very difficult to ski or walk across.

WILD SNOW • A very dry, fluffy snow that usually begins to fall during calm periods in the weather and extreme cold snaps. If the wind picks up, dangerous whiteouts can occur.

WIND-PACKED SNOW • The fallen (and accumulated) snow has been heavily compacted by strong winds. The pressure of the blowing wind causes a "cold-heat" hardening effect, which creates an excellent surface to walk on without breaking through. It's also one of the best ways to make igloo blocks.

CORN SNOW • Most common in early spring when changing temperatures continually thaw and freeze the accumulated snow. The texture is grainy and is more of a layer of ice crystals, separated by air space, than actual snow. It's sticky to ski across and very difficult to walk on without falling through.

ROTTEN SNOW • A dangerous circumstance caused by snow repeatedly melting and freezing on the upper layer (common on the south side of a hill), which in turn causes water to seep through to the lower layer. With the top layer acting as an insulator, the water on the bottom never freezes. The problem is, the snow may look safe to walk across, but it will collapse when you least expect it.

SLUSH SNOW • This is snow that has absorbed water from below. It can be spotted where the snow surface has a slight depression and in areas dark blue in color. Avoid such areas when crossing lakes and especially rivers – it's a good indicator there's a hole in the ice below.

The entire process of building a quinzee can take up to three hours, so start early. Digging in the snow is also a wet job, and wearing rain gear might be a good idea. And don't forget to store your shovel inside the quinzee in case there's a snowstorm through the night and you have to dig yourself out in the morning.

SNOWSHOEING

The class bully at my public school, Tommy Baker, would always tease me about being bowlegged. He'd yell out things like, "Hey Callan, where's your horse?" The heckling tormented me to no end; that is until the school's gym teacher, Mr. Finnigan, introduced our class to the sport of snowshoeing. The moment I lashed the snowshoes to my feet and then sprinted across the playground, passing my arch-enemy Tommy Baker (who had immediately taken a tumble in the snow), I knew my shortcoming was actually quite beneficial. At the end of the class "bowlegged Callan" had beaten "little brat Baker" on every snowshoe race Mr. Finnigan set up.

Of course, it's not essential to be bowlegged to snowshoe properly. It just makes the process of walking with snowshoes a lot easier. What is essential, however, is that you wear them. Snowshoeing is truly the best way to get around out there.

Snowshoe Styles

When going to purchase a pair of snowshoes don't worry so much about the manufacturer — they're all relatively the same. Be more concerned with the style of the shoe itself. For walking across flat, semi-open terrain, the proper style would be the Michigan or Algonquin snowshoe. It's the most common model, and is shaped like a teardrop, with its tail lagging behind to track a straight line and keep the tips out of the snow.

In hilly or mountainous country, the standard bear-paw style is more commonly used. With no tail, it makes walking easier. I also use the bear-paw in early spring for walking through deep, crusty corn snow.

The other main styles of snowshoe are the Ojibwa and the Alaskan. The Ojibwa is used for open areas, with its long length and upturned toe giving extra support and stability. The shoe's tip is pointed, looking like the back end of the Michigan or Algonquin style, and can actually help cut through the hard crust of snow or push away small saplings when walking in dense bush. The Alaskan is quite similar, except the toe is rounded.

All of these styles are made of wood and lacing. However, outdoor stores are now more apt to carry the new-age snowshoes made of lightweight plastic or anodized aluminum, equipped with mini-crampon bindings.

One of the best snowshoeing techniques books is Osgood and Hurly's *The Snowshoe Book.*

▲ *Michigan or Algonquin snowshoe design, Ojibwa or Alaskan design, new-age anodized aluminium design (right to left).*

Snowshoeing Tips

- Walking with snowshoes lashed to your feet is a lot like strolling down the sidewalk wearing a pair of sneakers, except that the width of the snowshoe forces you to swing each foot around in a semi-circular motion.
- Ski poles help you to keep your balance and assist you in getting up when you actually do fall down.
- Lurch forward on every step and let the snowshoe sink into the snow a bit to get a firm grip for the follow-through step.
- Make sure to also zigzag uphill and make good use of your ski poles.
- To turn, kick straight out (with the left leg if you're going left and vice versa if you're going right). Then twist 180 degrees with that leg and follow through with the other leg (ski poles will help you greatly here).
- Descend hills in a zigzag pattern and lean back a little. Make sure the bindings are tight enough to keep your toes in place. And if the slope is too steep, place one foot in front of the other, sit on the back snowshoe, and slide down.
- Be happy if you're bowlegged. It's definitely a plus.

Personally, I still prefer the wooden type. I find the plastic shoes way too cheap to depend on. The aluminum ones, even though they are lightweight and generally effective in moderate snow depths, are way too expensive. That said, however, I'd be hard-pressed not to rent a good lightweight pair if I only planned on spending a few days winter camping.

Having the perfect binding to hold your foot in place is critical; there's nothing worse than messing around with an awkward binding system when your hands are numb with cold. There's an endless assortment, ranging from lantern wick to a piece of inner tubing. The most common binding, however, is a combination of a wide toe piece and a leather heel strap with a cross strap over the instep. A single ski pole also comes in handy when trying to keep your balance in deep snow or trudging up and down steep inclines.

After the binding comes the boot. Oil-tanned moccasin boots worn with one light pair and one heavy pair of wool socks work well. A winter companion of mine raves about his pair of moccasins with the upper section of the boot made of thick canvas material. He purchased them from a Native living in the far North where the snow is always dry and crisp. In wet snow, however, his feet soon become soaked, and adding more oil just prevents his feet from breathing and they sweat uncontrollably. I find a good old pair of felt-lined boots with rubber bottoms and leather tops to be adequate. They're on the heavy side, give me blisters, and at times can be too warm to wear comfortably, but with an extra pair of interchangeable liners in my pack I haven't lost a toe from frostbite yet.

Safe Ice Guide

3 inches (5 cm) = extremely dangerous; don't even think about it
4 inches (10 cm) = okay for figure skaters and ice anglers
7 inches (18 cm) = just enough for snowmobiles
8–12 inches (20–30 cm) = can handle a small car or ATV

Take note that all ice should be considered unsafe at first. River currents, snow depth, and the amount of times the ice has thawed and then re-frozen can all be important issues.

Tips for Traveling on Ice

- Always walk in single file and well spread out when walking in groups.
- Stay clear of creek or river mouths where currents keep the ice from forming properly.
- Carry a long pole. You can use it to poke and check the ice as you go, and hold it horizontally in the event that you break through.
- Place ice grips around your neck or wear a sheath knife to help you crawl back out on the surface if you break through.
- If you happen to fall through the ice, try to remember to keep your arms stretched out. Quickly start breaking the thin ice around you. Then slide and roll on top of the harder surface. Make sure to keep low and your weight well-distributed. Immediately head for shore and get warm and dry as soon as possible.
- Of course, the best rule is to stay off ice any time you are in doubt of its safety.

Snow Words

The Inuit have over 100 words for snow. Here's the top ten list:

ANNIU • falling snow

TLAPA • powder snow

TLACRINGIT • snow that is crusted on the surface

KAYI • drifting snow

QANUK • snowflake

QANIR • to snow

NATQUIK • drifting snow

NUTARYUK • fresh snow

PIRTA • blizzard, snowstorm

KANEVVLUK • fine snow/rain particles

Swift

CANOE CAMPING

Everyone must believe in something. I believe I'll go canoeing.

HENRY DAVID THOREAU

THERE ARE LITERALLY hundreds of canoe manufacturers out there, each with an endless assortment of canoe models, as well as their own private classification system. On top of all that, there are those opinionated canoeists who also go out of their way to tell you you've bought the wrong boat the moment you bring it home. It's absolute insanity. Quite honestly, purchasing a canoe can be more stressful than buying a car. But like buying a car, the perfect scenario would be to own a dozen models. And just as golfers choose the best club to get the ball to the green, a canoeist would choose the best boat for the water to be paddled each trip.

Of course, acquiring a dozen or so canoes can be a little expensive, and storing them in the backyard tends to be a problem. I have eight canoes now, and I'm quickly running out of room. So for most canoeists, your best bet is to buy the most versatile canoe afloat — the quintessential tripper.

The most important elements that make up a good tripping canoe are the dimensions, shape and material.

◀ *A canoe is one of the best ways to get around out there.*

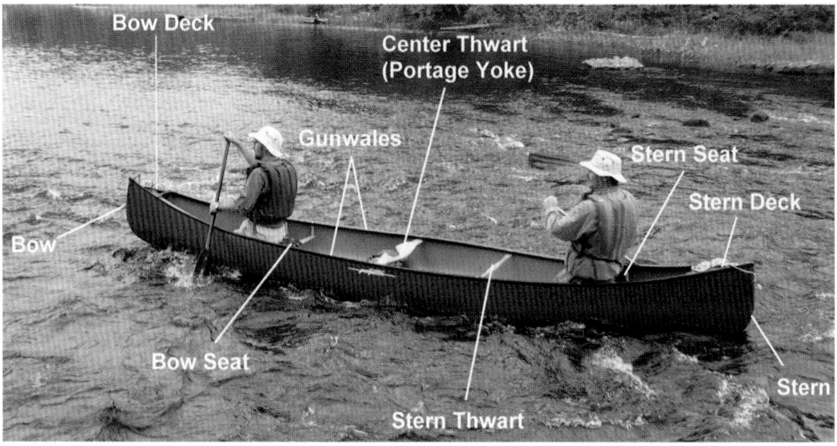

▲ *Parts of a canoe.*

CHOOSING THE RIGHT CANOE

Dimensions

This is the easiest to deal with. The minimum length of a tripping canoe is 16 feet and the maximum length is 18 feet. A 16-foot canoe gives adequate room for two people and gear for a week-long trip. However, if you're heading out longer or you need room for a third party (a young child or pet dog), then lean toward the 17-foot or even 18-foot. The tradeoff for the extra length, of course, is how well your boat handles on the water. A 17-foot or 18-foot canoe will be much faster across the water, but will be extremely difficult to turn and may sink like a submarine while shooting whitewater. The 16-foot boat will do much better in rapids and is far more maneuverable, especially while paddling down one of those constantly twisting streams, but will be slow across the lake and may even take on the odd rolling wave.

Shape

The shape of the canoe is a little more confusing. The width of an average tripper ranges from 30 to 36 inches (76–91 cm). But that's not really what counts. First, consider the entry line of the canoe. If the bow has a narrow entry line, then it will cut through the water nicely. However, it will also allow more water to splash up and into the canoe. A canoe with a blunt entry line will make the boat slower but will also tend to ride up on the waves and keep the bow person dry. If you paddle big lakes, some rapids, and you're not too concerned about how fast you go, choose the blunt shape.

Another part of the canoe's shape is how its bottom sits in the water. The flatter the bottom the more initial stability the boat will have, meaning it doesn't feel like you're going to flip over the moment you push off from shore. This shape, however, reduces your speed considerably and can be quite dangerous when out in rough water (the waves tend to splash over the gunwale easily). Then there's secondary stability. If the bottom of the canoe is more rounded, it will feel a little tippy at first, but you will have a much easier time moving across the water and be much safer when the size of the waves builds up. So, unless you're a complete novice and you'll never take the canoe away from the cottage dock, then go for the rounder bottom.

Depth is also important. The bare minimum is 12 inches (30 cm). But if you have a large load (up to three packs) and plan on paddling some whitewater or large lakes, then go for 13 or 14 inches (33 or 35 cm).

Finally, you have to look at the canoe's "rocker." It's the term used when dealing with the flatness of the overall canoe, as viewed from along the keel line. Basically, a boat made for extreme whitewater has more of a banana shape to it. This enables it to turn on a dime; however, it's almost impossible to go straight while paddling across calm water. A lake touring boat is close to dead straight from bow to stern. This allows it to track well. But don't try to turn quickly into an eddy or you'll end up missing the turn completely and going sideways down the river!

▲ *The "tripper" is the best overall canoe design for wilderness travel.*

TUMBLEHOME • a traditional term meaning that the sides of the canoe are widest just above the waterline (basically, it bulges out wider than the gunwales), which reduces stability but lets you paddle in a straighter line without much effort.

▲ *The beauty of a traditional cedar strip canoe is best understood by those who paddle them.*

Materials

Canoe materials are just as varied as their dimensions and shape. It's hard to believe that the choice of materials used in the construction of a canoe started with a walk in the woods. Now it seems everything is done in the science lab.

Weight and strength are the two major factors to consider when choosing the material to construct a canoe. Some materials create an almost indestructible canoe but are back-breaking on the portage; others are light as a feather but are as brittle as a potato chip. Here are some of the choices on the market.

Wood Living in Peterborough, a place thought to be the birthplace of the modern canoe, I've been told by many traditionalists that a canoe is made of wood and a boat is made of anything else. Even though wooden canoes are expensive, require far too much maintenance, are heavy when wet, and are at times far more fitting for a showcase than a wild river, I must admit it feels wonderful to paddle one.

Aluminum The aluminum canoe, or what was once called the "Grumman canoe" until the company closed down a few years back, is mostly used for institutional use, as it's durable and inexpensive. However, the aluminum canoe lacks the aesthetics of a wood-and-canvas canoe, they are pigs to carry on a portage, the bottom tends to stick when scraping over rocks, and there's a loud echoing bang every time your paddle hits the gunwales. But if looks mean little to you and you don't mind the possibility of announcing your arrival on the lake to every wild creature around, then the aluminum canoe is the choice for you.

Plastics Royalex is a type of plastic material consisting of a foam core sandwiched between sheets of ABS (acrylonitrile butadiene-styrene) with a vinyl surface. It's strong and flexible, making it the obvious choice for whitewater canoeists. Just pray the river you're running doesn't have too many lengthy portages; Royalex boats can weigh a ton. Thankfully, designers have worked hard in developing new, lighter models. They're not as durable, but you're not as likely to suffer from a hernia mid-trip.

Fiberglass Fiberglass was the most common fabric used for canoe construction a few years ago. Fiberglass creates a moderately tough, lightweight boat, and is made up of either strips of cloth or chopped glass mixed with resin and then sprayed into a mold. Some fiberglass models are superb and some are a joke. I'd stay away from the chopped glass types, they're cheaply made and not worth the hassle to have along on a remote canoe trip. In fact, I'd stay away from fiberglass completely, unless that's all your pocketbook can afford.

▲ *Royalex is the preferred material for playing around in rapids.*

Kevlar: Kevlar is more expensive than fiberglass, but it's lighter to carry and has added strength. Some manufacturers make up their own secret recipe of Kevlar and fiberglass. Some even make up their own Kevlar mixture and mold it around traditional canoe designs. But buyer beware: make sure you don't get swindled by any sales rep that doesn't know their stuff. I've only been happy with the Voyager Canoe Company in Millbrook, Ontario. The owner has the ability to blend chemistry with tradition extremely well.

TYING ONE ON

The odd canoe may be crushed in rapids or flipped over in high winds. But even if that happens, the repairs are usually manageable. It's on the highway, even before getting to the put-in, when the majority of boats get really smashed up — by not being properly tied down on top of the vehicle. To avoid this, make sure you take the time to properly secure your canoe. First, you need some type of roof rack. This can range from four square bits of foam placed between the gunwales and the top of the vehicle to a highly engineered system of clamps and bars. Then a series of ropes and tie-down webbing straps are used: two over the top, two to the front bumper, and two on the rear bumper. It's important to note, however, that it's usually the rack system, not the knotted rope that's holding the canoe in place, that gives way first. The worst I've ever seen was someone's entire truck cap lifting off, canoe and all, smashing into the windshield of another vehicle directly behind it. The canoe and even the rack system itself were properly secured; it was the cap of the truck that wasn't. Luckily, no one was injured.

▲ *"I told you we should have gone left!"*

BASIC PADDLING STROKES

Before we get into the basic strokes used in canoeing, it's important to note that, other than the J-stroke, all these paddling techniques need to be practised by both the stern and bow person. There are so many canoeists, especially men (sorry, guys), who place their inexperienced partner in the bow of the canoe and tell them to just paddle forward while they steer the boat. This type of partnership never works. The bow person actually needs to know how to steer the canoe more than the stern paddler, especially in whitewater. There's no way a canoe can successfully maneuver around a rock in mid-rapid by having only the stern person in control. It's a sure way to end the trip, and maybe the relationship.

Forward Stroke The idea behind the forward stroke is quite simple: position the paddle far forward and then plunge the blade into the water, pushing water back and propelling the canoe forward. But an hour of this "simple" motion and your arms will begin to ache and you'll start wondering if you're ever going to get to the other side of the lake.

To make the forward stroke more effective and produce more power with the least amount of strain possible, it's far better to make more use of your upper body strength rather than the arms themselves. This can be accomplished by twisting your torso, making the arm and shoulder on your paddling side extend as far ahead as possible, leaning your body slightly forward at the hips. Keep an eye on the position of your arms; the lower portion of the arm should almost be straight and your upper arm somewhat bent.

It is also important to note that while completing the stroke your lower arm should not go past your hip. If it does, you are wasting time and energy by actually lifting water up and pushing your bow down, like easing down on the brake of a car after depressing the gas.

Back Stroke The first stroke I mastered while running through rapids was the back stroke. It's the exact opposite of the forward stroke, obviously, and is used to slow your canoe down instead of pushing it forward — a crucial move that's needed when you're heading for something you don't want to hit, like a big rock. Pivot your upper body toward the center of the canoe, lean back, keep a sharp angle on the paddle when planting the blade into the water, and push the water toward the bow.

J-Stroke The problem with just completing the forward stroke is that as the canoe moves ahead, it will inevitably start to turn slightly away from your paddling side. What's needed then is a stroke that provides forward motion while keeping the canoe on a straight course. In my earlier years of paddling I used to adjust for this by twisting the paddle blade in toward the canoe after completing the forward stroke, treating the paddle somewhat like a ship's rudder. Somehow I had taught myself this technique, it worked well enough, and at the time it made sense. But then I took a canoe course and realized how ineffective my mode of steering was.

My instructor nicknamed my technique the "goony stroke," and noted how every time I twisted the paddle blade inward it was like putting on the brakes; however, twisting the blade outward, forming the letter J, did the opposite. The canoe is actually forced back on course without being pushed back.

To know you're doing the J-stroke properly, look at your hand gripping the top of the paddle after completing the stroke. If your wrist is bent down, with your thumb pointing to the water, then it's correct. If your wrist is bent up, with your thumb pointing to the sky, you're doing the goony.

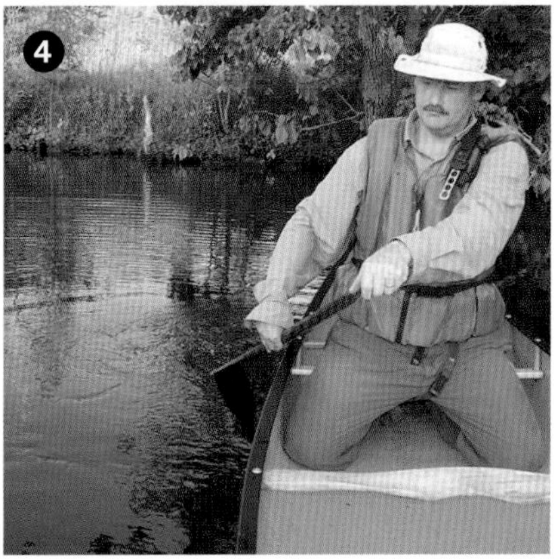

"I used to think it was a major tragedy if anyone went through life never having owned a canoe. Now I believe it's only a minor tragedy."

BILL MASON,

PATH OF THE PADDLE (1984)

Draw The advantage of the draw stroke is that it allows you to move your canoe effectively sideways and away from approaching obstacles. It is, therefore, no surprise that the bow person must become more proficient with this stroke than the stern paddler. Don't get me wrong, the stern person still makes use of the draw stroke to maneuver the canoe; it's just that it's far more efficient when used in the bow.

To produce a proper draw, place the paddle on the side you want to travel toward, with the blade facing the canoe. Reaching outward, plunge the blade into the water and push or "draw" the water toward you. If you are drawing on the right side of the canoe, the canoe will ultimately go right. When the paddle reaches the canoe, take it directly out of the water and repeat the process. Once you become an expert with this stroke, you can then advance by keeping the blade in the water after it reaches the canoe, turn it perpendicularly, and knife it through the water to repeat your draw.

Cross Draw The cross draw seems to be one of the most confusing for people, basically because it feels quite awkward to complete three-quarters of the way through. The stroke, which is usually done in the bow but can still be used by the stern paddler, is chosen when the canoeist wants to draw on the opposite side they are paddling on without switching hands.

First, position yourself as if you're about to complete a draw. Now, by pivoting at the waist, bring the paddle over to the other side of the canoe without changing the way you are gripping the shaft. Then draw the water toward you. At first you may think it would be easier and quicker to just switch hands and do a draw on the other side of the canoe. But the cross draw, when done correctly, is a far better option.

Pry The pry stroke is similar to the draw, except instead of pulling the paddle blade toward the canoe, you pry it away. It also forces the canoe in the opposite direction, so if you pry on the right side of the canoe, it will go left. Therefore, by combining draws and prys, you can move quite effectively without switching sides.

And as with the draw stroke, once you've mastered the pry stroke, you can then advance by keeping the paddle blade in the water, turning it perpendicularly, and knifing it through the water to repeat the pry.

Use Pool Noodles for Protection

The foam tubes used for insulating pipe, or better yet, pool noodles (used as a fun flotation toy), are an inexpensive and effective way to protect your boat from being marked up while stored on top of your vehicle. Cut a slit down the length of the tubes (a utility knife works well for this) and place them either over the gunnels of the canoe or on top of the roof-rack bars. To keep them secure, use good old duct tape or those self-locking plastic cable ties you get from the hardware store.

Forward and Backward Sweep The forward sweep turns the canoe away from your paddling side. Place the paddle blade alongside the canoe, as if you're about to complete a forward stroke. Now sweep the blade wide in an arc, forming a giant C in the water. The more forward you begin the sweep and the farther you end it will determine the turning ability of the stroke.

The backward sweep is in the exact opposite direction of the forward sweep and will propel the canoe in the opposite direction. So, if the bow person does a forward sweep and the stern person completes a back sweep, the canoe will go in circles. The same goes for combining other strokes to move the canoe side to side, like a draw at the bow and a pry at the stern or a cross draw at the bow and a draw at the stern.

> *"Love many, trust few, and always paddle your own canoe."*
>
> BUMPER STICKER

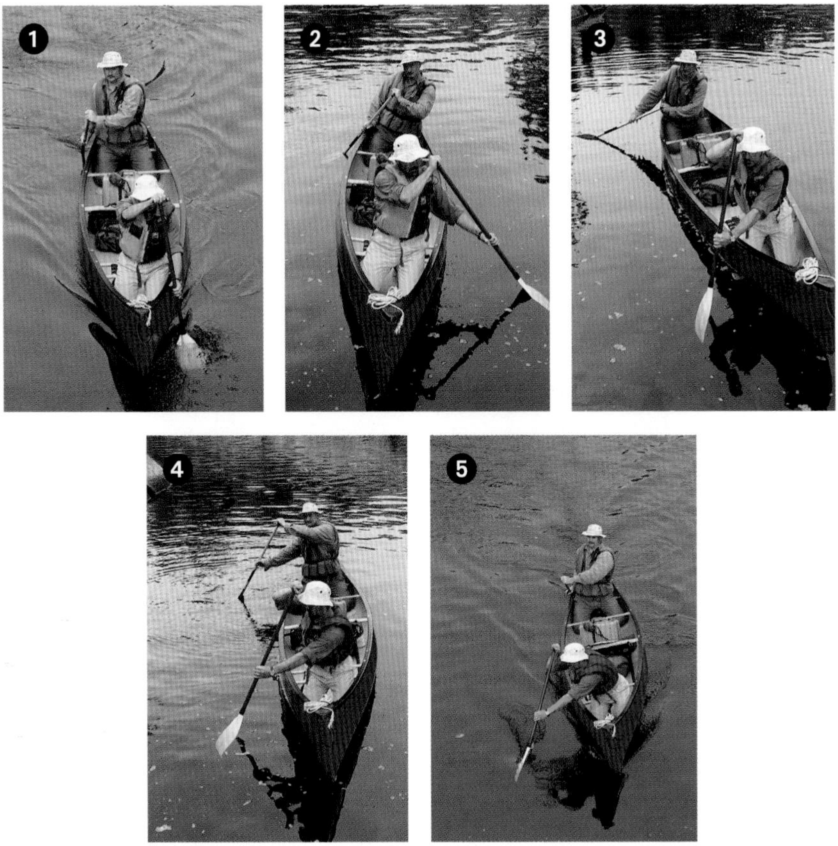

▲ *1. To keep the canoe in a straight line the stern paddler uses a J-stroke and the bow paddler uses a forward stroke. 2. To move the canoe sideways on the bow paddler's side, the stern paddler uses a pry stroke and the bow paddler uses a draw stroke. 3. To turn the canoe on the stern paddler's side, the stern paddler uses a backward sweep stroke and the bow person uses a cross-draw stroke. 4. To move the canoe sideways on the stern paddler's side, the stern paddler uses a draw stroke and the bow paddler uses a cross-draw stroke. 5. To turn the canoe on the stern paddler's side, the stern paddler uses a pry stroke and the bow paddler uses a cross-draw stroke.*

◀ *6. To turn the canoe on the bow paddler's side, the stern paddler uses a forward sweep stroke and the bow paddler uses a draw stroke.*

▲ *The key to tandem canoeing is being able to communicate with your partner. If you can't, then get a new partner.*

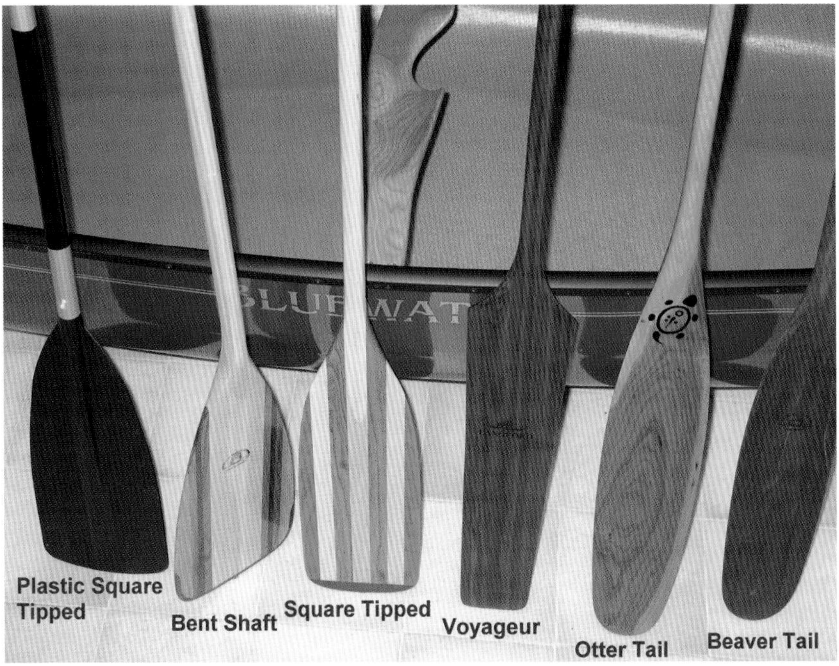

UP THE CREEK WITH THE RIGHT PADDLE

Considering that you are likely to paddle well over a thousand strokes an hour on an average canoe trip, which adds up to around eight thousand strokes per day or fifty-six thousand strokes per week, the paddle that you're using has to be one of the most important decisions that you make. The problem is, it's not all that simple.

What you first have to think about is what type of trip you're going on. The route, whether it's simple lake paddling, navigating down difficult rapids, or a combination of both, is what you will use to choose the various blade styles; each type is molded for the character of the canoeist as much as for the water course itself.

Beaver Tail Paddle

For general use (that being a trip that takes you from lake to lake), the old-fashioned beaver tail design works well. It's made from a solid piece of wood (usually maple, ash or cherry) and has a rounded end to it, like that of a beaver's tail. It's a great paddle to use for flat-water tripping, especially at the bow.

Otter Tail Paddle

For use in the stern, or especially solo paddling, the otter tail is preferred. It's similar in design to the beaver tail but extended somewhat, has a narrower blade toward the tip, and has a shorter shaft length.

Whitewater Paddles

For whitewater paddling you need a much wider, square-tipped blade to enable you to push lots of water in a real hurry. The previously mentioned touring blades are actually far more efficient when it comes to pushing water for the long term, as most of the blade length is under the surface and less friction occurs. The rounded tip also enters the water more easily. But to muscle your way through, it's far better to have a much bigger blade. It should also have reinforced tips to protect the paddle from sharp rocks. And for excellent control, the top of the paddle should have a T-grip. Avid white-water enthusiasts also opt for synthetic paddles made from fiberglass, graphite, Kevlar, or plastic. They're tougher than wood, but are also ugly as sin and take away the whole mystique of paddling. A laminated softwood paddle works just as well if you look after it.

▲ *No paddle is the perfect paddle.*

The grip on both the beaver tail and otter tail designs should be oval in shape and tapered slightly from the throat (where the blade reaches the shaft) to the grip. This makes the paddle far more comfortable and maximizes its strength over that of a rounded top. Just make sure that the long axis of the oval is perpendicular to the plane of the blade. If it's opposite to that, then the shaft will be very weak, and most likely the paddle will break.

For trips that have both flat water and whitewater, choose to bring along two different types of blades. After all, all canoes must be equipped with an extra paddle. So, when paddling solo use an otter tail most of the time and unpack the wide, square blade for navigating rapids. When paddling tandem, the stern paddler keeps using a beaver tail design throughout the trip, and since the bow person is far more important while navigating through rapids, they can change over to the square blade when flushing through the rough stuff. Also try using a bent-shaft blade in the bow and an otter tail design in the stern when there are lots of big lakes to cross.

Bent-Shaft Paddle

As for the new-age bent-shaft paddle, some canoeists love it, and some absolutely loathe the design. A canoe instructor I once paddled with is a faithful user of the bent-shaft. Being interested in seeing what all the fuss was about, I agreed to use one while out on our trip together.

While out paddling the instructor explained to me how first-time canoeists automatically attempt to travel in a straight line by constantly switching their paddles from one side to another. Paddling with a bent-shaft allows for that natural reaction, with the stern paddler hollering out the command "Hutt," to indicate the right moment for both paddlers to switch sides, allowing the canoe to stay on track.

He then displayed how, at the end of a stroke with a straight paddle, water is pushed up to the surface, slowing your progress. When a bent-shaft paddle surfaces, the blade is vertical; no water is pushed up, no speed is lost, and less energy is used. This allows the canoeist to travel much faster with less energy.

By the end of the trip, having tried out the newfangled technique the entire time, it became obvious that the instructor was right about everything he had pointed out. We moved much faster en route and never once wandered aimlessly across the lake. The design made perfect sense. But in all honestly, I couldn't stand it. I've never cared about how fast I go while I'm out there. With that kind of attitude you might as well stay home in my opinion. And every time he called out the command "Hutt," I went absolutely berserk. Needless to say, we've never paddled together since.

Sizing It Up

Sizing up your paddle is just as complicated as choosing the blade style. The traditional way to get the proper length of paddle was to line it up from your nose to toe. That doesn't work. The problem with this technique is that you are only interested in the length of the paddle between the grip and the throat of the shaft — the blade length is not part of the formula. It also does not take into account the kind of canoe you're using, the height of your seat, where you're seated (bow or stern), the length of your torso and arms, and the style of paddling you are used to.

The best way to measure the proper paddle length is to sit in your canoe and measure the distance from your nose to the water. You can also sit in the canoe while it's in the backyard and just position the paddle beside you, upright and upside down. Then measure the distance from the lawn to your nose. Both approaches don't help when you're standing in the aisle of an outdoor store trying to pick out the right paddle. So, try this instead. Grip the paddle with one hand on the grip and the other at the throat (where the shaft meets the blade). Then place it over your head. If your arms are perpendicular to your elbows, then it fits. If your arms are bent outward, then the paddle is too long. If your arms are bent inward, then the paddle is too short.

Keep in mind that this is not a definitive solution. For example, I prefer a longer shaft when solo paddling than when tandem. And in a difficult set of rapids, I'd rather use a much shorter shaft than usual.

▲ *A properly sized paddle can make or break a canoe trip.*

How you hold your paddle is important. Keep one hand always on top of the grip (which is why a nice rounded top is more comfortable than a T-grip). Your other hand grabs the throat of the shaft. The distance between your hand and where the shaft joins the blade depends on the type of stroke and type of blade. When in doubt, stay closer to the top of the blade for better control.

PFDS: KEEPING YOUR HEAD ABOVE WATER

Always wear a personal flotation device (PFD). It's as simple as that. You just never know when you might end up in the water with a head or other injury, and if you're unable to swim for any reason it will keep you above water. Just as important as knowing you should always wear a PFD is knowing how to purchase the right one for you. First, buy one that is comfortable. If it's comfortable to wear then you will have a tendency to keep the darn thing on. Stay away from the old-fashioned horse-collar types. They may keep your head above water, but they're incredibly uncomfortable, bulky, and not designed for canoeists. The vest-type jackets the coast guard label as a type III are the most widely used by avid paddlers.

It's also important not to determine your choice directly on flotation rating. A young child may need as much flotation as an adult. Think more of your body type than your weight. People with less body fat need more flotation. The average weight of an adult in water is 10 to 12 pounds (4.5 to 5.5 kg), so obviously a 140-pound (64 kg) man does not need 140 pounds (64 kg) of flotation.

Plastic zippers are better than metal for wear and tear, especially if sand sticks inside the teeth. Ties and straps are great but only as secondary fasteners. If the PFD is equipped with buckles as fasteners, make sure they are Fastex plastic buckles; anything else can be easily damaged when bumped around in rocky rapids.

The perfect PFD should fit snugly but not tightly to your body. Go PFD shopping dressed in your regular canoe clothes, zip up a life jacket and: (1) grab the back of the PFD and wrench it upward. Look side to side. Are you looking over your shoulders or is the PFD all you can see? If it's the PFD, the jacket is far too big; (2) sit on the floor and pretend to paddle down the aisle. If the PFD chafes under your armpits try another size; (3) now check to make sure the zipper doesn't touch your chin; (4) purchase the PFD you think fits, but keep the receipt. Now, put it on and jump into some deep water. If it keeps you afloat and you can easily swim in it, then great. If not, dry it out and take it back to the store for a refund.

▲ *If your PDF is comfortable to wear, then you'll wear it — plain and simple.*

ALL ABOARD!

There's not much chance of you falling into the drink while canoeing across a calm lake, just as long as you follow basic safety precautions, properly position your weight, and don't stand up and dance the jig. It's getting in and out of the canoe from dry land without flipping over that's the difficult part.

Most people prefer to put in and take out from a dock. That's their first mistake. You have more of a chance of getting wet using a dock than a beach or rocky shoreline. It basically gives you a false sense of security, and you're more likely to step improperly into the canoe. If you do choose a dock, make double sure to keep your body low and place your weight directly in the center of the canoe. It also helps to have the bow person get in first, since the front of the canoe is much wider and more stable than the stern. The stern paddler also holds the boat steady while the bow person sits on the dock alongside the canoe, and places one foot in, just forward of the seat and on the keel line. Then, continuing to keep their body low as possible, they place their hands on the gunwale and slowly bring their other foot into the canoe. The stern paddler then repeats the procedure while the bow person holds on to the dock to steady the canoe.

When boarding from shore, place the canoe into the water with the bow perpendicular to the shoreline and the tip of the stern resting on shore. Then, with the stern paddler sitting on top of the stern plate to steady the canoe, the bow person walks along the center line of the canoe, always staying low and keeping their hands on the gunwales. Now the stern paddler enters by placing one foot on the centerline, in front of the seat, then pushing off from shore with the other foot, making sure to keep their weight always along the centerline. Then away you go, dry sneakers and all.

THE PAIN OF PORTAGING

Let's face it. Portaging really hurts. Whether you are carrying over from one lake to another or avoiding a set of nasty rapids, each trail has some painful characteristic: slippery rocks, steep inclines, bug-infested hollows, boot-sucking mud, and wrong turns. And there's always that particular canoe mate who never seems to take their share of the load. So why do it? Well, it's one of those necessary evils that comes with canoe tripping. That brief moment of pain is the only thing standing in your way of absolute solitude. In the end, the moment you spot that bit of blue peaking through the thick canopy of green, and then realize that you're alone in this wonderful place, it all becomes worth the price.

▲ *Bill Mason said it best: "Anyone who tells you portaging is fun is either a liar or crazy."*

Ways to Relieve the Pain of Portaging

- Make sure there are no loose items dangling from the packs. Everything should be stuffed inside a large-volume canoe pack.
- When choosing your pack, look for a hip belt, chest strap, and a tumpline to lessen the sagging feeling a heavy pack can give; it's especially helpful while going uphill.
- Place a folded sleeping pad inside the back of the pack to keep jagged objects from poking into you.
- Practise carrying your packs around the block before attempting to drag them across a portage. If you're having problems, unpack and start taking out items you can do without.

Portage

The word "portage" is French for "to carry."
Portages are measured in meters, yards or rods.
1 meter = 1.0936 yards
1,000 meters = 1 kilometer = 0.6215 miles
1 yard = 3 feet
1,760 yards = 1 mile
1 rod = 16.5 feet or 5.5 yards (approximately one canoe length)
1 mile = 360 rods (5,280 feet)

- Avoid single carries when possible. Portaging twice across obviously takes longer, but injuries are less likely to happen en route and you'll be able to pack along a few luxury items.
- Try the "trip and a half." That's when both canoeists head across the portage, one with a pack and the other the canoe. Halfway along, the one carrying the canoe stops, puts their load down, and then returns for the second pack. The person carrying the first pack continues on to the end, and then returns for the canoe. If only one person in the group is able to carry the canoe, then just alter it so you both start off with packs, and one person goes back for the canoe. Either way, you are only walking the portage one-and-a-half times rather than three.
- Strap fishing rods along the inside gunwale of the canoe with bungee cords and make sure no lures are attached. There's nothing worse than having fishing line getting tangled up in brush or having a fish hook stuck in your gear, or worse, yourself.
- Strap the extra paddle along the gunwale with bungee cords.
- Assign each person in your group the equipment they are responsible for carrying across. This helps organize everything at the take-out and put-in as well as placing responsibility on each individual in case there's something missing at the end of the day.
- Splurge on either renting or buying a lightweight canoe. It's worth it.
- Learn how to single carry rather than shoulder the canoe with your partner. It's actually easier in the long run and fewer arguments will erupt (see portaging technique on page 283).
- Most canoes are factory-built now and generally come with a cheap yoke, which is placed smack dab in the center, creating poor balance. Having a custom-made yoke that conforms to your own shoulders is your best bet. Then place the yoke on the canoe yourself. Try to place it back a bit from center, making the canoe slightly tail heavy.

- A tump strap can help spread the stress of the load and stop the canoe from slipping down your back. Take note, however, that a tump may not be for everyone. Because the weight rests directly on the spine, strong neck muscles are essential.
- Try to occasionally drop one arm to your side, gripping the other side of the gunwale with the other arm, making sure it's outstretched and your elbow is straight. Then switch. This technique transfers the weight from one shoulder to the next and gives you a few extra minutes of pain relief.
- Avoid getting cramped hands by not holding the gunwales altogether. Instead, place a carrying bar in front of you, just within reach. This, of course, reduces the area for packs or a third paddler, so you may want to just simply tie a rope from the bow and grasp onto that to keep the canoe properly balanced.
- Pace yourself. It takes, on average, twenty minutes to portage about 1,000 yards (1,000 m). When carrying packs, one can generally suffer for at least forty minutes before having to stop and rest. But with the canoe you usually have to stop every twenty minutes and rest for five before continuing on.
- While on a trip with long portages, pack along a big bag of treats. At the end of each carry, celebrate by gorging yourself on candies or chocolate. It's amazing how the thought of having something sweet at the end of the carry may be the only thing that will push you to get the job done.
- Singing on the portage helps the time pass more quickly. Just make darn sure that the last song you heard on the radio before embarking on your trip was a good one. For some reason, that's usually the tune that's in your head for the entire trip.

And You Thought You Had It Bad . . .

While traveling the historic Grand Portage, Alexander Mackenzie noted in his journal that voyageurs would head off on the 18-mile (30 km) trail with two packages of 90 pounds each, and return with two more of the same weight, in under six hours.

Record-Breaking Portage

The record for carrying across Algonquin's Dickson–Bonfield Portage (measuring 5,802 yards or 5,305 meters) is forty-one minutes, set by Bill Swift Sr. while carrying a canvas-covered canoe and loaded pack.

Playing the Part of Mr. Canoe Head

To some, it's much easier to load themselves up with heavy packs and stumble across the portage than it is to balance a canoe over their heads. But I much prefer to choose the canoe. I'm not all that muscle-bound, and depend much more on technique than brawn. This is why the canoe is much easier for me to handle. Portaging, and most important, lifting a canoe over your head, is all about technique, not strength.

To properly lift the canoe up over your head, follow these steps:

- Start off by standing amidships, grasping the gunwale with both hands and tilting the canoe so the hull is pressed against your legs.
- Then, by grabbing the center of the yoke with your right hand, hoist the canoe up to your thighs. With the canoe resting on your thighs, reach over and grab for the far gunwale with your left hand, just forward of the yoke.
- The next part is the most important but also the most difficult. Begin swinging the canoe gently back and forth on your thighs like a pendulum. Then, with one fluid motion, flip the canoe over your head, with the yoke landing on your shoulders. Don't worry. Your head and shoulder will magically locate the yoke on their own. Just make sure not to hesitate. The weight of the canoe will be lighter the faster you flip. Remember right-left-right-flip and you'll be fine.
- At the trail's end, place the canoe "gently" down by using the opposite procedure, making sure to lower the canoe onto your thighs first to avoid smashing the hull against a rock.

Two Heads Are Better Than One

If you feel too uneasy about lifting the canoe over your head on your own, then do what's called a two-person lift, followed by a one-person carry. Have your canoe partner stand beside the canoe near the bow, and position yourself an arms-length away, somewhere between the front seat and the yoke. Then, both of you grab the opposite gunwale with your left hand and the other gunwale with your right. Flip the canoe over your heads, making sure the back end of the canoe doesn't leave the ground. Now, while your partner holds the canoe up, you slide backward and position yourself under the yoke. Once you have control of the canoe then your partner lets go and meets you at the end of the trail to help you unload, using the opposite procedure.

The same technique can be used on your own. Just flip the canoe over at the front without the aid of your partner. As long as the back end of the canoe keeps touching the ground you are not carrying the full weight until you slide yourself under the yoke.

Also, it is possible to have both paddlers carry the canoe together, even though there's a real danger of you and your partner not speaking to one another by the end of the portage. To keep the arguments to a minimum, make sure not to have the person in the front stick their head up inside the bow. Portaging then quickly becomes a game of blind man's bluff. It's best to have them place the bow plate on one shoulder, enabling them to see where they're going, and then position the other person under the stern thwart or back seat.

▲ *First rule of having your partner help you lift the canoe – don't make your partner the butt of all your jokes.*

Portage Etiquette

It was the day I got hit in the crotch with a paddle by a not-so-polite canoeist on a busy portage that I was forced to come to the conclusion that no portage etiquette seems to exist anymore. I was carrying a hefty 18-foot canoe down the path leading to Algonquin's North Tea Lake. She was carrying a paddle — just a paddle — yet she refused to give the right-of-way. We played chicken and I lost. When I reached the put-in I immediately pulled out my journal, wrote a list of rules for proper portage etiquette on a sheet of paper, and then stuck it on a tree for the next bad-mannered canoeist. This is what it read:

- When meeting someone coming the other way on the portage, the person carrying the canoe should always be given the right-of-way.
- All packs and canoes should be stored to the sides of the put-in and take-out areas. This prevents a traffic jam for others wanting to use the trail.
- If you're holding up others walking behind you, take a second to move off the trail and let them pass.
- If you have to relieve yourself, do it well off the trail, at least 300 feet (100 m) from the water source and any blueberry patch found at the put-in or take-out.
- Always double check the put-in and take-out areas for any garbage or forgotten piece of gear.
- Place any lost piece of gear found along the trail in plain view at either the take-out or put-in.
- Remember to say hello and give a smile to your fellow canoeists when passing them.

REFLECTIONS OF A RIVER RUNNER

During my early years of canoeing I avoided river tripping like the plague. I felt quite content paddling across calm water, instead of being flushed through foam and froth like laundry in a rinse cycle. Maybe I just had no interest in getting messed up with a group of over-enthusiastic river rats who just want to play in the rapids all day. But in my late teens I decided to see what all the fuss was about and headed downstream for the first time. The moment the current took hold of my bow and began dragging me along with it, I was completely hooked.

River running is totally different from canoeing a chain of lakes. The river takes you on a journey, gently floating you on its back one minute and then thrashing like an unbridled horse the next. Like many before me, my first battle with rapids was the biggest blooper of my time spent in a canoe. A friend had asked me to stand in for his regular bow partner for an annual canoe race on the local river. Neither of us knew enough about running wild rapids, but we pushed off from the starting point just the same.

Throughout the race we managed to grind over several gravel bars, thrust our way through yard-high haystacks, and bounced our way down boulder gardens and miniature chutes without flipping over once. We even traveled down the river backward after our canoe hit a rock and spun us completely around. Thinking back, it was pure luck that we survived the whole ordeal, not to mention receiving second prize.

Thankfully, I've learned from my past misadventures. Gone are the days when I blindly rounded each bend in the river and just hoped to keep the

Rating Rapids

The old-fashioned way to judge the difficulty of a rapid is using its given name; places labeled Hell's Gate or Suicide Run always had a well-used portage alongside them. Now we classify the difficulty of whitewater using a series of Roman numerals. Here's how it works.

CLASS I: Easy to moderate whitewater with an obvious route choice
CLASS II: Moderate to difficult whitewater but still has a recognizable and clear passage through
CLASS III: Difficult whitewater that requires initial scouting and advanced paddling skills (experience is essential)
CLASS IV: Extremely difficult whitewater that requires precise maneuvering – do not attempt while on a remote wilderness trip
CLASS V: Suicidal, plain and simple!

▲ *Class III rapids: they never had a chance.*

canoe straight and upright. It's now a ritual for me to scout every rapid before even thinking of attempting it. I constantly backpaddle going toward any rapid, slowing my approach, watching for upstream Vs, which indicate submerged rocks, and heading for downward Vs, which indicate a clear path. I also keep in control by practising effective strokes (draws, cross draws, prys, and ferry techniques) and by taking advantage of eddies so I can nestle in the calm of the storm before planning my next move. And when in doubt, I portage. And when I think I know what I'm doing, it's usually a sign that I don't, and I immediately sign up for a refresher course.

Trust me, to get a full perspective on river running and receive a three-dimensional view of any rapid, don't just believe in lady luck and sign up for some crazed canoe race. Head out with professionals who are humble about their skill. Only then will you truly understand the addiction — the feeling you get the moment the boat is at the brink of some run or is being tossed around a thick wall of water, and suddenly you realize there's no turning back. You are now at the mercy of the river gods.

Scouting

I think all canoeists go through that stage in life when one's personal arrogance gets in the way of common sense. I've known so many paddlers that have blindly run down dangerous rapids without scouting them first, simply because they're just too darn impatient to get out and have a good look first. I once witnessed a canoe mate, while paddling down the Colounge River in Quebec, run a technical class II dangerously close to a major waterfall. When I questioned his sanity, he simply laughed and said "Come on Kevin, I've never dumped on a class II. What's your problem?" Not surprisingly, he dumped in mid-rapid and luckily caught the throw bag we tossed him, which kept him from plummeting to his death.

On another occasion in Quebec I even cancelled a guided trip on day one of a week-long outing when the clients, who were completely stoned on cannabis at the time, refused to scout each and every rapid. They thought I was being far too safety-conscious. I thought they were being idiots and refused to guide them any farther.

However, the best example of how a canoeist's lack of patience can become a severe risk factor is one of my own immature actions. I was guiding the members of my publishing company, Boston Mills Press, on our annual canoe trip, and for the first time we chose a river route. I was partnered up with Noel, the managing editor. As we approached the first difficult

▲ *"Yep, I think it's runnable. But maybe you should go first?" Scott "Puffy Pants" Roberts scouts the rapid.*

rapids en route, a technical class II, I made the decision to run the set without scouting it first. I'm not sure if it was bravado, laziness, or just plain stupidity. I just know it was a big mistake.

Halfway down we found ourselves caught up in the current and tried to power toward shore. That failed miserably. Then we tried to eddy in behind a small boulder. That also failed, and it wasn't long before we found ourselves drifting sideways to the current, heading toward a miniature fall.

It wasn't a dramatic flip. Noel and I just slid sideways down a smooth piece of rock, miraculously staying upright until the very end. There was a brief moment of panic when Noel's foot became wedged in a rock and held him under, but he eventually recovered and we began swimming downriver after our packs and canoe. Thankfully, the only item lost was Noel's favorite baseball cap.

The rest of the group, who all had safely walked around the rapid on the well-marked portage, arrived at the put-in just in time to witness us coming ashore, looking like a couple of drowned rats. It was a humbling experience, to say the least. The important thing, however, is that I learned from it; I openly admit that I was totally wrong in not scouting that rapid first. Some paddlers take far too long to reach this stage — they make too many bad choices before developing good judgment in safety, and at times, aren't lucky enough to live through them.

How to Properly Scout a Rapid

- Take out well before the drop (using a back ferry to land is best) and pull the canoe well up on shore. Even tie the canoe off securely — you don't want to witness your boat floating by while scouting the rapids.
- Walk along the rapids with your partner, locating potential routes that both of you agree upon.
- Try to stay at river level when scouting. Rapids have a tendency to look easier from high above.
- Walk all the way to the base of the run, not only to note all possible routes, but also to see what's waiting for you at the bottom. If there's another set of rapids, and you end up dumping on the first set, chances are there will be no time to collect yourself before the second set.
- Make note of identifiable markers that can help point the way through (large boulders, overhanging trees, obvious Vs). Make sure these points of reference can be seen once you're at river level, as everything looks completely different once you're in the canoe and heading for all the foam and froth.
- Remember, even if one of the two canoe partners has doubts about an obvious route choice, use the portage. It's safer, and relieves the pressure on group dynamics.

PADDLING TECHNIQUES FOR WHITEWATER

Front Ferry Picture yourself paddling down a remote river. The twenty-year-old map you have brought along shows a portage to the right of a dangerous rapid. However, as you creep along the right bank until you're only a few hundred yards upstream from the drop, you discover that the map is wrong. The portage is actually on the left shoreline. What do you do?

The only safe way to reach the take-out on the opposite bank is to "ferry" your canoe across the current a safe distance upstream from the rapid. It's one of the most difficult tricks of river paddling, forcing your canoe to move sideways in the fast current, but it's the easiest way to deal with such a circumstance.

The front ferry, meaning the canoe is pointing upstream, is the easiest to negotiate. You first point the canoe on an angle, against the current, leaning toward the opposite shore. Then, with a series of power strokes, the canoe is taken out into the current. If the proper angle is kept, the force of the river should move you straight across the river. If you find yourself having to paddle hard and the canoe is moving quickly downstream, adjust the angle of the canoe so that the current is moving you sideways rather than toward the drop. It's the stern paddler's responsibility to keep the proper angle and the bow paddler's job to keep the canoe moving across. Stronger currents obviously require sharper angles and slower currents give you less chance for error. But the only way to get a good feel for what angle the canoe should be set at is to practise the technique over and over again on some local stream prior to your trip. This is definitely not something to try out for the first time while on some remote river.

Should You Move Faster or Slower than the Current?

The issue of whether canoeists should quicken their pace when navigating through rapids or reduce their speed to slower than that of the current is a simple one. The only time when ramming speed is appropriate is when you need to crash through large standing waves. The extra speed will actually give you more control and allow for less water to pile in. Any other whitewater maneuver (the other 99 percent of the time), is enhanced by going in slow motion. It's your only chance to have some type of control in a situation where it's extremely easy to find yourself out of control.

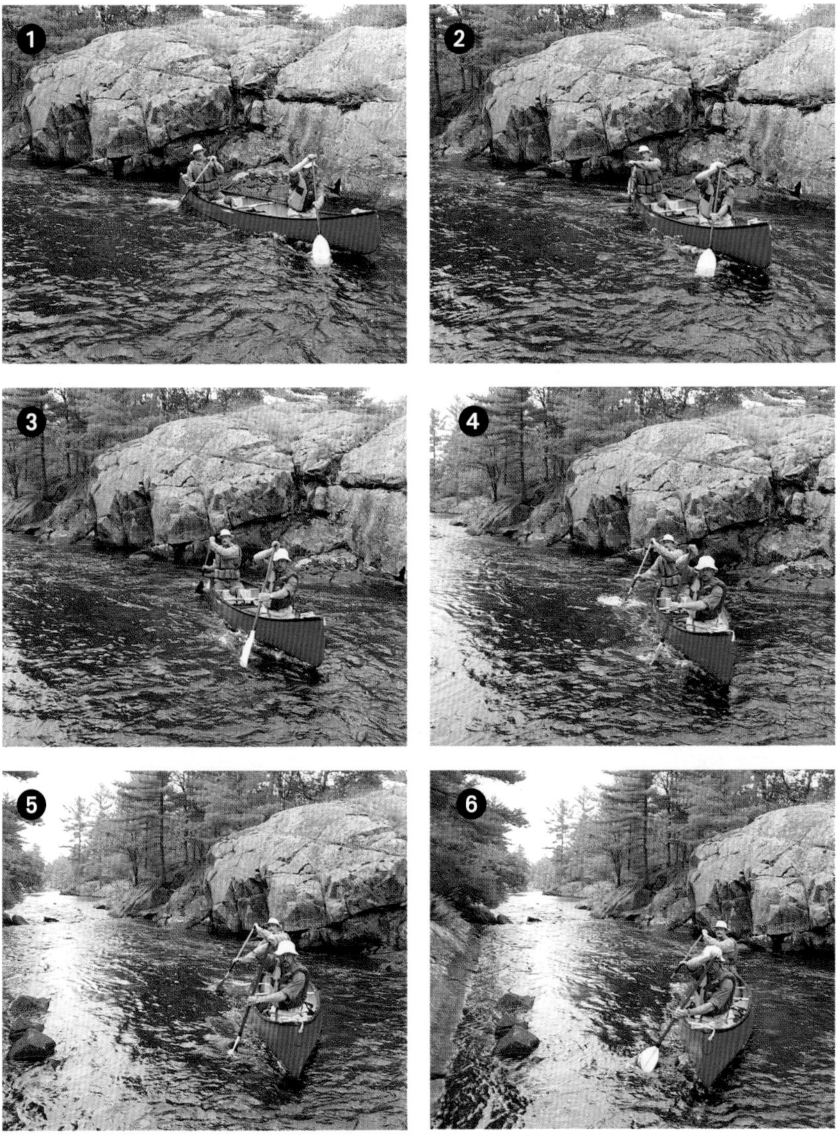

▲ *The front ferry, in which the canoe is pointed upstream, is the easiest to negotiate.*

> *"I always think rating rapids is sort of a silly thing, because if you tip over in a one, that's a five to you."*
>
> ROBERT PERKINS, *TALKING TO ANGELS*

Back Ferry The front ferry is a powerful maneuver. But it's the back ferry, a similar move except that the canoe continues to be pointed downstream, that's far more practical. It's also considered to be the most essential move for any whitewater paddler.

Most novice canoeists, when approaching a "sweeper," or a downed tree overhanging the outside bend of a river, will attempt to stay clear of the hazard by turning like a race-car driver, keeping to the inside track. The problem with this maneuver is that the main current is heading for the outside bend and will ultimately grab the stern of the canoe and take it broadside to the sweeper, pinning you against the obstacle.

So, when approaching a sweeper at a bend in the river you must do the unthinkable: head directly for it. Then, just as you reach the outside bend you back ferry the canoe to the inside bend. With the stern of the canoe pointing upstream, and leading away from the hazard, back paddle vigorously and the current will actually move you across the river away from the sweeper. To ensure enough control you should make sure that the canoe is moving considerably more slowly than the speed of the current.

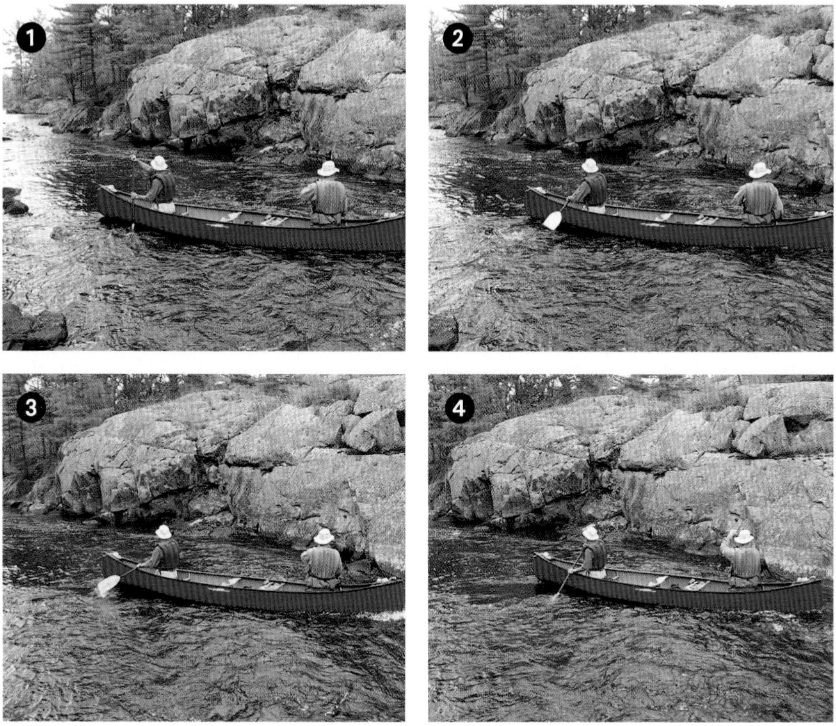

▲ *The back ferry.*

The Eddy Turn Behind every major rock or sharp bend in the river there will always be a place where the current suddenly changes direction and creates something called an "eddy." Canoeists use these calm sections of the river as an escape hatch from what's downriver. The eddy can provide a place to pull in, relax, and rethink your next move.

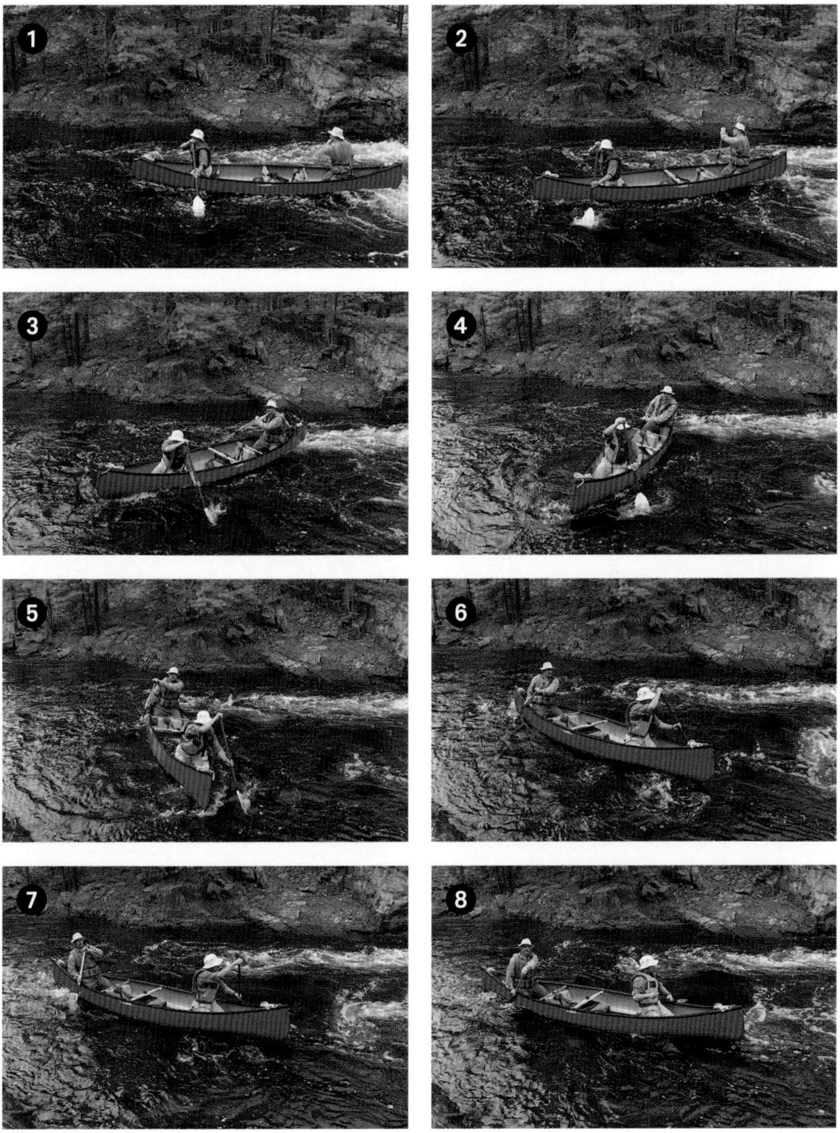

▲ *Entering an eddy.*

Getting your canoe into an eddy, however, is not an easy task. In fact, it's quite easy to miss the eddy altogether and find yourself heading downstream either backwards or broadside to the current.

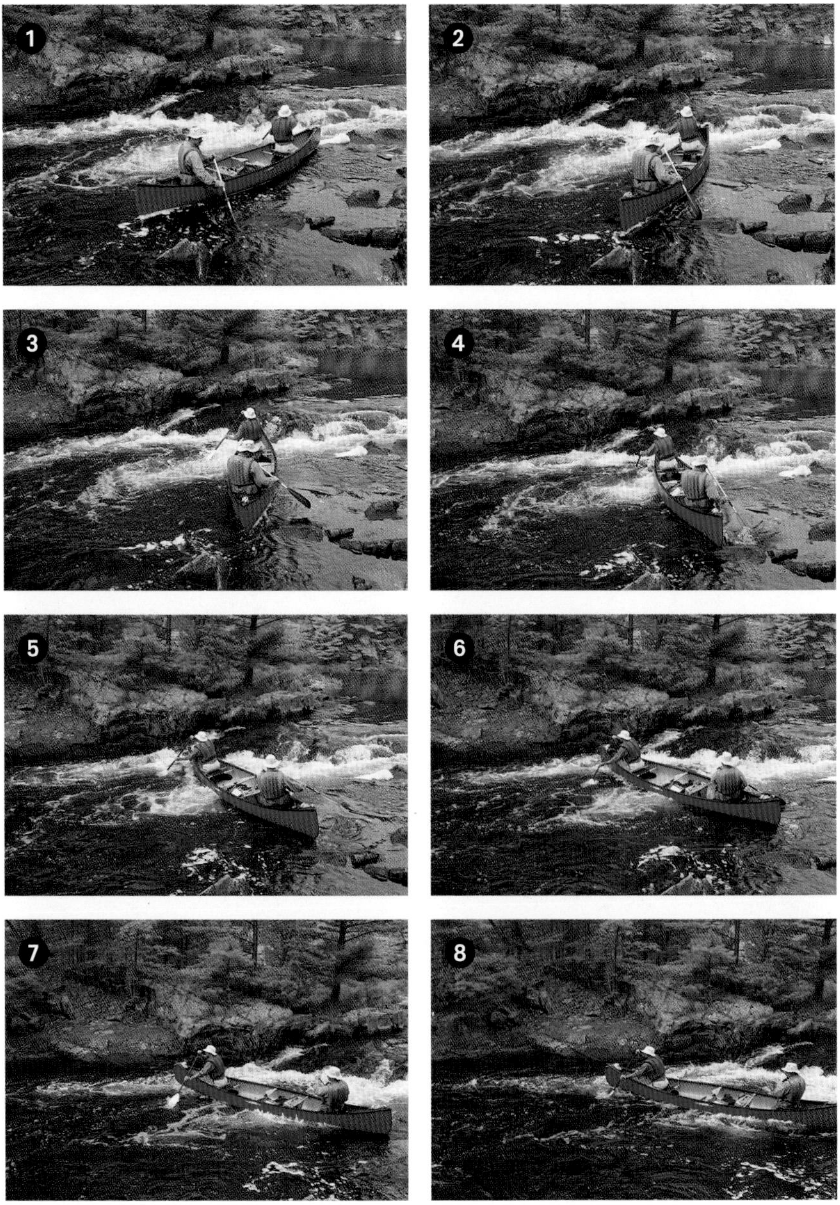

▲ *Exiting an eddy.*

To properly enter an eddy (paddling tandem) you must push the canoe, on a slight angle, toward the "eddy line" (a visible line in the water where the main current rushes around the side of the obstacle, and the calmer section, or opposite swirl, lies on the other). Now, with a strong outstretched draw or cross draw from the bow person and a wide sweep from the stern paddler on the opposite side, turn the canoe into the protected waters of the eddy. Catching the eddy is the tricky part. Don't wait too long to reach into the backward swirl or you'll miss it. You'll know if it's a success when the canoe spins around and enters the spot where the current flows back upstream and you come to an almost complete stop.

To exit the eddy, drive the canoe out into the current with a combined draw and high brace (leaning out downstream) at the bow and a sweep at the stern. The bow paddler maintains the brace right up until the canoe has pivoted around and is facing downstream. Do not hesitate during this maneuver or you'll find yourself swimming down the rest of the run — peeling out of the eddy requires more skill and balance than peeling in.

▲ *The canoe is one of the few inventions of man able to send us back to where we came from — the wilderness.*

The Art of Lining

Picture yourself approaching a set of rapids, with only a faint out-of-the-way animal trail heading up a steep incline as a portage. To make matters worse, the whitewater ahead is clogged with sharp pieces of granite, is rated at least a Class III, and has a couple of dangerous ledges. Making a safe run, especially in such a far-off setting, becomes questionable, even for the die-hard fanatic. So it's obvious that the best option is to tie your canoe and cargo on a short leash and walk it down like a pet dog.

This maneuver sounds a bit insane at first, but lining a canoe is an art form that has been practised for years. It shouldn't be taken lightly; however, after many years of trial and error on less remote trips I've learned that this technique can help transform a river thought to be unnavigable into the trip of a lifetime.

First you must choose between lining with one or two ropes. Lining with two ropes, attached to bow and stern, takes a little more rehearsing than just having one tied on to the stern, but it also gives you more control of the boat as it surges downstream. To attach your two lengths of nylon rope, which should be 27 yards and ¼ inch thick (25 m and 6 mm thick) some canoeists simply tie each piece to the bow and stern base plate. This limits your control over the canoe, however. I find the bridle knot (perfected by legendary canoeist Bill Mason) to be the best bet. Take a length of your rope and double back one end approximately 2 yards (2 m). Then knot both ends together in the center. Now place the two short ends of rope under the bow, so the knot is positioned under the canoe, right on the centerline, and tie the ends to the outer portions of the canoe seat. Repeat the same procedure with the other length of tracking line at the stern. With the main length of rope positioned directly under the canoe, you place the point of pull on the centerline; this prevents the canoe from tipping when you're pulling it across the current.

It is up to you whether to track the canoe downstream alone or with the help of a partner. Choosing to go alone means you're going to have to adjust both ropes, and this can be confusing at the best of times. But with a partner taking one end and you on the other, communication and coordination become essential. I've seen far too many arguments erupt from partners trying to line together. I choose to go at it alone. Lining solo you must adjust the two lengths of rope and regulate the angle of the canoe relative to the current. The force of the water will push against the canoe, skirting it back and forth and allowing you to place it in the desired position.

Having the stern pointed upstream and the packs weighing down the bow will give you more maneuverability and lessen the chance of the canoe digging into the water and swamping. Also try to avoid eddies where the canoe is forced upstream with the current — it may swing broadside when forced back into the mainstream and yank you into the drink. Also make sure not to get tangled in the rope. You can drown in an instant this way, which is why all canoeists should always have a sharp belt knife on them. Remember that lining is an art form, a technique where finesse and coordination beat out brute strength every step of the way.

▲ *Lining a canoe down rapids is truly an art form and must be practised well before your actual trip.*

THE JOYS OF KAYAKING

There is nothing — absolutely nothing — half so much worth doing as messing around in boats.

WATER RAT, IN KENNETH GRAHAME'S *THE WIND IN THE WILLOWS* (1908)

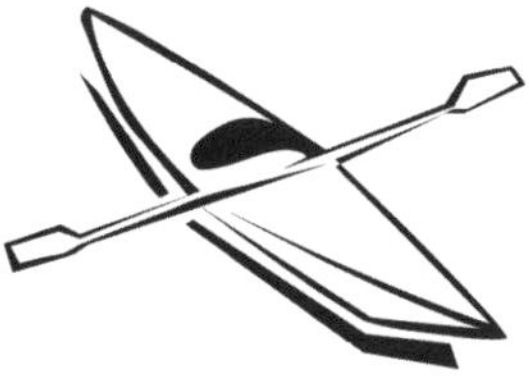

KAYAKING IS DEFINITELY on the rise. During the past five years, kayak sales have exceeded canoe sales by over 70 percent. And it's not that canoeing is a dying sport. Not by a long shot. It's just that more and more people are heading outdoors, and a good portion of them are now looking at the kayak as a way to get around out there.

If you think about it, the kayak has a lot of advantages over the canoe. With a lower profile (and a sealed top deck) the kayak stays much drier, making it far more navigable on large, choppy bodies of water and less influenced by cross winds. It's also narrower but feels stable. And there's less boat to push through the water, which means there's less effort for more speed. Probably the most important element, however, is its ability to allow the paddler to go solo, but not necessarily on a solo trip. Face it, one of the biggest skills required for tandem canoeists is communication between one another. Time on the water can quickly become extremely stressful if you're not getting along with the person sharing the canoe with you. With a kayak, however, you have the advantage of being on your own, propelling yourself along at your own skill level, and still enjoying the company of others while out on a trip. You could go solo in a canoe, of course, but the perception of solo canoeing is that it takes far too much skill to master. There are also such things as two-seated kayaks, but they've been given the nickname "divorce boats" by the paddling community, and basically collect dust on the outdoor-store shelves.

◀ *Playing in the rapids all day can definitely become addictive.*

> *"Kayaking is a form of waterborne locomotion in which the paddler sits, bent at the waist with legs outstretched, and uses strokes from a single, double-ended paddle to drag his or her butt across the surface of the water in a not altogether wholesome fashion. But they are our cousins and we love them like family."*
>
> NOEL HUDSON IN *STORIES FROM THE BOW SEAT* (1999)

▲ *Parts of a kayak.*

The canoe is still the preferred vessel for exploring a chain of small inland lakes, a remote river, or any place where portages are the norm. The one advantage the canoe definitely has over the kayak is that it's a lot easier to carry. I prefer the canoe — it suits my character more. I quickly get bored while paddling across big lakes and find it much more enjoyable to paddle and portage. But I'm certainly not anti-kayaker. Just give me a large stretch of open water and an antisocial, nonconforming canoe partner, and I'll be willing to switch in a second.

CHOOSING A KAYAK

Purchasing a kayak is not as overwhelming as buying a canoe, but there are a few things to consider before throwing your hard-earned money away. First, consider how you're most likely going to use it. Choose a boat that suits your ability, with a little room left over for improving your skill a notch or two. Second, make sure to test drive it. Check out its comfort level; the mold of the seat and the positioning of the thigh brace and backrest are crucial issues. And third, be familiar with at least the following terminology before going to the store.

Length There's the overall length of the kayak and there's the length of the waterline. The second measurement is more important. The length of the waterline is the section of the boat that sits in the water, which directly affects the speed and ease of tracking. Basically, a short kayak is easier to turn but will be slow. A longer kayak is quick and will be easier to keep straight.

Width The width, or beam, relates to the stability and the kayak's storage capacity. The wider the boat the more stable it is (and the more gear it can store). A wide boat is a good choice for a beginner. But remember, the wider it is the less streamlined and slower it will be.

Hull Shape and Rocker Like the canoe, the kayak's hull shape determines its initial and secondary stability. Initial stability means it has less rocker (amount of curve from bow to stern) and won't tip easily from side to side. It will feel much safer the moment you step inside the cockpit, and is an obvious choice for the first-time paddler. The more advanced you get, however, the more you're going to want secondary stability. Having increased rocker (the shape looks more like a banana) means you're able to easily lean to one side, which is a definite asset while paddling.

Depth and Volume More depth inside the kayak means more comfort. If you have long legs and big feet, make sure to take a close look at the depth of the kayak, or your time spent paddling will be absolutely miserable. Volume is also an essential element. High-volume boats mean more room to stuff your gear. Remember though, an empty high-volume boat is more than just a little awkward to paddle.

Types of Kayaks

General Recreation This is very stable kayak, user friendly, and very easy to maneuver. It's ideal for quiet-water paddling on lakes, ponds and slow-moving water. It's the shortest and widest design (this one is 12 feet by 26 inches), except for whitewater boats, and includes those "sit-on-top" models.

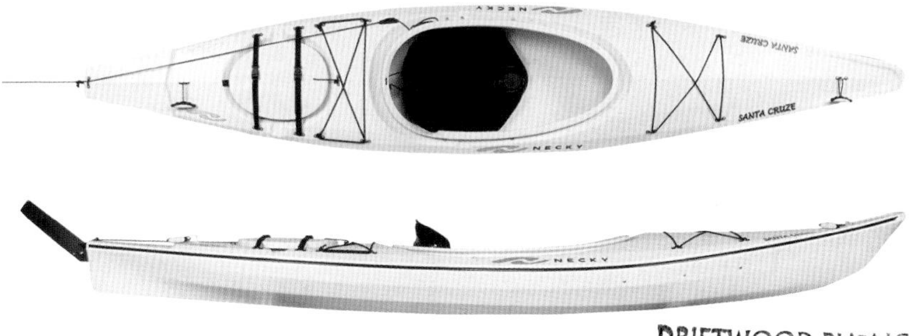

Day Touring This kayak, almost 13 feet long and 25 inches wide, is more streamlined and efficient than the general recreational kayak, with improved tracking ability, but it retains its stability. It has a medium length and a medium width, and is a good choice for long daytrips or even a bit of whitewater.

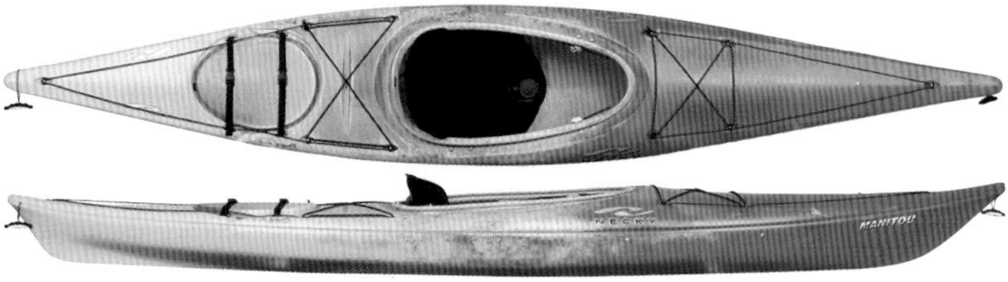

Touring (Sea Kayaks) This is a very versatile, efficient and stable kayak with good tracking ability. There's lots of leg room and large cockpits for getting in and out of and stowing gear. It's the longest and most slender (this one is 16 feet, 5 inches long and 22 inches wide) and a good choice for tripping and traveling across big open water.

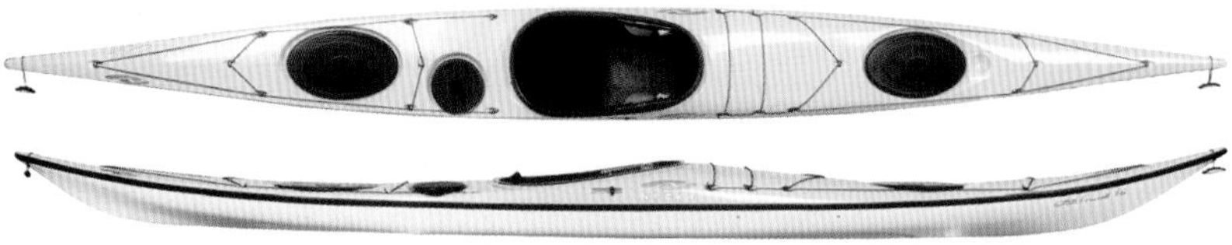

Whitewater This is a playful and responsive boat designed for moving through lots of technical whitewater but definitely not for extensive tripping or even going in a straight line. It's got lots of rocker and volume, which gives the boat its maneuverability. Basically, it's built for having fun.

Wear Protection

Before placing the kayak on your roof rack, make sure to put a nylon cover over the cockpit. This will greatly improve the fuel consumption of your vehicle.

MATERIALS

Plastic This is a low-cost product that can be abused, which usually makes it the choice for novice paddlers. It's also the best material for whitewater kayaks. Plastic is definitely durable. But it also makes the boat heavy and much slower on the water than any other product.

Fiberglass/Kevlar Both materials, fiberglass and Kevlar, produce a much finer line of entry and a sharper edge, making the kayak a dream to paddle. Kevlar is the preferred choice, though. It may more expensive than fiberglass, but it's a better material and makes the lightest boat to haul around.

Wood Just as in a wooden canoe, wooden kayaks are the most beautiful to look at and the nicest to paddle. The only down side, apart form the overall cost, is the maintenance required. However, if you're truly dedicated to the art of kayaking, a wooden boat should be your preferred choice.

Airalite This is a new hull material introduced by Perception Kayaks. It's stiff, durable and light, like a traditional composite kayak, with a similar appearance, but it costs a lot less. It's definitely a material to look into when shopping for a new kayak.

HOW DOES IT ALL FIT?

A huge downfall of the kayak, if you're planning on long trips, that is, is its inability to carry heavy loads. It's not that the boat can't handle the weight, it's just that there's no place to put it. Unlike the canoe, where everything can be stored in a couple of hefty packs and then thrown in, gear for kayak tripping has to be stored separately in waterproof sacks, ranging from the size of a lunch bag to the size of a grocery bag, and then stuffed into the kayak's storage areas.

Make sure you have compensated for equalizing your bow and stern, and watch out that the kayak doesn't constantly lean to one side. Also, make sure to practise loading everything back home first and keep to a routine while packing and unpacking each and every day. Finding a place for the tent has to be the worst, and it's best to pack the tent's components disjointedly throughout the boat. The poles fare well along the seat in the cockpit and the tent and fly are placed into individual bags. Having the tent fly separate can actually be a huge advantage when you want to pull it out during your lunch break to dry out the morning condensation.

Where to Stuff It?

BOW • clothing, sleeping bag, sleeping pad

STERN • food, tent, tarp, stove, fuel, cook set

COCKPIT • tow rope, sponge, waterproof daypack filled with things like sunscreen, snacks, first-aid kit, water filter, and sunglasses

DECK • maps, compass or GPS, camera, water bottle, spare paddle

PFD (PERSONAL FLOTATION DEVICE) • whistle, matches or lighter

▲ *Rolling over in a kayak is not as dangerous as you might think.*

CAPSIZING IN A KAYAK

Rolling over in a kayak is the most feared event for inexperienced kayakers. But it's not as dangerous as one would think, and the one thing that seems to help paddlers fight this phobia is to make sure to practise a "wet exit" over and over again before the initial trip. Once you've tried it successfully in a safe environment, it will seem like second nature to you if you do manage to flip over in rough seas. To exit, simply roll forward and out of the cockpit. The spray skirt is quickly and easily removed by pulling the grab loop directly in front of you (be sure the grab loop around your spray skirt is always ready to be used and easy to get at). Don't panic. Even if you don't manage to pull it off while submerged, somersaulting forward should do the trick anyway. Also, hold on to your paddle. You're definitely going to need it once you're upright again. But you can also use it to help with the exit by pushing upward and against the front deck.

> *"Even at the very bottom of the river, I didn't think to myself, 'Is this a hearty joke or the merest accident.' I just thought, 'It's wet.'"*
>
> EEYORE, IN A. A. MILNE'S *WINNIE-THE-POOH* (1926)

How to Get Back In?

The paddle float is the best self-rescue device after a wet exit. There are two main types: a urethane-coated nylon bag that is inflated by a few puffs of air, or a rigid square block of foam. Which ever the type, this is how it is used:

- The paddle float is first slipped over one of the paddle blades.
- The kayak is rolled back over (reach across to the far side of the cockpit and then lean back and roll the boat over).
- The paddle is positioned perpendicular to the kayak, with the blade without the paddle float tucked under the deck rigging behind the cockpit. The paddle now acts as an effective outrigger.
- While facing the kayak, the person pushes himself or herself up and onto the back deck (this is the most difficult part), placing the closest foot to the paddle over the paddle shaft and then into the cockpit.
- The next foot is then placed over the paddle shaft, and with a strong kick, the rest of the body is finally maneuvered into the cockpit and then twisted around to face the bow.
- The outrigger is then placed on the front deck to keep the kayak steady, the spray skirt is secured, and then the extra water is pumped out with the bilge pump.

ESSENTIAL KAYAK GEAR

Personal Flotation Device (PFD) It's obviously essential to wear one, but make sure to buy a proper kayak PFD with lots of room under the arms to limit chafing.

Double-Blade Paddle Paddles used for kayaking are doubled-bladed, with the average length being 85 inches (216 cm). Kayaks for whitewater need a shorter blade length and touring kayaks need a longer blade. They come in many materials (aluminum, fiberglass, wood), but lightweight carbon fiber is the preferred choice. An extra paddle attached to the deck is also a must.

Paddle Leash You definitely don't want to lose your paddle, especially while caught up in high winds and rough seas. The paddle leash, bought at any outdoor store, attaches your paddle to your wrist or kayak and will keep the paddle with you if you happen to flip over.

While at camp, you can place your cooking stove inside the cockpit of the kayak to make an effective windscreen. Just make sure to place some type of base underneath the stove so you won't burn a hole through the boat!

Pierre Berton said that "a true Canadian is one who can make love in a canoe without tipping." I think if you can make love in a kayak without tipping, you are a superhero.

Spray Skirt Skirts are made to keep you and your gear dry. They're made of high-density neoprene or nylon and neoprene and attached to the top of the cockpit with a specially designed rubber band. Just make sure to practise a wet exit and know how to release the strap.

Deck-Mounted Compass A compass is an extremely important tool needed for offshore kayaking, and having one mounted directly on the deck in front of you makes navigation a heck of a lot easier.

Paddle Float An essential self-rescue device for wet exits. It allows the paddle to act as an outrigger while you maneuver your way back into the cockpit.

Bilge Pump A bilge pump, combined with a sponge, is essential for getting rid of excess water, especially after a wet exit.

Day-Tripping Gear

- PFD
- whistle
- flashlight
- paddle (with leash) and extra paddle
- spray skirt
- pump or bailer and sponge
- buoyant rope, 50 feet (15 m)
- compass (GPS) and waterproofed navigation charts for the area
- tidal charts (if applicable)
- rain gear
- sun hat
- sunscreen
- sunglasses
- repair kit (a roll of duct tape will do fine)
- first-aid kit
- survival blanket
- matches and/or lighter
- paddling gloves
- toilet paper
- water bottle
- extra change of clothes stored in a waterproof bag
- camera and/or binoculars
- extra footwear (neoprene booties or sandals work well)
- knife
- common sense

KAYAK STROKES

The Forward Stroke The forward stroke does exactly that — it propels you forward. It's also the stroke you use 95 percent of the time, which is why it's important to do it right. A good forward stroke drives the kayak forward smoothly using the least energy and imposing the least stress on your body possible. Start off grasping the paddle with both hands, about shoulder length apart. Make sure to keep a fairly loose hand grip. This will greatly reduce the tension placed on your wrists and eliminate blisters from forming. The stroke itself is then broken down into three phases: catch, propulsion and recovery.

For the catch phase, sit up straight, lean forward, and place one blade into the water as close to the side of the boat and as far forward as possible. For forward propulsion, smoothly push the blade through the water until it is parallel to the boat's waterline. Make sure to twist your torso to make full use of your stomach and leg muscles and take some pressure off your arms and shoulders. Now, recover the blade from the water and repeat the process with the other blade.

The Reverse Stroke The reverse stroke is simply the exact opposite of the forward stroke. Begin with the paddle positioned at your hips, and then push the blade toward your toes. Repeat the maneuver on the opposite side. The stroke is an obvious way to travel backwards but it's mostly used as a breaking or stopping stroke. If you need to stop the kayak's momentum then place one blade in the water beside your hips, then do the same on the opposite side. Repeat this procedure until you come to a full stop. Be careful, however, not to place too much pressure on the paddle or you'll become unstable.

▲ *For a proper forward stroke (left), smoothly push the blade through the water until it is parallel with the boat's waterline. The reverse stroke (right) is the exact opposite of the forward stroke.*

During the forward sweep (left), the paddle blade creates a wide arc, well out from the side of the kayak. The back sweep (right) is the exact opposite of the forward sweep.

Forward Sweep The forward sweep is similar to the forward stroke except the blade is drawn back in a wide arc, well out to the side of the kayak, and the retrieval of the blade is done when the blade reaches the rear end of the kayak. The beginning and end of the stroke are the most effective for turning the boat, and the action in the middle keeps the boat in motion but has little to do with turning. Make sure to keep rotating your torso throughout the entire stroke, and tilt the kayak slightly to help emphasize the turn.

Back Sweep The back sweep, or reverse sweep, is the exact opposite of the forward sweep. By doing this stroke the kayak will turn toward the stroke side. Begin by rotating your torso toward the stern. Then place the blade to the side of the boat and sweep it out and forward in a wide arc. The stroke ends when the blade reaches the bow.

Stern and Bow Rudder Stroke It's quite possible to keep on a straight path by using the forward stroke and continually compensating on each side by either applying more force or easing up on the stroke. Now and then, however, you must correct yourself with either the stern or bow rudder stroke. The stern rudder stroke is applied by placing one end of the paddle

Average Stroke Rate

Each forward stroke propels the kayak approximately 2 to 3 feet (1 m). The average stroke rate of an intermediate paddler is around 60 strokes/minute. Therefore, a kayak can move 120 to 180 feet/minute (60 m/min).

▲ *The stern rudder stroke (left) will push the bow in the same direction as the blade is placed in the water. The draw stroke (right) will move the kayak sideways and in the direction of the side you are paddling on.*

in the water alongside the stern. This simple action, done while propelling the kayak forward, will push the bow in the direction of the same side in which the blade is placed in the water. The only problem, however, is that the stroke slows down your momentum. Slicing the blade away from the kayak after each stroke will help. The bow rudder stroke, which is similar to the canoeist's cross draw, is the more effective but harder to do (you become very unstable and have a good chance of flipping over). Begin by rotating your torso and placing one of the paddle blades in the water up at the bow. This action makes the paddle parallel to the kayak and also forces your opposite forearm to be placed across the deck and horizontal across your chest. By rotating the paddle blade slightly away from the kayak, the boat will turn in the same direction the paddle is on.

Draw Stroke Just like paddling a canoe, the draw stroke moves your kayak sideways. By turning your torso so you're facing the water beside you, hold the paddle vertical to the water and at an arm's length away. Then place the blade into the water and push toward yourself. This will move the kayak in the direction you are paddling in.

How to Beach a Kayak

First, line up with the beach, back paddle, and take a good look at how the breakers are crashing against the beach. Then, start paddling toward shore, riding the front of a wave. Make sure to keep your body weight forward and keep just ahead of the breaker, or the next wave will come crashing down on your lap and make life extremely interesting. Once you reach shore, get out as quickly as possible.

Some traditional canoeists may mock kayakers, yet the kayak does the same thing as the canoe — it gives the person who paddles it a sense of freedom.

FLEMING

THE LAST WORD

I went to the woods because I wished to live deliberately, to front only the essential facts of life, and see if I could not learn what it had to teach, and not, when I came to die, discover that I had not lived.

HENRY DAVID THOREAU, *WALDEN* (1854)

JUST RECENTLY I WAS ASKED to be on a radio talk show. The idea was to have the listeners call in and explain why they like to go camping. It was to air live, which made my stomach cramp up a bit a few minutes before the show. But I was still quite excited about the prospect of having strangers phone in from all over the country to tell why they loved spending time in the woods so much.

The very first caller, however, started the show off by stating that she absolutely hated it. The caller explained, in great detail, that she was too "princess-like" to spend her holidays in the wilderness and seriously wondered about the sanity of people who do spend time out there. I panicked, of course. This wasn't what I thought would happen. This wasn't good. I had promised the producer, who also had a dislike for camping out, that a lot of people actually did like spending time sleeping in the woods and that it would be easy to fill up a full hour. Now, only five minutes into the show, all we had was someone who loathed it with a passion, some dead air, and another fifty-five minutes of live radio to fill.

I must confess that I was a little taken aback by the caller. It's not that I'm unaware that some people just don't get it; that the idea of spending a night on the cold, hard ground is no match for a soft bed, room service and a spa. But I had to ask her before she hung up, "Have you even tried it?" Of course her answer was no. In fact, her reply was: "There's no need. I know I would hate it. I mean really, what's there to like?"

Well, that simple statement lit the boards up. We had hundreds of callers reply, all of them totally disagreeing with the first caller, and all of them having spent at least one night sleeping in the woods. Some gave reasons relating to historical and cultural values. Others raved about the intrinsic aesthetic properties of wilderness camping. And some claimed it had therapeutic and even spiritual significance. And all agreed that wild, faraway places inspire you, that they make you strong, both physically and mentally, they teach you to be humble, they make you happy, and they definitely make you less "princess-like."

A camping trip can be a painful, nerve-racking ordeal — and the most peaceful, uplifting and self-satisfying thing you've ever done. Of course, the only way you will ever understand this is to go camping yourself.

ACKNOWLEDGMENTS

This was a difficult book for me to write. Every time I thought it was done, all the possible bits of advice, recommendations and guidance given, some friend or even complete stranger would suggest something else to add. I eventually had to just stop writing the darn thing and hand it in to the publisher, knowing that the book was incomplete. My thanks therefore go to those who gave me their two cents worth up until the night before the deadline. The names, of course, are too many to list or have left my memory, but you know who you are (or at least will recognize the advice I stole from you when you read the book).

I'd also like to thank the individuals who generally traveled with me in the outdoors. It's not easy tripping with a writer who's consistently working on a "how to" book, always snapping photos and badgering everyone with questions about their gear choices. Thanks to the camp regulars: Andy Baxter, Scott Roberts, Mike Walker, Doug Galloway, Peter Fraser, Kevin Foley, Hugh Banks, Kip Spidell, Nancy Scott, Boris Swidersky, Ashley McBride, my dog Bailey, and especially my wife, Alana, and my daughter, Kyla.

Special thanks to the gang at Boston Mills Press (John Denison, Noel Hudson, Kathy Fraser, Mary Firth), not only for being an awesome publishing company but also for being great tripping partners. Thanks also to Jane Gates for her editorial work, and Kevin Cockburn and Andrew Smith of PageWave Graphics for their design work.

Thanks for the use of their photos to David Harries (waves, page 221; kayaking Georgian Bay, page 311) and David Hendrey (black spruce, page 241).There's also the staff at Wildrock Outfitters, Jim Stevens at Eureka Packs and Tents, Bill and Anne of Ostrom Packs, Glenn Fallis from Voyageur Canoes, Old Town Canoe, and Necky Kayak; I've bothered them all nonstop for information and also the odd piece of gear during this and every other writing project I've done. I consider all of these people friends, not just business partners.

And last, but definitely not least, I would sincerely like to thank the wilderness I have tried so desperately to spend most of my life exploring — it has made me who I am today.

BIBLIOGRAPHY

Bell, Patricia J. *Roughing it Elegantly.* Eden Prairie, Minnesota: Cat's-paw Press, 1994.

Buckley, Dave and Beth. *At Home in the Wilderness.* New York, Ashford Outdoor Media, 1994.

Bennet, Doug and Tim Tiner. *Up North.* Markham, Ontario: Reed Books Canada, 1993.

Chester, Quentin and Jonathan. *The Outdoor Companion.* Australia: Simon & Schuster, 1991.

Dennis, Jerry. *From a Wooden Canoe.* New York: St. Martin's Press, 1999

Golad, Frank S., ed. *Sports Afield Outdoor Skills.* New York: Hearst Books, 1991.

Greenspan, Rick and Hal Kahn. *The Campers Companion.* San Francisco: Foghorn Press, 1991.

Harvey, Mark. *The National Outdoor Leadership School's Wilderness Guide.* New York: Fireside, 1999.

Hodgins, Carol. *Wanapitei Canoe Trippers' Cookbook.* Cobalt, Ontario: Highway Book Shop, 1982.

Hostetter, Kristin. *Don't Forget the Duct Tape.* Seattle, WA: The Mountaineers Books, 2003.

Jacobson, Cliff. *Boundary Waters Canoe Camping with Style.* Merrillville, Indiana: ICS Books Inc., 1995.

Jacobson, Cliff. *Camping Secrets.* Merrillville, Indiana: ICS Books Inc., 1987.

Jacobson, Cliff. *Canoeing and Camping Beyond the Basics.* Merrillville, Indiana: ICS Books Inc., 1992.

Jacobson, Cliff. *Canoeing Wild Rivers.* Merrillville, Indiana: ICS Books Inc., 1984.

Kesselhiem, Alan S. *The Lightweight Gourmet.* Camden, Maine: Ragged Mountain Press, 1994.

Kimber, Robert. *A Canoeist's Sketchbook.* Post Mills, Vermont: Chelsea Green Publishing Company, 1991.

Kraiker, Rolf and Debra. *Cradle to Canoe.* Erin: Boston Mills Press, 1999.

Lanken, Dane. "Learning to Love Leeches." *Canadian Geographic.* July/August 2004.

Mason, Bill. *Path of the Paddle.* Toronto: Key Porter Books, 1984.

Mason, Bill. *Song of the Paddle.* Toronto: Key Porter Books, 1988.

McGuffin, Gary and Joanie. *Paddle Your Own Canoe.* Erin: Boston Mills Press, 1999.

McHugh, Gretchen. *The Hungry Hiker's Book of Good Cooking.* New York: Alfred A. Knopf, 1995.

McTaggart, Bonnie and Jill Bryant. *The Wilderness Cookbook.* Toronto: Second Story Press, 1999.

Mears, Ray. *Bushcraft.* London: Hodder & Stoughton, 2002.

Meyer, Kathleen. *How to Shit in the Woods.* Berkley, California: Ten Speed Press, 1989.

National Outdoor Leadership School. *NOLS Cookery.* Harrisburg, Pennsylvania: Stackpole Books, 1974.

Patterson, Freeman. *Photography of Natural Things.* New York – Toronto: Van Nostrand Reinhold, 1982.

Sparkman, Rick. *Woodlands Canoeing.* Fredericton, New Brunswick: Goose Lane Editions, 1998.

Tawrell, Paul. *Camping & Wilderness Survival.* West Vancouver, BC: Gordon Souls Books Publishers Ltd., 1996.

Townsend, Chris and Annie Aggens. *Encyclopedia of Outdoor & Wilderness Skills.* Camden, ME: Ragged Mountain Press, 2003.

Websites

www.blazingpaddles.on.ca/tips/wet_tent.htm

www.paddling.net/guidelines/

www.earlham.edu/~peters/knotlink.htm

www.poisonivy.aesir.com

www.myccr.com

www.backpackinglight.com

www.adventurework.com

INDEX